Pru & Me

Pru & Me

TIMOTHY WEST

MICHAEL JOSEPH

PENGUIN MICHAEL JOSEPH

UK | USA | Canada | Ireland | Australia
India | New Zealand | South Africa

Penguin Michael Joseph is part of the Penguin Random House group of companies
whose addresses can be found at global.penguinrandomhouse.com.

First published 2023

004

Text credits: Timothy West, *A Moment Towards the End of the Play: An Autobiography*
(Nick Hern Books, 2010); Timothy West, *I'm Here, I Think, Where Are You? Letters From
a Touring Actor* (Nick Hern Books, 1994); Timothy West, *Our Great Canal Journeys: A Lifetime
of Memories on Britain's Most Beautiful Waterways* (John Blake, 2017); Teresa Ransom,
Prunella: The Authorised Biography of Prunella Scales (John Murray, 2005)

Picture credits: Inset: p. 2 (*bottom*): © Bristol Evening Post, 1941; p. 4 (*top and bottom left*) © Srdja Djukanovic;
p. 6: © The Telegraph Media Group Limited/via Mirrorpix, 1966; p. 7 (*top*) © Daily Express/
via Mirrorpix, (*bottom right*) © John Lomas; p.15 (*bottom left*) © Sheila Lovell, 2000

Set in 13.5/16pt Garamond MT Std
Typeset by Jouve (UK), Milton Keynes
Printed and bound in Great Britain by Clays Ltd, Elcograf S.p.A.

The authorized representative in the EEA is Penguin Random House Ireland,
Morrison Chambers, 32 Nassau Street, Dublin D02 YH68

A CIP catalogue record for this book is available from the British Library

HARDBACK ISBN: 978–0–241–62955–0

www.greenpenguin.co.uk

Contents

Work, Work, Work

Growing Older

Great Canal Journeys

Fin

Introduction

'You know we've always regretted not being able to get married in a church,' Pru said to me one day. It was late 2003 and we were staying just outside Chichester with a friend of ours, the now late Canon John Hester.

'Yes,' I replied, not knowing what was coming next.

'Well, why don't we have a blessing in a church? Not the whole ceremony, of course – just the vows.'

I knew immediately that Pru's suggestion was not something that she had simply plucked out of thin air, and that she had probably been considering it for quite some time. As such, and despite it coming as a surprise to me, I felt it deserved my full and wholehearted support. As King Lear says, 'O, reason not the need.'

'What an excellent idea,' I replied. 'As we're here, why not ask John if he'll officiate?'

'All right then, I will.'

Canon John had been a friend of ours for many years. As chaplain to the Chichester Festival, he was well known among the acting community and in 1985 had been appointed Canon and Precentor at Chichester Cathedral. When we first met John back in the 1960s, he fascinated us. Hailing originally from Hartlepool, he was rector of Soho from 1963 until 1975 and acted as chaplain to at least fifty strip clubs. In one of his obituaries in 2008, it was claimed that he had once declared that a striptease performance is 'a display of beauty, sipped and its bouquet savoured, as one might do with a rare and delightful wine'. Always a very liberal man, he had also been one of the few clergy in the Anglican Church to openly support and applaud Monty Python's *Life Of Brian*, which the majority labelled blasphemous. But it was in the theatre where John's heart truly belonged. In 1942 at the age of fifteen his father had taken him to see a performance of *Macbeth* starring John Gielgud and claimed that afterwards he'd been hooked.

John shared our enthusiasm and as well as offering to take the ceremony himself, just as we'd hoped, he suggested his local village church as the location – St Andrew's in the charming village of Oving. 'I'd keep things low-key if I were you,' he said. 'Just a few of your nearest and dearest. Then afterwards we can go off for a bite to eat.'

We happily accepted John's suggestions, so it was all systems go.

'Happy?' I asked my new fiancée.

'Oh, very,' she said. 'A perfect day.'

When Pru and me were married in 1963, such was our financial situation that the suit I wore had seen much better days and was somewhat ill-fitting. Although we didn't choose anything too elaborate, this time round we made up for it by purchasing something especially for the occasion – myself a new suit that actually fitted me, and Pru a white trouser suit with a longish coat. My daughter Juliet was in charge of Pru's hair and make-up and when they joined me in the dining room at home in Wandsworth, prior to us leaving for Chichester, Pru looked, as she always does when she dresses up for a special occasion, effortlessly stylish and incredibly beautiful.

'You could at least have made an effort,' I said jokingly. 'You look marvellous, darling.'

'It's all Juliet's doing.'

'Now, Pru,' I said. 'Today is not a day for self-effacement.'

'Sorry, darling, shall we go?'

Pru's devotion to me was matched only by her devotion to the service. For as long as I have known her, she has been a robust defender of the 1662 Book of Common Prayer. When it came to us preparing the service, this is where we found the text.

'Whatever the English speaker's faith,' Pru once said to me, 'if they don't understand the Book of Common Prayer then they are not going to understand English. It's the language that inspired Shakespeare and we dismiss it as old-fashioned at our peril. It gives everyone a chance to take part in a beautifully written play.'

As well as with each other, we also discussed the service with Canon John Hester and Pru confessed to him that her regret at not having been married in a church had very little to do with the traditional trappings and our apparel.

'I wasn't really bothered about the white dress,' she said. 'Although it would have been nice. It was the service that I wanted. The Solemnization of Marriage. "I take thee to my wedded husband, to have and to hold from this day forward, for better for worse, for richer for poorer, in sickness and in health, to love, cherish, and to obey, till death us do part, according to God's holy ordinance; and thereto I give thee my troth." It's that word "cherish", isn't it?' Pru

said. 'I can't think of a better word to describe the relationship between a husband and wife.'

My own favourite part of the service is when it states
that marriage is ordained for the mutual society, help and
comfort that the one will have of the other.

When Pru and me got to say these beautiful words
in front of John and the handful of people we invited, it
somehow brought us even closer together. And not
because of what the ceremony represented. Having already
been together for over forty years at the time, we knew
exactly how much we meant to each other, not to mention
what we and our union meant to our friends and loved
ones. This, as I said before, was about the service. About
us, Tim and Pru, who had already experienced so much
together and had so very much to be grateful for, now
taking part in this beautiful service.

Background

'I am Yorkshire. You, my dear, are not!'

Pru

You'd never know by looking at us, but Pru is some eighteen months my senior. It must be the genes, I suppose. She was born Prunella Margaret Rumney Illingworth on 22 June 1932 in the village of Sutton Abinger in the county of Surrey. According to Pru's late brother Timmo, who was born a couple of years after her, she was very late arriving and her mother, after becoming tired of the enquiring villagers, decided to play a trick on them by dressing up the family's diminutive cook in a bonnet and shawl, putting her in a pram and then pushing her around the village.

'Ooh, can we look?' cooed the locals.

'But of course, come round . . .'

'AAAAH!'

Pru must have had hundreds of stand-ins and understudies since then, but the cook was her first.

Pru's mother, Bim, as she was known, was born in 1903 and was the youngest of four children: the eldest, Freda, having been born some thirteen years earlier. Bim was actually christened Catherine but had been nicknamed 'the bambino' before birth, which was eventually shortened to Bim. Like Pru, Bim had dreamed of becoming an actor from an early age. Starting off at school, she eventually won a place at the Royal Academy of Dramatic Art, which back then was a great achievement.

Mainly due to financial constraints, Bim was forced to leave RADA after just one term and later moved to Harrogate where, as the only unmarried daughter, she was forced to care for her dying mother. When her mother eventually passed away, Bim was able to resume her theatrical ambitions and promptly joined the Liverpool Playhouse, home to the extremely prestigious Liverpool Repertory Company.

Starting off as an acting student, having to take all manner of jobs backstage with the occasional small part thrown in, Bim eventually became a permanent member of the company, joining future luminaries such as the great Robert Donat, who would go on to win an Oscar for his masterly performance in the celebrated film, *Goodbye, Mr. Chips*. In fact, Pru told me many years ago that one of Bim's first roles as a permanent member of the cast at Liverpool was as Hermia in a production of *A Midsummer Night's Dream*, with Robert Donat as Oberon and Diana Wynyard as Titania.

After remaining with Liverpool Rep for a couple of years, Bim moved down to London where she promptly fell in love with a friend of her flatmate. The flatmate, called Eileen, had been invited out for a drink by a companion and, not knowing him quite well enough, she asked Bim to chaperone her. Within an hour of them meeting, Eileen and Bim had swapped places. Eileen was thrilled with the new arrangement, as she'd decided that he wasn't quite her type, and Bim was even more delighted as she had decided he was. His name, by the way, was John Illingworth. Of medium height, he was always very dapper and had a small, neat moustache. He also wore a silk cravat in bed with his pyjamas on, which I always found rather exciting.

John and Bim were married on 5 September 1930. Less

than two years later, at approximately 9.30 p.m. on 22 June 1932, Pru appeared. Late, and already having been understudied by a cook, as we have established. After Timmo was born in March 1934, Bim and John decided to buy a house of their own and managed to scrape enough money together – £600 to be exact – to buy a newly built five-bedroom house in Dorking. Neither she nor John had much money of their own. John, who had fought in the trenches during the First World War, was working as a sales manager when they married and earned just enough money for them to get by.

Anyway, let's shift our attention to Pru.

I managed to dig out a few of her old school reports the other day and the headmistress at her first school, a Miss G. E. Short, commented that during her first term there Pru was wholehearted in all she undertook. 'She is intelligent,' stated Miss Short, 'and her sense of humour and fun make her a delightful member of the group.'

What an astute woman.

The following year, Pru's form-mistress noted that her reading was 'quite exceptional'. However, in the summer of 1938, Pru was reported as being rather untidy and 'fond of her own voice'. I'd have thought that normal for a six-year-old, wouldn't you?

A few months later, in December 1938, Bim and John received word from the school that included the comment, 'Prunella possesses a good sense of humour and is able to appreciate the ridiculous. She is also a reliable, capable and happy little girl and enters fully into school life.' Despite her only being six at the time, that really is Pru to a tee.

Pru's favourite lesson at school, at least in the early years, was English and until quite recently she could remember her very first reading lesson vividly. A Miss McGill was the teacher, and at the start of this lesson she stood in front of the blackboard and told the class a story. It was all about a Mr and Mrs Smith, and Miss McGill used objects around their house to help spell out words.

'I remember Miss McGill saying that there was a dog by the fireplace,' Pru told me. '"D". Then there was a baby in a cot, "B". Following that there was a clock on the mantle-piece, "C", and then Mrs Smith asked Mr Smith where her hat was, which resulted in a "H". That's how they taught us in those days.'

When war was declared in 1939, Pru's father John was keen to re-join the army, but at forty-four he was too old to be called up. After acting as a special constable for a while he volunteered for army service and was eventually accepted. 'I think he rather enjoyed army life,' Pru once observed. 'In fact, he probably preferred it to the civilian variety.'

One of Pru's earliest memories of the war was when a small time bomb landed at the bottom of their garden, which fortunately was deactivated by the local bomb dis-posal unit before detonation. Their new home, which her parents had named Broomhills, was situated right under-neath an enemy flight path and Pru remembers them all being terrified. The effect this had on her parents was quite profound. The war may only have been a few months old but, with the threat of an invasion looming and John about to disappear, Pru's parents decided to put the house on the market. Such was their eagerness to sell up, however, that they ended up letting it go for just £400, which meant a

£200 deficit. That's about £20,000 in today's money. Much of the initial £600 had been borrowed and this caused them innumerable problems.

Help eventually came in the form of Freda, Bim's eldest sister. She and her husband Gordon had moved up to a village called Kirkburton near Huddersfield at the start of the war and they invited Bim, Pru and Timmo to live with them. They stayed there for almost a year before moving again to the West Country to be close to where John had been stationed with the Pioneer Corps. Pru still remembers her aunt and uncle's telephone number, incidentally, which was Kirkburton 74.

West Yorkshire, and the many happy years she spent there during her childhood, had quite an effect on Pru and to this very day she considers herself to be a Yorkshire-woman. I was actually born in the county of Yorkshire (Bradford, to be exact) but because it was not my home, and I have never spent a great deal of time there, my wife does not deem me worthy of the title of Yorkshireman. '*I* am Yorkshire,' she says grandly. '*You*, my dear, are not!'

Although Pru and her brother Timmo were fortunately kept well away from the country's most dangerous areas in terms of air raids during the war, as soon as they stepped on a train, they became vulnerable. Pru has just one recollection of this.

The family had moved from Huddersfield to Buck's Mills in Devon, and thanks partly to a wealthy and generous relative, Bim was able to send Pru and Timmo to her old school, Moira House. Situated in Eastbourne originally, Moira House had been forced to relocate to Windermere after the war started and, in the summer of 1942, aged just ten and eight years old respectively, Pru and Timmo had to make the journey there from Devon alone.

'First we had to get from Exeter to Huddersfield,' Pru told me. 'I remember standing on the platform at Exeter, clinging on to Timmo's hand for dear life and then hearing the words, "Illingworth, passengers to Windermere via Leeds and Carnforth." Timmo said, "That's us," tightening his grip. The two of us were petrified.'

In total, their journey took well over a day (after reaching Windermere they had to catch a taxi to Bowness and then a ferry across the lake to the school) and Pru said that afterwards she became quite agoraphobic. 'I never really got over that journey,' she claimed. 'It left its mark.'

When Pru left Moira House in 1948, with eight As on her School Certificate, she was elated, as were John and Bim. 'The only person who wasn't very pleased was my boyfriend,' she told me. 'I think he was quite appalled!' Pru's Uncle Gordon, who she'd spent so many happy times staying with up in Yorkshire, wrote a tribute to his niece's academic success in the form of a poem.

> Hang out the banners, and flaunt the washing too,
> For Prunella Illingworth has gotten through.
> Blow, blow the trumpet, the clashing cymbals clang,
> Prunella Illingworth's got through with a bang.
> Eight blooming Alphas she took in her stride – !
> All Moira House is bursting stays with pride –
> As are old Miss Ingram and Swannee River too
> Grin with delight at A. Talfas Pru.

Quite unsurprisingly, Pru's prowess *a la academia* led to pressure from both her family and from her former school that she should sit the entrance exams for Oxford and Cambridge. Pru, however, had very different ideas and informed her sponsors and supporters immediately that she would be applying for a place at the Old Vic Theatre School. 'Everyone was frightfully miffed,' she said. 'But only at first.'

When Pru arrived for her audition for the two-year course she did so brandishing a letter of commendation from the headmistress of Moira House, who happened to have worked with the principal of the Old Vic Theatre School. Not that she really needed it. Immediately after delivering the second of her two audition pieces, which was a passage from Thornton Wilder's *Our Town*, she was offered a scholarship. A grant from Surrey County Council would eventually cover Pru's living expenses, but only after she had been grilled by the Surrey Grants Board.

'They sat behind a table and looked carefully at my School Certificate results,' she told me. 'Then the chairman spoke. "Miss Illingworth," he said. "Two writers, Shakespeare and Shelley. What would you say the difference is between them?" "Well," I replied, rather surprised by the question. "I suppose you could say that Shakespeare was a classicist, whereas Shelley was a romantic, wasn't he?" They conferred for a moment. Then, "Very interesting,' agreed the chairman. "We think you are admirably suited for a dramatic career." And I got the grant.'

Pru's memories of her time as a student are quite a mixed bag. Thus far she'd led rather a sheltered life and despite her being the daughter of an actress (Bim gave up acting professionally after marrying John but continued for many years as an amateur) she'd always been made to feel that showing off, which is quite an essential ingredient if you're going to make it as an actor, wasn't the done thing. 'My mother wasn't a very flamboyant person,' said Pru. 'And although I wanted to be an actress, I was extremely inhibited and considered it wrong to show off. Again, that parental thing, that one must think about other people. It takes quite a long time when you're a bit immature, or very immature – which I was – before you can sort out the morality of being an actor.'

Pru went on to say that, contrary to popular belief, the best actors are not selfish people. 'They have to be extremely modest and un-self-centred, I think. On the other hand, you do have to have a certain instinct for performance, and I found it very difficult to sort out in my head what the ethics of acting were.'

Pru's drama school equivalent of the nightmarish journey from Exeter to Windermere with Timmo was the dreaded 'End of Term Note Sessions', which involved the tutors telling the students exactly what they thought of their work. Taking anything up to ten hours, each critique would be delivered in front of the entire class, and many would end up leaving the sessions crying. 'I once left a session in absolute floods of tears,' Pru told me. 'And was found several minutes later by two tutors curled up on the floor. They whispered some words of comfort to me, I remember, but they had no effect whatsoever. The sessions were pure purgatory.'

Pru graduated from the Old Vic Theatre School in 1950 and immediately set about trying to secure her first engagement as a professional actor. Unfortunately, in addition to a general lack of confidence, which she has suffered from all her life, Pru was riddled with self-doubt, and particularly regarding her abilities as an actor. Even so, instead of allowing that to hinder her chances of doing what she loved, she immediately set about utilizing some of the contacts she had made at drama school, not to mention some of the admirers.

'I had no agent to find work for me,' she said. 'So, I borrowed tuppence, and I phoned Denis Carey, the director of the Bristol Old Vic.' Denis, together with many other theatrical luminaries, had attended a showcase at Pru's drama school towards the end of her course, but she had no idea whether or not he would remember her. 'Fortunately, he did,' said Pru, 'and after inviting me down for an interview he offered me a job as an acting ASM.'

Pru's favourite story from her time as Assistant Stage Manager at the Bristol Old Vic involves her being scolded by the actor Lawrence Harvey, who she would later appear with in the Academy Award winning film *Room at the Top*. You have to start somewhere. Lawrence had wanted Pru to feed him a line during the show, but Pru's mind was elsewhere.

'I was a hopeless ASM,' she said, 'because while I was on the book, I was fascinated by what was happening on stage and didn't keep my eye on the script. I remember Lawrence, who was our leading man and ever so popular, suddenly shouting, "Darling, for God's sake will you please feed me the bloody line!" I was mortified.'

I'm going to move on to my own origins in a moment, but before I do, allow me to tell you a very quick story about Pru's first engagement on leaving the Bristol Old Vic, which relates to a television show for which she eventually became quite famous. It was December 1951 and, during a moment of boredom while she was staying at her parents' house, Pru decided to contact another luminary who had attended her end-of-course showcase.

'I did it on a whim, really,' she said. 'The agent was called Ronnie Waters and he worked for the agency called Al Parker Ltd., who at the time was one of the biggest and most influential theatrical agents in the country. I'm surprised I had the courage to do it really, as normally I wouldn't have dared.'

As luck would have it (actually, it was more down to talent than luck) Ronnie remembered Pru from the show and had been impressed by her performance.

'I couldn't quite believe it, but he actually remembered me and had even remarked to one of his colleagues afterwards that he thought I had promise. Or at least, that's what he said to me. You never know with these people.'

I have a feeling that Ronnie was telling the truth, as a day or two after signing Pru as a client he called her up to see if she'd be interested in joining a weekly repertory company, at the Connaught Theatre in Worthing, to be exact. To those of you who are not familiar with weekly rep, the actors of the company rehearse next week's play during the day, while performing the current production in the evening, not forgetting occasional matinees. It's just as terrifying as it sounds, I'm afraid, although you do get used to it. I really loved it, and so did Pru. Which was just as well really, as that was all that was really on offer at the time for actors who were starting out.

When Pru arrived at the Connaught Theatre she immediately made friends with the ASM. 'He's only about my height,' Pru said in a letter to Bim. 'But he's ever so sweet and has been very welcoming. He's called Andrew Sachs.'

Me

All right, now it's my turn.

I was born on October the twentieth in the year of our lord, 1934. As you already know, despite being told I was unworthy of the title Yorkshireman, I was born in Bradford (which is in Yorkshire, I understand). My father, Lockwood West, was on tour with a play at the time so was not present. My mother, the actress Olive Carlton-Crowe, had also been in the company.

They had met some seven years previously in a production of *The Ghost Train* by Arnold Ridley. Ridley was a playwright primarily, but ended up having a successful second career as an actor, most notably playing Private Godfrey in the situation comedy *Dad's Army*. The reason I mention him is because in 2018 I was asked if I'd like to reprise the role made famous by Arnold for three 'lost episodes' of the sitcom. Produced by UKTV for their channel UK Gold, they starred Kevin McNally as Captain Mainwaring, Robert Bathurst as Sergeant Wilson and Kevin Eldon as Corporal Jones. They were great fun to make.

It's hardly surprising, but I have no clear memory of living in a permanent home until 1939, when I was four years old. It would be well over a decade before my father became a 'West End actor' and, although he and my mother were constantly in work (just like Bim, my mother

13

gave up acting professionally after having children), they were always on tour or in regional rep and lived either in theatrical digs or in rented accommodation.

A small house in Ealing is the first place I remember not having to pack my bags and leave after a week or two. It was just a street or two away from my maternal grand-parents' home and my one abiding memory of living there is watching my father, who had managed to secure no less than six months' worth of engagements within just a few miles of Ealing (there were quite literally dozens of thea-tres there in those days – Hippodromes, Empires and Lyceums), happily setting off to whichever venue he was appearing at on his brand new Raleigh bicycle.

In May of 1939 my sister Patricia arrived. Four months later, amid the first rumblings of global hostilities, it was decided that my mother would take the two of us to the West Country. My father, in the meantime, utilizing some contacts, attempted to secure a position with a repertory company in Bristol, the idea being that as soon as he had achieved this objective, he would find some accommoda-tion and then send for us.

My mother had taken my sister and I to a village in South Devon called Bishopsteignton, and when war was eventually declared busloads of bewildered evacuees immediately began arriving there. One morning, while my mother and I were out walking, one such bus pulled up and dispatched twenty or so familiar-looking youngsters. 'I recognize them,' said my mother. 'Oh God, they're from your school, aren't they?'

Not only had the evacuees – who were walking in a line, all with labels hanging round their necks and clutching their gas masks – attended the same school in Ealing as me, but we'd been in the same class. My mother looked on aghast. While we were living off the fat of the land (we were staying on a farm that appeared to have an inexhaustible supply of bacon, sausages, eggs, milk and butter) my former classmates would have to be content with whatever sustenance the rigidities of local rationing allowed.

As we awaited news from my father, my mother, racked with guilt, decided to move us all from the safety and abundance of the farm, where I was blissfully happy, to a set of dingy rooms off the High Street. This, I'm ashamed to admit, resulted in me throwing a rather substantial and prolonged tantrum. But not because of the change in our diet, although I did miss the sausages and bacon. The father of the farmer who had been hosting us owned the local transport company, which consisted of a fleet of four buses. I'd become friendly with three of the drivers (the fourth, a Mr Banham, thought me a 'bloody nuisance') and they had allowed me to inspect their vehicles and go for a ride in them. For a five-year-old with an interest in mechanical transportation this was just the best thing in the world.

The result of my ire was that one morning I attempted to kill my sister. Now I'm fairly sure I didn't *mean* to kill her, but if that was the case I had a fairly good go at hiding it. I released the brake on her perambulator while our mother was in a shop, and sent it speeding down the hill towards a busy crossroads. There weren't too many cars around in those days, but it was still a highly dangerous situation. Fortunately, some heroic soul ran into the street and managed to prevent my sister from reaching the crossroads. It was a near thing by all accounts, although I'm sure she quite enjoyed it.

Fortunately for everyone concerned, my father sent for us about a week later, and on arriving at our new flat on Clarendon Road, Redland, Bristol, all thoughts of buses and runaway perambulators quickly evaporated when, much to my exultation, my father greeted us by unpacking a brand-new wireless set.

My father's favourite part of acquiring any new electronic appliance was to ponder at length over its instructions. It is akin, I suppose, to a small child ignoring the brand-new television that their parents have proudly unpacked and crawling into the box, there to revel in the wonders of polystyrene. Faced with even a trivial task such as opening a tin of sardines, my father would remove the tin from the cupboard, elope with it to his favourite chair, switch on the standard lamp, reach for his spectacles, light a pipe most probably, and then study the vessel intently. Happy was the man.

(My mother, on the other hand, who always treated any kind of instructions, written or otherwise, with utter contempt, would attack the tin with the sharpest object she could lay her hands on and would not desist until she had drained the olive oil and got at the sardines.)

Once the wireless was operational, we all sat down as a family and happily surrendered our imaginations to the seemingly infinite geography of radio drama. We repeated this exercise every evening for several weeks and I remember it as being a rare period of family stability, after a hitherto nomadic and unsettled childhood.

As the war progressed it became clear that my father,

Harry, as he was known, who was able-bodied and not in a reserved occupation, would soon have to swap his position with the Rapier Players at the Little Theatre Bristol for one with a different organization either in the army, the fire service or the war reserve police. I'm unsure as to whether he had any say in the matter, but he eventually became PC46, 'C' Division of the Bristol Constabulary. He adapted to his new life with ease, as the comradeship of the police force was not unlike that of a theatre company in weekly or fortnightly rep. Of course, there were physical dangers; it was part of a policeman's duty to stand guard over any unexploded bombs, and Bristol was quite often strewn with them. That wasn't his main duty, however. And thank heavens for that.

After learning about my father's peacetime occupation, he was soon asked by his superiors to start organizing a series of morale-boosting shows, which he ended up scripting, directing and starring in. I actually made debut in one of these shows. A pantomime, no less, in 1943, in which I played 'small child'.

The biggest problem my father encountered while staging these shows was accumulating necessary properties, and he and his stage manager, a fellow constable, eventually developed a highly effective method of doing this. While patrolling the streets looking for blackout infringements, my father would familiarize any offenders with the penalties the law was bound to exact, and his assistant would cast an eye over the house and grounds in search of props for their new production. On discovering such an item, my father would then 'persuade' the offender to deliver the item to the police station – on loan, of course – in return for their misdemeanour being forgotten about. It's commonly known as bribery and corruption, I believe.

As the son of a police constable, I used to worry that my father might fall subject to some terrible injury while tackling a wrongdoer. In those days, a policeman's sole weapon was a wooden truncheon that was concealed in a special long pocket in his trousers. But my father used to abandon this in his locker at the station in order to conceal hard-to-come-by items, such as bottles of HP Sauce, large candles and bicycle pumps. Anything that would fit, basically.

As with Bim and John, every last penny of my father's £3.10 weekly salary was accounted for, except that instead of it being enough for us to get by on, there always seemed to be a shortfall. Fortunately, he was later able to supplement his salary with an occasional BBC schools broadcast – the BBC having moved that department from London to Bristol. The switchboard operator at his police station, who had been a regular patron of the Bristol Little Theatre, offered to act as his agent and if a job came in from the BBC while he was on the beat, she would contact him via one of the police telephone boxes.

'46C!'

'Hello Harry, I've got a job for you. 2.30 tomorrow afternoon. I managed to get them up to four guineas. Usual terms?'

As I once suggested to my father, given the way he used to eulogize about some of his experiences during the war, I am of the belief that it was the happiest period of his life. Alas, not so my mother. In addition to her having been forced to give up the stage after my sister was born, she had spent the majority of the war years having to deal with my father's unconventional work and sleep patterns while bringing up two young children, not to mention dealing with things like rationing and air raids. She had a miserable time, I'm afraid.

So, what of my own recollections? Well, I had a very different war, that's for sure. Bristol was terribly badly bombed during World War Two and one of my most vivid memories is waking up and finding my bedroom ceiling suffused with a bright pink glow, which gave the effect of a rather beautiful sunrise. It was only when I got out of bed, walked over to the window and drew open the curtains that I realized it was actually the middle of the night and the whole of Bristol was on fire. The sky was an unearthly, hideous pale pink, thick with choking smoke.

But it wasn't all bright ceilings, hell-like infernos and impending Armageddon. While ensconced in an air raid shelter one evening with a friend of mine called Melody Davey, a worldly-wise fellow a few years our senior, named Stuart Hodder, lit a candle and explained to us, by means of a rather crudely drawn diagram, the wonders of pro-creation. I remember feeling quite underwhelmed by the revelation, and so I decided to keep it to myself. But not so Melody. She had been horrified and so had informed her mother, who arrived that evening at our house to discuss the incident, clutching a letter that she intended to hand to Stuart Hodder's mother. Such was the seriousness of the issue that Mrs Davey had donned a hat and a pair of fresh white gloves and intended to deliver the letter in person. I never did find out what happened, more's the pity.

Unlike Pru, who was every inch the model student while

at school, I was the complete opposite. At primary school, this was down in no small part to the fact that our head-mistress, Miss Torrens, scared the absolute living daylights out of me. Built like a prop forward, she wore tweeds, enormous black shoes that must have weighed a couple of kilogrammes each and could have crushed a medium-sized dog, and a black, thick, bristly moustache. I was absolutely terrified of the woman and even when she wasn't in the class, I'd be listening out for her size elevens. The only thing that ever tempered my fear of Miss Torrens was the presence of her deputy, the fragrant and softly spoken Miss Heath. I was deeply in love with Miss Heath and when she was appointed the leader of my local Wolf Cub Pack I joined like a shot. Alas, my prowess as a young Wolf Cub was about as successful as my prowess as a scholar and while the other boys in my pack all rose through the ranks and became Scouts, I remained where I was. Older than everyone else, larger than everyone else, and notice-ably less decorated than everyone else.

Given what I've just told you, you'll be hardly surprised to learn that things did not improve during the second half of my schooling. In fact, if anything, things were a good deal worse. Bristol Grammar School was the estab-lishment lucky enough to have me as a pupil, and the majority of my time there was spent in the company of Mr Pitt, the head of the prep school. Less visibly ferocious than Miss Torrens, he more than made up for this with an unyielding penchant for sadism in the form of corporal punishment. What I found particularly distasteful about Mr Pitt's leaning wasn't quite so much the act itself, more the time which he took to complete it. Having announced that he would deliver six of the best he would dispense his first – WHACK! – and then start playing with his calendar before returning to the fray and dispensing another one –

WHACK! After that, he would stroll over to the window and look out over the playing fields. 'Going to be nice weather for the house matches, I think,' he would remark languorously. WHACK! Now back in the room, conversation might turn to the play he had seen at the Little Theatre that week. 'I enjoyed *George and Margaret*, and thought your father very good. Be sure to tell him I said so, West.' WHACK! After that he would attempt to light his pipe, scrabbling around in his tobacco pouch and breaking several matches in the process. 'Ah, that's got it,' he would say, drawing on it happily. WHACK! Finally, something would catch his eye on the cover of the *Western Daily Press*. 'What's this? Unity in Bristol Churches? Tributes by the Dean? What a load of . . .'

WHACK!

'Well, I think that'll do now, West. Off you go.'

Things couldn't go on like that, so I decided to take drastic action by simply not going to school. Every morning I would set off on my bicycle in the direction of Bristol Grammar, and then turn off and spend the day pedalling and exploring. One of the first spots I visited was the notorious Christmas Steps, a narrow Dickensian alleyway that climbed up from the Tramway Centre. This, so I'd been informed, was an area riddled with sin and debauchery. Marvellous! I frequented the steps for several hours every weekday for at least a fortnight, looking very sophisticated, but apart from spotting an old copy of

Health and Efficiency, the popular naturist magazine, and being grunted at by several people, I remained disappointingly uncorrupted.

After deciding to postpone my voyage of depravity – at least for the time being – I started spending my days watching the ships unloading timber at Cumberland Basin and then cycling up to Royal York Crescent, where I'd gaze through the handsome Georgian windows. I forget how long I got away with my truancy but one day it caught up with me and I was expelled. I remember my father sighing when he heard the news. 'I suppose we'll have to find him another place,' he said.

About the same time, another pupil was expelled from the same class as me, and for exactly the same offence; a tall, fair-haired boy named Glover, whom I had never spoken to and only knew by sight. Very many years later, when I was having a drink in the bar at the Arts Theatre, I spotted, out of the corner of my eye, a tall man with very fair hair. I had known the actor Julian Glover just well enough to say hello to, but now that he had his hair bleached and cropped for his part as the Knight in John Osborne's *Luther*, things suddenly clicked into place.

'Don't tell me,' I said. 'Glover, 2B, Bristol Grammar School?'

'Good God, yes,' he said, looking quite astonished. 'Wasn't it terrible?'

'Yes, wasn't it just? I'm so glad we escaped.'

We've been firm friends ever since.

Although the two events weren't related (or at least I don't think they were), not long after being expelled from

Bristol Grammar School my family and I moved from Bristol to South Ruislip in London, where I was put in the care of a Mr O. A. LeBeau at John Lyon School in Harrow. Far more entertaining than Mr Pitt, Mr LeBeau was also a great deal less flagellant, which was a relief, and instead put his efforts into causing all manner of explosions or noxious demonstrations during chemistry classes. I remember quite vividly my classmates and I being showered with fragments of broken glass and clambering on each other's shoulders to force open a window when a heavy, dark-coloured gas rolled over the benches in sinister, foul-smelling clouds. The only other subject Mr LeBeau took was divinity, which I think must have helped him to reconcile the potential consequences of his dangerous experiments.

I attended John Lyon School (on and off) for about three years and by far the most significant thing to happen to me there was being introduced, via the English master Mr 'Sammy' Cowtan, to the wonders of Shakespeare.

'You're never going to understand any of this,' he said to the class, 'until you feel what it's like to say those words, and to have those words said to you. Clear all the desks to the edge of the room, we're going to get up and do it.'

Then he'd cast the play, and we'd begin; erratically at first, and then gradually, as we used the space between each other and allowed ourselves to breathe, the language did begin to work its magic.

Sammy Cowtan must have been at least sixty years of age and was bald, portly and bespectacled. Even so, every time we endeavoured to perform one of the Bard's masterpieces, he always cast himself in the lead female roles. This, he explained to me later, was to prevent the inevitable giggling embarrassment that would occur when two teenage boys were required to perform a love scene.

To be fair to Sammy Cowtan, every lead role he ever played in our classes he did splendidly. His Cleopatra was beguiling, and his Rosalind superbly lovesick. Only his Juliet let him down a bit, but we forgave him. The main thing was that he never failed to make the class appreciate both the excitement of the story and the power of the language.

About this time in the West End, something was happening that sought to identify the whole Shakespeare canon in sequence: the Michael Benthall Five-Year Plan at the Old Vic Theatre.

I saw many of those performances: in the first year Richard Burton as Hamlet, Paul Rogers as Macbeth, then, in 1955, Virginia McKenna as Rosalind and John Neville as Richard II. Just too early for Sam and Joe to benefit, but the list carried on until December, then continued until May 1958.

OK, just a few more paragraphs on me, then we'll get back to Pru.

Any decisions about what I might do with my life on leaving school had to be deferred until I'd done my National Service. While I was waiting for the summons, however, I managed to secure the position of Box Office Manager at the Frinton Summer Theatre in Essex. My job there was quite simple – tear out the tickets, take the money, mark up the seating plan, cash up at the end of each evening and, most importantly of all, engage the usherettes. Why they left this task for me to deal with I have no idea but instead of arguing with my slave-masters I selflessly ploughed ahead and gave it my all. The competition among the young women of Frinton to perform this function was surprisingly fierce, which put me in a position of considerable power. One exceptionally attractive applicant invited me to join her in the laurel bush at the back of the theatre so she could demonstrate her suitability. She was duly employed four nights a week, much to the displeasure of several other young hopefuls who made me aware of the fact, rather loudly, that their rival's persuasive talents were recognized (and appreciated, I should imagine) as far afield as Clacton.

In the end, I didn't do my National Service. With the scheme now coming to an end, the army were looking to excuse as many of the final intake as possible and when they found out that I had been prescribed a drug called phenobarbitone to combat migraines, they discharged me, just like that. With eighteen unexpected months suddenly at my disposal, I set about trying to find a job. The first opportunity to come my way was via a producer I'd met at Frinton who offered to introduce me to the people in charge of the Repertory Company at Leatherhead. Incredibly, I turned him down. Why? Well, I'd been appearing in several amateur shows and my mother and father, whose opinion I trusted, had been far from complimentary about my performances. They had also made it quite clear that they would rather I took a different path; one that was far removed from the theatre.

Much to my parents' joy and relief, I managed to secure a position as a salesman for an office furniture company in Holborn. Much to my parents' frustration, however, it didn't last very long – before they could start promoting me, I answered an advert to be a quality control engineer in the Records and Tapes department at EMI. As a lifelong fanatic of classical music, this should have been my dream job. There was just one thing holding me back, however, which was the fact that I actually *did* want to work in theatre.

Several months later, after I'd turned twenty-one, my chance to pursue this dream arrived one evening after a performance of Thornton Wilder's *Our Town* at the *Sunday Times* Drama Festival in Bristol. While visiting the gentleman's lavatory I found myself standing next to Harold Hobson, who was the drama critic at the *Sunday Times* and had been head of the judging panel.

'That was very good,' he said. 'Tell me, are you going to take it up professionally?'

Slightly perplexed, I stared into the white porcelain in front of me, searching for guidance. ARMITAGE SHANKS, it advised me firmly.

'Yes,' I said. 'Oh yes, certainly.'

Love and Marriage

The following passages cover the period from when Pru and me first met in 1961, to our having children and then finally moving into the home of our dreams in unfashionable Wandsworth.

Meeting Miss X

'Oh dear. I could have sworn he was gay. I really am most terribly sorry.'

'Oh, don't be! He'll be most amused when I tell him.'

'No, you mustn't! Oh please, Tim. Promise me you won't.'

'Sorry! I'm afraid I must!'

'Oh, you are awful!'

I had been acquainted with the up-and-coming actress, Miss Prunella Scales, for all of five minutes before she informed me she had assumed my father was gay. Pru had played opposite my father in a production of *Pride and Prejudice* for the BBC – he as Mr Collins and her as Lydia Bennet – and while discussing the show with her she had made the remark to me about Lockwood West without even considering the possibility of us being related. Apparently, he'd decided to give Mr Collins a rather camp performance. My father found it wildly amusing when I told him and informed my wife-to-be, of whom he later became very fond, that he considered her observation a compliment.

'I'm so terribly sorry,' she said. About a hundred times.

This all happened way back in July 1961. She and I had been cast in a poorly written and altogether improbable BBC play entitled *She Died Young*, which had been subtitled by the cast *And None Too Soon*. Pru was to play a bishop's daughter who gets debauched by one of the leading actors and I, who had to make do with one solitary line (par for the course in those days), was to play a Regency buck. The line, incidentally, was, 'Can't say I blame him, sir. Damnee, she's a morsel!' Subtle, then.

The production was doomed to failure for a number of different reasons. As I said, the script was a real stinker but, as if sensing that this abomination should never see the light of day, every time we tried to record the damned thing the BBC electricians went on strike. 'Sorry, everyone,' the assistant director would say. 'Nothing happening yet, I'm afraid. You may as well go for a walk or something.' As well as sparing the British public's eyes and ears, this turn of events, or should I say non-events, forced Pru and me to spend rather a lot of time together.

'*Times* crossword, Tim?' she'd suggest, after we'd been informed of yet another delay.

'OK then,' I'd reply.

Immediately we'd find somewhere quiet and over a packet of Polo mints we'd complete roughly half of *The Times* crossword, tease each other mercilessly and laugh a great deal.

I used to be mad about waistcoats in those days and actually had quite a smart collection. I'd started wearing them while I was doing A levels (they complimented the derivative poetry I used to write) and they used to amuse Pru no end.

'Which one are you wearing?' she'd say with breathless

anticipation after having hurried from the bus station to the studio.

'Ta da!' I'd reply upon removing my coat.

'Oh, you wore that one on Monday,' she'd complain. 'What about the nice green and red one. Be a love and wear that one tomorrow, would you?'

At this point in time, Pru and me were just friends. A mutual attraction existed but I was in fact already married (although unhappily so) and had a young daughter named Juliet. We did, however, flirt quite a bit and this soon caught the attention of our fellow actors.

'Be careful,' one of them said to me. 'People are talking.'

'Let them,' I remember saying in reply.

Around this time, I recall Pru and me going to the cinema one afternoon to watch a film called *The Grass is Greener* starring Cary Grant, Deborah Kerr, Robert Mitcham and Jean Simmons. I don't remember much about the film, except for the fact that its subject matter was unrequited love and infidelity, which I must admit made us both feel rather uncomfortable. Worse still, the female character involved in the affair, played by Deborah Kerr, eventually renounced her love for Cary Grant's character and returned to her family. Oh dear.

Had Pru and me not been falling for each other I doubt very much whether our friendship would have remained intact, least of all progressed. Scandals of any kind were to be avoided at all costs by young and ambitious actors, as they still are today, and Pru and me were acutely aware of this. Even so, our burgeoning yet unfulfilled adoration for one another compelled us to continue sharing Polo mints, flirting, teasing, laughing and failing to complete *The Times* crossword.

As the strike went on, a decision was finally made to postpone the recording until the beginning of August and so we each went our separate ways. Sadly, by the time we were called back I'd been offered a part in a touring production of a Brian Rix farce entitled *Simple Spymen*. So my one solitary Regency line, alas, would have to be articulated by somebody else.

I still have the postcard that Pru sent to me after learning of my fate. It reads:

Shattered you're not with us – paralytic tedium of it all now totally unrelieved . . . Returning fresh to this script is to realize anew the unspeakable (in every sense) banality of every single line. Hope your play is fun. Do ring up when you get back and come to dinner.

As sad and despondent as we both were at this turn of events, it sparked an ongoing communication which, over time, propelled us into the forefront of one another's minds. With a scandal still threatening to engulf us, however, Pru decided to write in a disguised hand, adopt a *nom de plume* and pretend to be a fan of mine. After we'd managed to steal some time together in Oxford, she wrote:

Dear Mr West,

I thought you were lovely in Oxford this week. I saw you several times, oh you were good. It made all the difference to my life. Of course, you have just the sort of character I like, and you certainly do it well, don't you?

H. Green (Miss)

Far from being loyal to H. Green (Miss), Pru used to change her pseudonyms regularly and it got to a point where I couldn't always tell the difference. In November 1961, while on tour in *Simple Spymen*, I wrote to Pru from Pacitto's ice cream and coffee bar in Stockton-on-Tees regarding one such anomaly. Although a welcome one.

Yes, well. Rather cheered this morning by receiving a fan letter purporting to be from Mrs Angiolina Tabone, Gili's Dispensary, Sleema, Malta, and containing some raffle tickets for a local school playing field. If this is you really, I'd rather you didn't tell me, because it's the best thing that's happened this week.

That day in Oxford was one I shall never forget for as long as I live. The weather was charming and after having lunch in a pub we went down to Folly Bridge and took a punt on the River Cherwell. She talked about her boyfriend at the time, Robin, and I told her a bit about my wife, Jacqueline. It was a polite exchange, and we were careful not to touch on the thing that we knew was happening to us.

As my relationship with Pru flourished, albeit remotely and in Pru's case sometimes incognito, my marriage unfortunately disintegrated. Jacqueline and I had married very young, and it had become apparent early on in our relationship that she suffered from what then were known as 'emotional highs and lows' and which today is called bipolar disorder. As a result, she had to be hospitalized on a sadly regular basis. There was nothing I could do. We had a young daughter, Juliet, who became my priority.

Pru accepted this situation philosophically and with good grace. Pursuing a life as an actor is, of course, a transient and unpredictable endeavour. As a consequence, we are quite often better disposed at coping with unresolved issues. Out of sight, out of mind, as they say. Although I would sometimes divulge certain details about my domestic situation, it never affected my relationship with Pru for the very simple reason that we spent so little time together. It wasn't through want of trying, though. Good heavens no.

On our fiftieth wedding anniversary, almost ten years ago, we estimated that we had probably spent less than half of that time in each other's company, such is the lot of a brace of jobbing actors. Nevertheless, there's no doubt that the nature of our profession has enhanced our relationship. When we are apart, we miss each other wildly and write letters or make telephone calls, and when we are together, we always have plenty to talk about. It works for us. Always has.

Pru is almost as proficient at the sadly near-forgotten art of letter-writing as she is at acting, in terms of both talent and also application. And at solving *The Times* crossword, at which she was always so much more adept than I was. Her command of the English language is perfect. At the start of our relationship, she would write to me almost every day, sometimes twice. It was our form of texting or emailing, you might say, and had there been four or five post deliveries a day (and enough time to write the letters) there would have been millions of other people just like us ready to take advantage.

I'm digressing slightly here, but one of my very favourite letters from this period was the one that Pru wrote to me during the interval of a show that I came to watch. It was a light comedy (light on comedy, that is) in three acts called *The Marriage Game* and I'd travelled down from London to Eastbourne specially to see it. Or specially to see Pru. It was a good play. Afterwards, this is what she wrote to me.

> *This is the first letter I've ever written to someone under the same roof. If you still are, that is. Well, at least you are seeing it in the worst conditions audience-wise we've suffered so far. We're all quite hysterical, as must be only too painfully apparent. Poor love, I'm so sorry, it's much less agonizing with a really rousing house. Act II. Oh no, really. The moment Rex kissed me, an old woman in the third row of the stalls shrieked, 'That's right, get in.' In Eastbourne! . . . Or was it perhaps, 'Get him.' Don't know, feel ghastly, so false and self-conscious and theatrical. Darling, THANK YOU for coming all the way and sorry it wasn't a better show for you. And thank you for the nice lunch.*

There were just two challenges that this ancient form of communication presented: the crippling cost of paper and where to put all the letters received. Bearing in mind we probably spent no more than two days a month together, this could amount to anything between twenty-eight and forty letters each month.

'I've just been going through the drawers of my desk,' Pru said in one such letter. 'This means opening them one by one, taking a despairing look inside and shutting them again as quickly as possible. The second long one down is crammed to the point of total inertia!'

Affording paper was an easier problem to overcome, at least for Pru. Radio was still in its pomp and in the early 1960s she was never off it.

'The only drawer that isn't stuffed full of your letters is stuffed full of radio scripts,' she went on. 'If I cut off the bottoms, which I can use for telephone messages (always the thrifty hussif), the result is exactly the same size as the extremely expensive Kingsize Bourgeois Bond. So there!'

These daily letters to each other became our lifeblood as they were our only insight into how we were feeling and what news each other had.

'Wish you were here,' Pru wrote one day while some-where on tour. 'It's a cold clear autumn day and everything smells marvellous and I miss you. The more I think about it the luckier I feel to have you and the more terrifying it is to know I haven't really. I am very, very SLOW about some things, and still can't believe that this is actually IT.'

Her next letter which arrived by the next post read, 'I have just realized that I wrote to Sir John G. [Gielgud] last week asking to read for "Lucy", a part that doesn't exist – at least not in *The School for Scandal*. Have written frivolous letter admitting mistake, but don't suppose anyone's going to audition an actress who doesn't know the difference between that and *The Rivals*. Darling, going to post this now, though shan't have yours till this p.m. in London.'

Sadly, I must have been late posting my reply so when my letter didn't arrive Pru put pen to paper.

'Oh WOE,' she wrote. 'No such letter from you today.

Determined not to ring up.' The following day, however, all was well again. 'Much better today. Two lovely letters just arrived!'

The longer this went on the more painful it became and so meeting up became an obsession. Train timetables were an indispensable part of our luggage and we managed to contrive a series of Sunday assignations at crossing points in our two schedules. If she was playing in Bristol, for instance, and was about to move to Sheffield, and I had left Manchester and was going to Coventry, we would meet in Birmingham. On the occasions when a diversion like this wasn't possible one of us would take a nocturnal train, stay for the day, and take a nocturnal train back again.

Talking publicly about our relationship still wasn't an option as, despite her being quite well at the time, nothing with Jacqueline had been finalized. It had to be settled, however, and soon. Pru felt isolated and as much as I tried reassuring her that there was no blame to be apportioned, it made little difference. She was, I'm afraid, rather in turmoil.

In an effort to resolve matters with Jacqueline I spoke to my solicitor who advised me that the easiest route in bringing an end to all this was to let Jacqueline divorce me for adultery with a 'person unknown'. For a moment I wondered if he'd forgotten which one of us he was representing, but he explained that, providing I didn't contest it, that would be the quickest and easiest way to get a divorce.

'But how am I going to get caught committing adultery with a person unknown?' I asked him.

'I'll arrange everything,' he said. 'Jacqueline's solicitor

will hire an enquiry agent who will catch you *in flagrante delicto.*'

The arrangements were conducted in a very civilized manner and when I spoke to Jacqueline about it, we laughed uproariously for a good hour.

'Well, you're an actor,' she said. 'It'll be a bit like one of those farces you've been appearing in.'

Strangely enough, after having managed to persuade Pru to take on the role of the 'person unknown', we set about arranging a venue for our tryst. The most suitable option seemed to be a hotel in Cheltenham while I was rehearsing one of the aforementioned farces. *Simple Spymen* again, to be exact.

When the time came, the private investigator got in touch to say that he was going to have trouble making it to Cheltenham.

'Perhaps I could save you the trouble by providing evidence that could be noticed by the chambermaid,' I suggested. From whom he could later take a statement.

'No, that won't do at all,' he told me. 'Hotels give strict instructions to their chambermaids that they are to see and hear nothing. Would you want your staff giving evidence in a divorce case when they should be making beds?'

He had a point, I suppose.

We finally fixed a day when the agent could come and surprise us.

'I can be there by about 9.30 a.m.,' he said.

'Too late, I'm afraid. My person unknown is off up to London for the day. She'll have left the hotel about half an hour before.'

'No matter,' exclaimed the agent. 'The physical presence of Miss X –' as he insisted on calling her – 'is not
obligatory. Nor, for that matter, is yours.'

'Really?' I enquired.

'Twin indentations on the pillows will suffice,' he said.
'Though perhaps an item of ladies' night apparel would
just serve to clinch matters.'

Jacqueline was right, this was akin to a farce.

Later that day Pru went off to Marks and Spencer to buy
a matter-clinching class nightgown and on the morning
that we were supposed to 'give evidence' I draped it over
the bed, thumped both pillows several times and went off
to rehearsal.

At the time, Pru and me had been in love with each
other for many months. Desperately in love, as a matter of
fact. Despite this, our situation had been so complex and
fraught with trepidation that neither of us had dared to
make a declaration to each other through fear of com-
pounding things. Or, worse still, losing each other forever.
We were terrified.

It's fair to say that Pru had to bear the brunt of all this
far more than I did. On the face of it, my own situation
was probably the more challenging of the two but because
I wasn't on tour quite as much, I was able to enjoy the support of my friends far more. Pru, on the other hand, had
to make do with a daily letter from me reassuring her that
everything was going to be all right. One of her letters
from this period chips away at my heart to this very day.

*Still frightened of accepting responsibility for something I can't help
regarding as a major disaster, although it may be a wonderfully*

good thing all round. I am a COWARD. No, actually, it isn't entirely that, it's the feeling that perhaps in this case one might be behaving in a horribly selfish and inhuman way, grabbing what one wants for oneself without any regard for two people in a very much weaker position.

I replied:

Being a terribly unsure person in lots of ways, I nearly always require to feel RIGHT. In the sight of others, I mean. Want to have the approval of absolutely everyone . . . So, I don't quite understand your attitude about requiring to be completely wrong over the whole thing in everybody's eyes. Where have you found the strength to withstand such censure? I admire it very much.

Despite me trying to make light of the situation, Pru's solitude and sense of guilt affected me in a way I had never known before. I'd been controlled for far too long by my domestic situation and professional reputation, and I'd had my fill of it. I was in love with Miss Prunella Scales, and I didn't care who knew.

God Speed My Love, the Girls Say Hello

The only competition I faced after Pru and me became a couple was from Peter Sellers, of all people. Six months into our relationship, Pru got offered a part in a film he was appearing in, *Waltz of the Toreadors,* alongside the marvellous actress Margaret Leighton. Peter played a retired General who, after retreating to Sussex in order to write his memoirs, comes unstuck when his womanizing past begins to catch up with him. Ahem. Pru played one of the General's daughters whom he thoroughly dislikes, and although I don't remember enjoying the film very much when I went to see it, it did rather well at the box office.

'The strangest thing happened to me today,' Pru said, after returning from Pinewood Studios one day. 'Peter Sellers asked me if I'd like to have dinner with him.'

'Why on earth is that strange?' I asked her. 'He doesn't know that you and I are together.'

'Yes, he does! I told him yesterday.'

'What, so this isn't the first time he's asked you?'

'Good heavens, no. This must be the fourth or fifth. It's all a bit bizarre as I'm playing his daughter.'

'Well, are you going to accept?' I asked, teasing her. 'After all, he's very famous and probably quite rich.'

'I haven't decided yet,' said Pru, teasing me back. 'I'll be sure to let you know, though.'

During his final ten years on earth, the only part of Peter Sellers' existence that potentially exceeded the volatility of his love life was his film career, in that he made some very strange choices and some appalling films. Strangely enough, my own endeavours in the film industry have also been, shall we say, rather hit and miss, and in 1974 I agreed to appear in a film starring Peter called *Soft Beds, Hard Battles*. This too was an absolute shocker, and my only memory of making it is witnessing first-hand Peter's unorthodox way of courting the press. After falling in love with a member of the unit, which he did frequently, he would invite them out for dinner, as he had Pru and most probably hundreds of others. Once that was achieved, he would then get someone in his entourage to inform the members of the press that an assignation was taking place. Nothing strange there, I hear you say. It's called 'playing the game'. Be that as it may, what separated Peter's behaviour from that of a press-hungry celebrity was that, as he was leaving the restaurant, instead of posing for photographs he would berate them for invading his privacy and call them all the names under the sun. He really was quite a strange man.

If you try to ignore the farcically convoluted trysts, generalized turmoil and a divorce, mine and Pru's was actually quite a happy courtship. Eventful, but happy. Both of us were on tour almost constantly during that period and when Jacqueline and I finally agreed to part (she too had fallen for somebody by then – her lodger, who, incredibly, was actually called Roger) I was able to move from the family home in Wimbledon to a bedsit in Turnham Green.

It was plain and nothing special – a bed, a desk, a cup, a few plates and a handful of knives and forks – but it was comfortable.

Whenever the owner of the house in which the bedsit was situated, a Mr Pritchard, heard me closing my door behind me he would stop whatever he was doing, meet me at the bottom of the stairs, tell me I was looking rather tired and then enquire as to whether my bowels were functioning normally. Before I could answer he would exclaim, 'I have been as regular as clockwork for over fifty years. Did you know that? Seven-thirty every morning. You can set your clock by me.'

I remember telling Pru about this unfortunate conversation one day and she immediately made a suggestion.

'Well, why don't you then?' she said.

'I beg your pardon?' I retorted.

'Get up at seven-thirty and see if it's true. Why don't you? You'll hear the flush.'

I tested Mr Pritchard for the best part of a week, and he was absolutely on the dot. Most impressive.

Unlike the poor soul who was in love with her, Pru lived in a light, well-furnished and generously proportioned flat in Flood Street, Chelsea. She shared it with three other girls who were surprisingly tolerant of my presence. This, I soon found out, was because they had already learned to embrace the swinging sixties and had devised a system whereby, if ever one of their parents called by unexpectedly while their daughter had company, the person answering the door always had an arsenal of plausible and well-rehearsed excuses at the ready.

On the rare occasion when I wasn't touring, I would

often do odd-jobs around the flat such as wallpapering or putting up shelves. In addition to voicing their thanks and appreciation, Pru's cohabitants would often furnish me with all the latest scandal. Far from doing the decent thing and turning a deaf ear to these revelations, I became a professional gossip and was eager to hear the next instalment. It was akin to being embroiled in my own personal soap opera, in a way, with each girl enthusiastically delivering their own storyline. It was wrong of me, but sometimes I'd mix things up a bit by repeating a piece of gossip to one girl that had been confided to me by another.

'Did you hear that Mary's got a new boyfriend?'

'NO? Really? That was quick! Who is he?'

'Oh, I'm not at liberty to say, I'm afraid.'

'Oh, go on Tim! I'll tell you about Joan's latest indiscretion if you do.'

'All right. It's Ken who works in the pub. She's seeing him again tonight. Now then, about this indiscretion?'

It was an absolute delight.

I ended up renting a room from a friend of the girls' called Douglas Dryburgh, who lived just around the corner in Tedworth Square. As well as bringing me closer to Pru (at least when we were both in town) it helped to ensure that I remained well informed!

If Pru and me ever wished to and we had the time, we could probably fill several books with our touring escapades. The 1950s and 1960s in particular were especially abundant in this regard, and for a variety of different reasons. For a start, there were the digs, or lodgings as they were sometimes known. These days they're much harder to find but back in the fifties and sixties every actor would have had in their possession a national catalogue of land-ladies, the great names of the touring circuit: Mrs Treacy in Nottingham, Mrs Cairns in Edinburgh, Mrs Munday in Glasgow, Mrs Hellewell in Blackpool, Mrs Blakemore in Wolverhampton and so on.

The most renowned was Mrs McKay who owned and ran an establishment called Astra House (the Home to the Stars) in Manchester. Her hilarious malapropisms used to have Pru and me in fits and they were renowned throughout the profession. 'I've got that Allan Cuthbert-son coming next week,' she told Pru. 'I hear he's a bit pendatic.'

I used to question Mrs McKay about all the famous guests she'd had to stay and one day she confided that an archaeologist from Israel had once resided at Astra House (the Home to the Stars) while making a documentary for Granada Television and had shown her the 'Deep Sea Rolls'.

Years later Mrs McKay managed to expand Astra House by taking out a mortgage on the property next door and I asked her one day whether any of her rival proprietors had considered following suit. 'Oh no, love,' she said pursing her lips. 'They don't have the cholesterol.'

Letters that were written while on tour would, more often than not, begin with a description of our current accommodation and I thought it might be of interest if I included one or two examples. Here are two from Pru that she wrote to me while on tour in *The Marriage Game*, fol-lowed by one she wrote to Bim some years earlier.

In Eastbourne . . .

Have a comfortable ground-floor bedroom, with only three kinds of wallpaper and four kinds of chintz, the usual neo-Jacobean rocking wardrobe, dressing table, running H&C (Ascot), one of the most lurid linoleums in my entire experience of touring, and, final luxury, a large modern gas stove in the corner in case the notices are bad. An army of binmen arrive at 6 a.m. and perform a dustbin routine just outside the window, but I think this is a once-weekly occurrence.

In Brighton . . .

Good digs, nice landlady, cat, two boxers (one in twilight of gestation) and a parrot. Tend to fall violently in love with boxers (no, no, the DOGS, you fool) and am sorely tempted to bespeak one of the puppies. My room has a vast double and two single beds. It does seem a waste.

In Oxford . . .

It's not much of a place (the digs, not Oxford) but madly convenient. There are legions of undergraduates living here and we all have breakfast at a refectory table in the basement. My room is tiny, and I have to do all the washing (clothes, not me) at the theatre, but digs are so awful in Oxford (as far as I can make out every other building is a brothel), that I am very lucky.

Here are two from me, including just one example of how we used to take our revenge on unscrupulous landladies, which happened in Newcastle. But first, a threat of home-lessness in Wilmslow, which I wrote in 1962 while on tour with Andy Sachs in *Simple Spymen*.

There are no such things as theatrical lodgings in Wilmslow. After a whole wet Sunday of searching, Andy and I felt we were faced with three alternatives: to commute nightly from Manchester, to take out an overdraft to stay in Prestbury, or to set fire to the theatre. In the end we went and had a drink in a pub and pleaded with the landlord, who obligingly turned his sons out of their bedrooms for us. Only two more weeks of the tour to go, then back on the dole. I haven't been able to save much out of £22.10s a week. Hey ho.

And Newcastle . . .

A good week in my favourite touring theatre, the Newcastle Theatre Royal, was somewhat marred by the most appalling digs. Fiona Walker, Hazel Coppen, Neil Stacey and I were all together, and agreed that forty-five shillings a night without breakfast for a filthy room with damp sheets and continual rudeness from the landlady was not to be borne. We had to stick it out for the week, though, because there was absolutely nowhere else, but before we left, we put into operation a device from my father's touring days. Hazel went out early to buy a pair of kippers and a screwdriver, and then while Fiona held the landlady in the kitchen in argument about the bill, Neil and I went into the front parlour, unscrewed the back of the Rexine sofa, inserted the kippers and screwed it together again. The only sadness is, of course, that we shall not be around in a week's time to savour that mature effect.

But it wasn't just the digs and/or the proprietors that could be disagreeable. The theatres could be too, on occasion. I remember being in Blackpool one year over Christmas. I was sharing digs with an actor called Harry Rowson, who was playing King Rat in the pantomime on the South Pier. On the first night, the heat from the stage lighting had melted the snow on the roof so that water had then poured through the flies.

'The actual heating has broken down,' I wrote, 'and audiences sit in their overcoats and gloves. The six chorus girls dance in thick woollen stockings, and my friend wears a selection of pullovers under his rat costume. I've offered to go to a matinee, but he says not to. He has the most appalling cold, and I'm getting it.'

My next letter amused Pru no end when she received it and, over the years, she's asked me to repeat the story often.

While on tour in *Simple Spymen* I often shared digs with the company manager, Bertie Parham. He was about seventy years of age and reminded me very much of a popular comedian from my childhood called Leslie Henson. Bertie seemed to regard me as his natural contemporary in the company, presumably because I was playing a character about his age (but at least twice my own). This is from my letter to Pru.

Bertie has been in the business a very long time. And he is very informative. Somewhere – Leeds, I think it was – our landlady asked us to sign the visitors book and then turned back the pages to show us names of the famous performers she'd had to stay in the past. I noticed that some of the signatories had added the initials 'L.D.O.' after their names, and I wondered what this stood for. 'Licentiate of Dramatic Orthodoxy' seemed unlikely, so I asked Bertie. 'Coded information,' he told me. 'Landlady's Daughter Obliges.'

Next on the list we have travel, which for many decades was the bane of every touring actor's life. Trains were frequent enough, but they were often slow and many of the more provincial lines could be somewhat unpredictable. I suffered this on many occasions, but never more entertainingly than while I was on tour in Farquhar's *The Constant Couple* and an adaptation of E. M. Forster's *A Room with a View.*

Rather an extraordinary journey here. Engine failure meant we missed our connection at Barrow-in-Furness, but they announced that a train which should have been going just as far as Millom, a few stations up the line, would be extended to Workington, which suited us. When we got to Millom, Richard Cottrell, John Warner and I, we seemed to be waiting rather a long time and I got out to investigate. There was no one on the platform and there was no one else on the train. There was also nobody driving the train or guarding it, nor was there anyone inside the station building, or in the road outside, or anywhere in sight. The rooks cawed in the elms. The church clock struck 6.30. A little way down the line was a signal box, and I walked up to it. The signalman was there all right, having a cup of tea and seemed surprised to see me. I explained our situation. Nobody had told him, he said, nor as far as he knew had told anyone else, that our train was supposed to go any further. The driver and guard, he assumed, had cycled home. There was, however, another crew due to arrive on the next up train, to take our train on an Outward Bound excursion to Ravenglass, leaving at 7.20. I walked back to the train, and when the new guard appeared he kindly suggested there was no real need to wait till 7.20 and if we cared to go and have a drink in the village pub, he'd come and fetch us as soon as the Outward Bound boys had

*been rounded up. So we went to the pub, and that's where all the
boys were, playing a fruit machine called Super Jolly Taverner.
We tried to chivvy them back to the station, and they all thought
Richard, who insisted on introducing us as 'strolling players', quite
hilarious. We finally got them on board and reached Whitehaven
at 8.30 – thank God we didn't have a show that night. Nowhere
to eat in Whitehaven at all, but as we walked up the hill, very
cross, we were met in the road by a farmer's wife who asked us if
we were hungry, and took us in for some minced lamb, macaroni
cheese, fresh strawberries, home fruit cake and tea.*

On 23 December 1961, while appearing in Blackpool, I
received a letter from Pru informing me that she and her
newsworthy cohabitants in Chelsea were intending to
throw a party on New Year's Eve. 'Please come if you can,
darling,' Pru said. 'We're all dying to see you.'

I'd already been on tour for several months and, with
several more months ahead of me, I sat down with the
relevant train timetable to see if it might be possible. We'd
been booked for two weeks in Blackpool, playing twice on
Christmas Day, and as the intervening Sunday was New
Year's Eve, I could travel down to London on Sunday
morning and then head back the following day in good
time for the show. Pru was delighted when I told her, by
letter, of course.

'We will meet any train you'd like to catch,' she wrote
in reply. 'Sitting-room bed will be free for thee. Sweater
finished, not actually made for two, though you might not
think so.'

The party was a great success and at some point, in the
wee small hours, after having talked so much I never had a

chance to overdo it on the drink, thank the lord, I crept sleepily into bed. Pru woke me at seven o'clock in the morning with a cup of tea.

'You have to catch your train, darling. Would you like me to open the curtains?'

'Go ahead,' I said, reaching for the cup and saucer. 'I'm actually feeling OK. What a marvellous evening, though. Well done all of you.'

As Pru opened the curtains she gasped. 'Oh dear,' she said taking a step back. 'Tim, come and look.'

Despite still lying prostrate on the bed, I could see from where I was that the usual vista across Flood Street had been whitewashed. 'Oh, blast. Is there a lot of it?' I asked reaching for my dressing gown.

'Yes, I'm afraid there is. Oh dear.'

Not only was the ground outside buried underfoot but the snow was still falling heavily. 'Put the radio on, would you?' I asked Pru.

The news, when it came through, was not good. There were no main line trains out of Euston at all. 'What on earth are you going to do?' asked Pru.

'I've no idea. Find some huskies? I'll have to get there somehow.'

Anxiously, I rang Paddington station. Western Region trains were severely curtailed, but some were still running. In those days there was a service from Paddington to Birkenhead, so if I could catch a train there, I'd be able to cross the Mersey to Liverpool, catch another train to Preston and then another to Blackpool. It would be quite a journey, but it was worth a try.

'All right, there's a train at ten past nine,' I said, after putting down the receiver. 'Which gives me just under two hours to get to Paddington.'

'It's only a couple of miles,' said Pru. 'Even in the snow you should be able to make it in under an hour.'

Actually, it took me closer to an hour and a half, such was the severity of the snow. London seemed all but deserted and as I walked from Flood Street to the King's Road, before venturing north onto Sydney Steet, I spotted a dozen or so stranded cars, four or five pedestrians and a visibly disconsolate police constable taking refuge inside a shop doorway on the corner of Chelsea Manor Street.

When I finally reached Hyde Park, I was met by deep snow that had all but covered the gate leading onto West Carriage Drive. There was no time to try to clear a path so after prizing open the gate I accepted my fate and walked directly into the drift. Fortunately, my time was not yet up and after emerging triumphant through the other side I ploughed on – literally – circumnavigating the Serpentine and continuing north along Lancaster Gate before turning left onto London Street, and there it was, Paddington station.

When I finally reached Paddington, and after purchasing my ticket and ensuring that my train was running on time, which it was, I broke the habit of a lifetime and called Pru.

'You made it then?' she said.

'Well, at least as far as Paddington,' I replied.

'Yes, of course. Silly me. God speed, my love, the girls say hello. I'm just in the middle of writing you a letter. You might receive it within the month.'

'"Ful ofte in game a sooth I have herd saye," as

Geoffrey Chaucer once said. I'll call you when I get to the theatre. Bye, darling.'

As the engine came to life and slowly began hauling the series of cumbersome carriages westward, the deluge of snow, which had begun some six or seven hours ago, continued apace. Our progress was hampered continually by frozen points, but we finally pulled into Birkenhead station almost seven hours later at four o'clock. When I arrived at the ferry terminal, I was told by a guard that the next crossing would be in just over five minutes, which led me to believe, momentarily at least, that my luck might be changing. Alas, as I alighted onto the landing stage on the Liverpool side of the river fifteen minutes later, I could see immediately that the only activity at the taxi rank was a burgeoning queue of people. There was only one thing for it. I would have to run to Lime Street.

The snow was falling harder than ever and when I arrived at Lime Street station, exhausted and wet through, I looked hopefully in the direction of the departures board. A train was due to leave in ten minutes according to the board but when I went to purchase my ticket the gentleman serving me didn't seem very confident.

'It's fifty-fifty at the moment, sir,' he said. 'If I were you, I'd start thinking about alternative modes of transport.' We were back to huskies again.

The train from Lime Street to Preston eventually pulled out of the station at about ten to six and managed to crawl as far as Ormskirk, before giving up the ghost.

'Sorry, ladies and gents, but we won't be going any further,' said the guard. 'There'll be no more trains from this station this evening.'

I was desperate to call Pru but knew that she'd worry so decided against it. What on earth was I to do, though? I'd never been to Ormskirk before and even if I had, the entire town was hidden under a blanket of thick snow. Just keep moving, I said to myself.

I tramped aimlessly through the streets of Ormskirk for about half an hour until I finally came across a garage, in the forecourt of which stood a taxi with chains fitted to its wheels. Glory be! After tracking down the driver I pleaded with him to take me to Blackpool. At first, I think he thought that I'd escaped from some kind of asylum but after explaining my position and the history of how I had arrived at his establishment he gamely agreed to have a go at transporting me to the theatre.

We can't have gone more than a couple of miles before we ran into a snowdrift. My second of the day. 'Sorry, mate,' the driver said apologetically. 'It'd take us a couple of hours to dig our way through this. I'm going to have to turn back.' I looked at my watch. It was already a quarter to seven and with Blackpool being about forty miles away we'd never have made it anyway. Blast!

After turning around, we drove back to Ormskirk. 'Could you drop me at a pub?' I asked the driver. 'I need to call the theatre as soon as possible and then after finding a bed for the night I'll need a stiff drink, or two.'

Bertie, our company manager, was furious when I told him, and rightly so. After all, I had committed the worst sin in the book as far as an actor is concerned. I had missed a performance. Absolutely nothing, short of death or serious illness, excuses us from missing even an entrance, let alone a performance. I've certainly never done it since.

The plain fact is, however, that given the time allowed I should never have gone to London in the first place, and I felt deeply ashamed of myself.

'You do realize that Maurice is scared of acting?' said Bertie. Maurice Baring, my understudy, was a retired ballet dancer and he was indeed terrified of acting. 'He'll have a heart attack when I tell him.'

I got on very well with Maurice so hoped very much that he wouldn't actually have a heart attack.

With the help of the driver, who I now looked upon as being my own guardian angel, I managed to find not only an extremely comfortable bed for the night but also a more than satisfactory evening meal. It was all far more than I deserved but what could I do?

By the following morning the snow had abated somewhat, and I was able to get to Blackpool, although it still took me the best part of three hours. The first thing I did when I arrived at the theatre, after I'd sought forgiveness from Bertie who was waiting for me at the stage door, was take a bottle of champagne and a thousand apologies and thanks to Maurice. According to Bertie he'd been brilliant, despite the fact that no more than twenty or so people had been able to brave their way to the theatre.

'It was all fine in the end,' said Maurice. 'In fact, I wasn't terrified at all. I'd rather not have to do it again, though, if it's all the same to you.'

'You have my word, Maurice,' I vowed.

The following day, the letter that Pru had written during the start of my ill-fated journey arrived at my digs. My word, it was a tonic. Not only because I'd been feeling slightly despondent post my return to the theatrical fold and was in need of a boost, but because Pru made a suggestion in the letter that would bring us closer together.

Darling heart,

Thank you from all of us for coming and for all your help and hard work, and thank you from me for the record, washing up this morning and coming at all. Here is your collar. Found in Mary's room by a FASCINATED Mrs Cole [the cleaner]. She found Jean Marie's waistcoat in Nicky's room too. Can't decide whether this will shock her into giving notice or give her such a vicarious thrill that she will decide to stay after all. Still can't get over your success les girls. No, that sounds insulting. Are you Well Known Lady Killer? Joan says you should come and live here. I suppose if Nicky goes abroad, you could, come to that.

Yes, I thought, as I read the letter. What a good idea.

I Think the Lady Has Already Retired, Sir

P ru and me had decided to get married while my divorce from Jacqueline was going through. In fact, unless my memory is playing tricks on me, the catalyst for the conversation was the 'Miss X' episode. Rightly or wrongly, I had offered to be the guilty party in the divorce, which had shone a spotlight directly onto my relationship with Pru. We made each other very happy and given what we'd had to go through, I thought we deserved the right to start making a few plans of our own.

We chose the ring while we were down in Brighton one day. There's an area there called The Lanes, a labyrinth of narrow roads and squares situated between North Laine and the seafront. It was famous then for its jewellery shops (and still is, so I believe) and Pru and me spent several hours looking for an engagement ring. We eventually settled on a sapphire and diamond ring that we found in an antique shop. Pru had wanted an emerald, but unfortunately my coffers wouldn't run to it. The cheapest emerald engagement ring we'd managed to find had been £15, which was about £5 over my budget.

'This one looks rather nice,' said Pru, after spying the sapphire in one of the more archaic-looking emporiums. Her countenance as she gazed at the piece reassured me that her enthusiasm was genuine, so without any further ado I checked the price (£8.10s), sought out an assistant, and then handed over the money.

I fully appreciate that the customary way of going about this, at least in those days, was for the would-be groom to purchase the ring independently and in secret and then propose to his bride-to-be at a suitable time and loca-tion, but we were adamant that we wanted to do this together. After all, we'd already decided that we wanted to get married and bearing in mind what an engagement ring was going to signify, it was an experience we wanted to share.

The significance of us buying the ring together was, I'm afraid, to the detriment of me performing any kind of actual proposal and after two or three weeks I still hadn't officially popped the question. Then, one Sunday after-noon while we were on our way to visit my parents, we stopped at some traffic lights on the outskirts of Brighton.

'So, can I wear my ring now?' asked Pru.

'What are you talking about?' I said.

'My engagement ring. It's been sitting here in my hand-bag for almost three weeks.'

'Oh, good heavens!' I said. 'I completely forgot. Yes, of course. Of course, you can. My word, I suppose I'd better propose, really. Erm, Pru darling, will you marry me?'

Funnily enough, my decree absolute had come through the previous week, so it was perfect timing.

'Oh, at last!' she said. 'You're making an honest woman of me. Yes, of course I will.'

I took the ring and after putting it on Pru's finger I went to give my beautiful bride-to-be a kiss. Just as I did so the traffic lights turned to green. 'Sorry, dear,' I said, leaving poor Pru with her eyes closed and lips pursed. 'The kiss will have to wait.'

'Oh, bother!'

On the various occasions when Pru and me have been asked about our wedding day the conversations tend to be quite short, for the simple reason that there really isn't very much to tell. After becoming engaged, officially at least, at the traffic lights in Brighton, we'd gone about our business as usual, and we were both extremely busy. I was rehearsing a play called *Gentle Jack* starring Dame Edith Evans and Kenneth Williams, and Pru was rehearsing a new situation comedy starring her and Richard Briers called *Marriage Lines*. Once again then, and to my eternal shame, I had forgotten that getting engaged was supposed to be a penultimate act and not a final one. It was a colleague in *Gentle Jack* who reminded me.

'Have you and Pru set a date then?' he asked.

'For what?' I enquired.

'The big day. You know, your wedding?'

'Oh, yes, that. No, not yet. We've been a bit busy.'

That evening I spoke to Pru, and we decided that we should put wheels in motion. She would have loved to have had a church wedding but with me being a divorcee it wasn't feasible. That being the case, we decided to keep things as low-key as possible, choosing once again to focus purely on the significance of the occasion.

We called Chelsea Register Office and the first date they had available that suited us both was Saturday 26th October, 1963. 'That'll do,' we said. In addition to us, the bride and groom, we had two witnesses present – Pru's friend, Betty Turner, and Pru's cousin, Stephen Kaye. By the time the wedding took place the first series of *Marriage Lines* had gone to air and Pru had become a household name. The fact that she played a newlywed in the show was not lost on the press and resulted in several headlines light-heartedly accusing Pru of swapping her current television husband for a new one. You know the kind of thing. Fortunately, though, the ladies and gentlemen of the press stopped short of gatecrashing the ceremony and everything went according to plan. After the service, which seemed to fly by, we had a few photographs taken outside the venue and then went for lunch at a marvellous restaurant we used to frequent called Prunier's, which is, alas, no longer there. This was a slightly more inclusive affair as in addition to me, Pru, Betty and Stephen, both sets of parents were in attendance.

Questions had been asked by our families beforehand as to why they nor anyone else had been invited to the ceremony and the answer to that was simple. With Pru being thrust into the public eye all of a sudden and with me being a divorcee (and a recent one at that) we had absolutely no clue what the reaction might be should the press and public get wind of our marriage, and moreover no idea of the effect that this might then have on our families and friends. Once we had explained this to them they were fine about not attending the ceremony, and the lunch afterwards was as joyous and celebratory as we had hoped it would be.

I'm sure this isn't the norm in these circumstances, but our honeymoon was a great deal more eventful than our wedding, at least in terms of what is worth recalling in a memoir that I'm assuming will not be sold from a high shelf.

Because of our hectic schedules, we simply didn't have time for what you might call a conventional honeymoon – two weeks in Paris, for example – so after much discussion and phoning around we decided to spend two nights at the Compleat Angler Hotel in Marlow, Buckinghamshire, which is approximately thirty miles from Chelsea. Not very exotic, I admit, but it was on the River Thames, was quite comfortable so we'd been told, and had a good restaurant and bar.

We kept the confirmation letter from the hotel, which reads:

Dear Sir,

We thank you for your letter and have much pleasure in confirming your reservation of one double bedded room with private bathroom for the nights of Saturday and Sunday, 26th and 27th October.

We have also reserved a table for two persons for dinner on the Saturday evening.

Looking forward to receiving you at the Compleat Angler and assuring you of our every endeavour to make your stay comfortable and enjoyable.

Yours faithfully,
Mr Michael A. Bentley, General Manager

What we hadn't been told about the Compleat Angler Hotel was that it was renowned for being – how can I put it? – an establishment favoured by those who might be indulging in some extramarital activities. Dirty weekends, in other words. The irony was that this was the first legitimate weekend Pru and me had ever spent together. We realized the moment we walked through the door – the guilt in the air seemed almost palpable. The guests all appeared to be rather flushed, which I suppose could have been for a variety of different reasons, and instead of talking normally everyone spoke in hushed tones, as did the staff. Throughout the entire weekend Pru was referred to as 'the lady', as in, 'the lady is waiting for you in the bar, sir.' The only thing they didn't do was follow it up with a conspiratorial wink. You could have inserted your marriage vows into every menu and left confetti on the tables, but the waiter would still have approached you discreetly and murmured, 'I think the *lady* has already retired, sir.'

The first thing we did on returning from our clean but dirty weekend was to find our own place to live. It took a while but a few months later we moved into a top-floor flat in Battersea, which was just over the river from where we'd been living in Chelsea and not too far from where we live now. The flat was situated just south of Battersea Park in a building called Albert Palace Mansions in Lurline Gardens. As well as being situated up five flights of rather steep stairs, the flat was not in very good condition. Even so, the rent was cheap and because we were quite young and relatively fit the stairs didn't intimidate us too much. Unlike the move itself. I forget how long it took exactly (I must have exorcised it from my memory) but because we couldn't afford to employ a removal company, we had to carry all of our belongings down Flood Street, over the Albert Bridge and through Battersea Park. About a mile and a half as the crow flies.

The biggest problem we had after moving in was with pigeons that had managed to get in through a ventilation hole and had nested under the bath. We didn't quite know what to do initially and so for the first couple of weeks or so we let them be and cohabited. They had to go eventually, of course, and I remember Pru feeling rather guilty about disturbing them. Unlike me. I don't mind sharing a bathroom with other people, but I've always been funny about pigeons.

Marriage Lines

Apart from us finally living under the same roof, the biggest change to our circumstances in the immediate term after getting married was Pru becoming a household name all of a sudden, thanks to *Marriage Lines*, and therefore instantly recognizable to a large proportion of the general public. Written by a nice man called Richard Waring, *Marriage Lines* had been created as a vehicle for her co-star Richard Briers, who had come to prominence the previous year in a sitcom based on a novel by Henry Cecil called *Brothers in Law*. Richard Waring had both written and starred in several episodes of that particular show and was of the opinion that its star, Richard Briers, had a bright future ahead of him. He certainley did.

Marriage Lines tells the story of a newly married couple, George and Kate Starling, who, after returning from their honeymoon, move into a new flat and begin their life together. It really is that simple and sees them learning how to cope with the ups and downs of married life. Pru got the part of Kate Starling thanks to Richard Briers, who became a great friend of ours and would eventually be godfather to our son, Sam. Pru had appeared with Richard briefly in a television play of some sort and fortunately he'd remembered her. I don't think she was quite sure whether or not to accept the part at first. Despite what we actors are always working towards, which in the main is

remaining employed as often as we possibly can, not everyone is comfortable being thrust into the limelight, and
especially in a show that could potentially result in you
being typecast.

Pru's career prior to us meeting each other had been
quite different from mine. On leaving the Old Vic Theatre
School she had been engaged by various repertory companies, had appeared in several pantomimes and, in 1954,
had been cast in a play by Thornton Wilder called *The
Matchmaker*, which transferred from the Edinburgh Festival to the Theatre Royal Haymarket in London and then to
Broadway, no less. I understand that the play featured on
Ed Sullivan's TV show, which was partly responsible for
it transferring across the pond. Pru had quite a time of it
over there and when we first met she used to talk about it
a good deal. Bearing in mind she was only twenty-three
and had never been abroad it must have been quite an
experience.

Pru and the company of *The Matchmaker* set sail on
Cunard's RMS *Media* and I remember her saying that it
was great fun. After walking around the funnel a few times
each day she would meet the captain who would grunt at
her approvingly and then take her onto the bridge. 'Sea
voyages give one the most deliciously suspended irrespon-
sible feeling,' she said in a letter to Bim. 'I eat, sleep, sew,
write letters and purr.' Her first opinions of the new continent, however, were a little more mixed. 'The first sight
of the New York skyline against the stars as you come up
the Hudson River is one of the most beautiful man-made
phenomena I've ever seen,' she said. 'The Statue of Liberty, however, is quite horrid, I think, even floodlit.'

The first thing she did after settling in was to go sight-seeing with a friend of the family called Louis Connick. I'm not quite sure about the circumstances but Louis, who was from New York, had stayed with the Illingworths during the war (possibly to help out Bim) and had become good friends with Pru. His mother had an apartment on Park Avenue, so although digs had been offered to Pru she decided to stay with the Connicks, at least initially. 'The apartment is very nice,' she wrote. 'Lots of double doors and brass filigree fingerplates and veneer and madly good furniture.' The following day Louis took her sightseeing.

Yesterday, which was a gorgeous day, dry and clear under an even blue sky fading to white over the horizon all round, we went on the roof of a hotel called the Beekman Tower and looked over the city. It's much redder than I expected, not white and staring at all, but incredibly clear and knife-edged in every shade of pink and brown and orange and cream.

Pru's two favourite stories about the play itself involve her being insulted by the director, although unintention-ally, and being told off by the leading lady, very much intentionally. The director was Tyrone Guthrie, one of the great originators of British theatre who had a reputation for speaking his mind. He only gave Pru one note during the entire run of *The Matchmaker* (in which Pru played the niece of one of the main characters played by Lee Mon-tague), which was given to her after a show one evening very early on in the run.

'I came down from my dressing room on the top floor, running to catch a bus home to Battersea,' she would tell me, 'and as I passed him outside Dressing Room One, he said, "Do something about your make-up, dear; looks like three raspberries on a plate."' She'd go on to explain that, 'when you have a round face like mine, you make as much as you can of the features so that they take up as much room as possible.'

The story regarding the leading lady, who was the formidable American actress Ruth Gordon, was a great deal more serious, and involved Pru missing an entrance one evening. I think I've already demonstrated the significance of an actor missing an entrance (or in my case an entire performance) and, although I can obviously empathize with Pru, I have absolutely no sympathy. She was halfway through a costume change one evening (not even a quick change, apparently) and the usual tannoy announcement requesting her attendance in the wings did not occur. Being 'off', as it's referred to, is bad enough. Being off for the leading lady, however, is another thing altogether. Pru went to Miss Gordon's dressing room after the show and, as well as apologizing, she vowed to change in the wings from now on.

'I'm glad to hear that,' said her leading lady. 'The first thing I'm going to teach in my drama school is that not everybody can act, but everybody can *get* there.'

While in New York, Pru also attended classes at the Herbert Berghof Studio with the great American actress and teacher Uta Hagen. Hagen had originated the role of Martha in the very first production of Edward Albee's *Who's Afraid of Virginia Woolf?* and had later been blacklisted from Hollywood for her association with Paul Robeson. Uta became Pru's mentor, and they remained close friends until Uta's death in 2004.

Even more impressive than Pru's appearances on the stage during these early years are her appearances on the big and small screen. Starting off with four episodes of *Pride and Prejudice* in 1952, she went on to make five films, one of which was the hugely enjoyable and successful *Hobson's Choice* starring the great Charles Laughton, in which Pru played one of his daughters (rather well, I might add); one episode of a very popular series called *Television World Theatre*; two episodes of a series called *Champion Road* starring William Lucas; two episodes of *BBC Sunday Night Theatre*; seven episodes of *The Secret Garden*; three episodes of *ITV Playhouse;* and five episodes of a new and extremely popular soap opera based in Manchester, which I will come on to later.

Incidentally, I recently came across an interview Pru did with the *Guardian* many years ago in which she talked about her screen-test for *Hobson's Choice*.

> *Hobson's Choice* was only my second film. At the screen-test, David Lean sat behind the camera and asked: 'What's your name?' In character, I said: 'Vicky Hobson.' He said: 'Where do you live?' I said: 'Manchester. I work in the shops.' He asked: 'Have you got a boyfriend?' And I smiled all over and said: 'Yes, his name is Freddy Beenstock.' I couldn't stop giggling. I was terribly impressed – a director like David Lean coming to the screen-test of a minor character. And I got the part.

The aforementioned engagements had brought Pru into contact with people, conditions and attitudes that were, quite frankly, alien to me at the time. I'd made no films, my two television appearances had been fleeting, and my theatrical engagements had consisted largely of regional tours and seasons with companies playing weekly or fortnightly repertory. Eventually, once audiences had witnessed things on television such as solid-looking walls, furniture that they didn't recognize and a butler who looked like a butler and not a heavily made-up nineteen-year-old, the end was in sight for repertory companies. It's not that I hadn't been looking to broaden my experience, by the way. Indeed, I'd estimate that almost every waking hour I hadn't spent treading the boards in a provincial theatre somewhere, I'd spent pounding the streets of central London looking for something else.

Nowadays, the casual actor is rarely seen on the streets of central London. Or at least in the daytime. Soho used to be awash with us and if you weren't recording a voiceover in one of Soho's innumerable recording studios, advising the general public which deodorant to use or what car to purchase, you'd be attending auditions or invading offices belonging to producers or agents.

From eleven o'clock every morning the area between Charing Cross Road and St Martin's Lane would be literally teeming with actors. The day would begin with a frothy coffee, as they were known – the precursor to the cappuccino – and a gossip in the bar at the Arts Theatre, which is where Pru and me made our West End debut together in *The Trigon*. Snippets of news about new productions that were currently being cast would be exchanged and would eventually lead to an exodus up the road to Cambridge Circus, around which were situated the offices of a large number of reputable, and some less reputable, theatrical agents. These people didn't always keep a list of clients and, when a production company called about a role for which they needed an actor, the agent would simply wait for the inevitable stampede up the stairs. Then they'd select someone who they thought fitted the bill, negotiate an almost invariably derisory salary (from which they would deduct ten per cent), and inform the lucky actor about the role they'd be playing and instruct them where they had to be and when.

That was just the 'haves', however. What of the 'have nots'? Those who had not struck lucky would begin to feel that they had done more than enough work for one day and retire to one of a number of different pubs for a libation of some kind. Often somebody would come in carrying what appeared to be a script for a play, and after selecting a table in the far corner, would sit and study it closely, occasionally raising their eyes and mouthing silently to themselves. After all, the most important thing after getting a job, a friend once said to me, was *looking* like you had one.

In those days a substantial number of actors lived in the West End, and one such was a friend of mine called Richard Huggett. Also a playwright, Richard had an apartment on Old Compton Street in Soho and used to invite me around for dinner every Thursday. On one evening he asked me if I liked vegetables, and I assured him that I found them most agreeable. Over the following weeks then, that became the usual fare, and we had all kinds of dishes. Vegetable stew, vegetable curry and what have you. Then, one Thursday afternoon while I was walking down Berwick Street just as the market was closing, I saw

Richard on his hands and knees collecting the debris from beneath the stalls. My supper! I arrived that evening armed with some fish and chips and told him that from now on I'd bring sausages and would chip in for the veg.

No Rest for the Wicked

After Christmas I went straight on tour and Pru started rehearsing the next series of *Marriage Lines*. I should probably have mentioned this earlier, but I actually had a part in the first series of that show. I played the chap who sold George and Kate their flat and, when I first started reading the script, I got my hopes up about becoming a regular. The character, who was called Bob, appeared to be relatively interesting and I remember saying so to Pru.

'It looks like we might be working together for a while.'

'Really, darling? Oh, that's marvellous.'

Two pages on my excitement was tempered somewhat by a line from George Starling that read: 'Poor Bob, he's gone to South Africa for seven years.'

'False alarm, darling,' I shouted. 'I'm afraid I'm off to South Africa.'

'Well, do be careful,' she replied.

Pru and me sat down and watched a few episodes of *Marriage Lines* the other day and although the performances are fine and some of the humour has aged quite well, the attitudes in general are, at best, slightly archaic. Pru's character Kate, who doesn't work, is incredibly naive and despite being rather sweet she just burns the food, fails to iron her husband's shirts properly, and bursts into tears every five minutes. The exasperated George mainly takes refuge in the pub with his pals, and when he eventually comes home his hapless innocent of a wife cries once again, apologizes profusely and he forgives her. Oh, dearie me.

Pru once said of the character, 'I don't really approve of Kate, to be honest with you. She's a much better housewife than I am but she's terribly one-dimensional.' I couldn't agree more.

Rehearsals for each episode ran from Tuesday to Friday and then on Saturday morning they had a technical run-through. On Sunday they'd do the recording and, on that day, Pru could be at the studio for anything up to twelve hours. The show would be taped and shown the following week and after having Monday off it would be back to rehearsals on Tuesday.

As I was rarely working on a Sunday I'd always try to get to a recording, and I remember both Richard and Pru usually being absolutely terrified. The audiences, who had been selected apparently, but from God knows where, used to queue up outside their dressing room windows, which meant that Pru and Richard could hear their comments as clear as day.

'As if we aren't nervous enough,' I remember Richard complaining, 'without having to listen to somebody saying, "I never liked Richard Briers in *Brothers in Law*. I hope he's funnier this time."'

Despite it being quite challenging sometimes, Pru and Richard ended up making forty-four episodes of *Marriage Lines* over five series and the same number of years, and it became one of the most popular sitcoms of the sixties. From our own point of view, it provided us with a regular and not insubstantial income, which meant that, by the end of 1964, and with the help of my own emoluments, which I'm happy to say were improving steadily, we were able to purchase our first house together, the address of which was 18 Lillian Road, Barnes. Situated just south of Hammersmith Bridge, it was an easy walk to the underground station and had two good-sized bedrooms, a small kitchen, a small bathroom, a decent-sized lounge, a tiny but easy to maintain garden and the use of a garage. Not that we had a car at the time, but nevertheless it was good to have the space.

Incomes notwithstanding, we still had to take out quite a sizeable mortgage in order to buy the house, which made Pru's parents extremely nervous. As I explained earlier, they had lost a fortune on their own house at the start of the war and unfortunately, they'd never recovered. Indeed, John and Bim were never in a position to purchase a property of their own again, and in their twilight years Pru had to help them out.

'But you'll have all that debt hanging over you,' said Bim. 'Please think twice about it. It was almost the end of John and me.'

They became so worried about us being able to afford the mortgage that in order to allay their fears we had to sit down and explain to them why we were confident of being able to do so and what would happen if we ever couldn't. It was similar to our meeting with the bank, come to think of it, except the interrogation was considerably more forensic!

In January 1965 I was invited by the Royal Shakespeare Company to go to Stratford-upon-Avon for an entire season. I had already appeared in several productions for the company at the Aldwych Theatre in London and had enjoyed every moment. As I would be working in Stratford for almost ten months, digs were out of the question and so I ended up renting a cottage in a small village just outside the town called Tredington.

'I'm not sure I like the idea of being all alone in London for ten months,' Pru said when the offer came through.

'Then why not come with me?' I suggested. 'I'm sure you could find a job in the Midlands just for a few months.'

Fortunately, television hadn't quite finished off the practice of visiting your local theatre on a regular or semi-regular basis and, after making several telephone calls, Pru was eventually offered the role of Hermione in Birmingham Rep's forthcoming production of *The Winter's Tale*. On being informed about our working holiday in Warwickshire, Bim and John were straight on the phone.

'But how will you afford the mortgage?' they asked. 'Surely you can't afford to keep two places going.'

Bim and John actually had a point here, as although at a stretch we could probably afford to pay the mortgage and the rent on the cottage, it would leave us with little disposable income, least of all some money to put by for a rainy day, as is often an actor's wont.

'We could always rent out the house,' suggested Pru. 'After all, we don't have much furniture, and we'd be taking the majority of our personal effects with us.'

The furniture that we had accumulated since purchasing the house had either been given to us by generous relatives or had been bought second-hand (eminently expendable, in other words), so we decided to rent out the house in Barnes, furniture and all, for the duration of our secondment.

'Oh, I think that's very sensible,' said Bim. 'We shan't have to worry now.'

Pru moved back to London a few weeks before me, and before I joined her I got to meet one of my absolute heroes, although in somewhat bizarre circumstances. The company I had been performing with included Glenda Jackson, Janet Suzman, Michael Pennington and Paul Scofield and, to be perfectly honest with you, by the end of the season we were all starting to get a little bit tired and emotional. Furthermore, the popular idiom 'Leave the best to last' had been somehow overlooked by whoever had planned the season, as we were concluding our tenure there with the never-popular *Timon of Athens*. I don't know what it is about that play. It just never seems to catch on. Paul Scofield was incredible in the title role, and it was directed by John Schlesinger. How on earth could a production like that be anything but a roaring success, we all thought?

Poor Pru suffered the brunt of all this from me in a letter.

The season is too long and there's a feeling of despondency among the company, of hopes disappointed. In March, everyone's optimistic. They're going to get wonderful notices, the cottage is idyllic, there's a romantic liaison waiting to flower, the cricket team will triumph. October comes and the notices haven't mentioned them, the cottage roof leaks, the actress has gone off with somebody else and the cricket team's lost every match. Timon is not the success of the season, but then I suppose it never is. At a matinee last week,

76

Paul came off after one scene and said, 'Take a look at that man sitting by himself in the front row. I'm sure it's Buster Keaton.' So, we all looked when we had a chance, and the likeness was indeed uncanny. After the matinee I went for a walk through the town and called in at a pub I'd never seen before. There, sitting at a table in the corner, was, undeniably, Buster Keaton. I went up to him. 'Mr Keaton?' I asked. 'What?' He seemed surprised. I said that Mr Scofield thought he'd spotted him in the audience. 'Yes,' he said, 'I was in the vicinity, and thought I'd better see some Shakespeare.' 'Did you enjoy it?' I asked, insanely. He considered this, 'Not much,' he said finally, and went back to his drink.

The final play of the season was *Hamlet*, starring David Warner. I wasn't in that. I remember thinking to myself, why on earth couldn't he have come to see *Love's Labour's Lost*?

Soon after arriving back in London, Pru started having dizzy spells. 'I know what it is,' she said to me almost nonchalantly over the telephone. 'I'm pregnant.'

I must admit this took me by surprise somewhat. 'What? Really? Are you? How on earth do you know? Have you seen a doctor? Oh, good lord!'

'No, no, darling, calm down. I meant I *think* I'm pregnant.'

'Well, why on earth didn't you say so?'

Pru made an appointment to see a doctor and phoned me again a few days later to confirm that she was indeed pregnant. 'I knew I was,' she said. 'It's good news, though, isn't it, darling? Are you happy?'

'Absolutely,' I confirmed. 'I couldn't be happier.'

Pru had just started rehearsing a play called *The Birdwatcher* for the Hampstead Theatre Club when this happened and was also making a new series of *Marriage Lines*. This meant that, by the time our new baby arrived, they would already be a veteran of the stage and the small screen, although in utero. With regards to *Marriage Lines*, you could almost have accused Pru of going 'method', as her character in the show, Kate Starling, had fallen pregnant several weeks earlier as part of the storyline and Pru had been made to wear padding. When she started to show in real life that was no longer necessary, but a problem was soon to occur.

'I wonder what will happen when Kate gives birth,' I said to Pru one evening.

'What do you mean?' she asked.

'Well, when is Kate due to give birth in the show? The next couple of weeks? And when are *you* due to give birth? About six weeks? That means there'll be a month when Kate won't be pregnant in the show, but *you* will be in real life. Rather heavily. Sorry, darling, I didn't mean to worry you.'

'Well, you have,' moaned Pru. 'Oh dear, what are we going to do?'

'Let Richard Waring and the BBC worry about that,' I said. 'It's their problem. Not yours.'

Fortunately, only one episode of *Marriage Lines* was due to be made between me dropping the truth bomb and Pru giving birth, but it still presented a problem. Pru was supposed to be sitting up in bed with her newborn baby for the majority of the episode, but when they rehearsed it the bump was still evident.

'What did they do?' I asked her after the recording.

'They cut a big hole in the mattress, which meant I sunk into it.'

'And did it work?'

'Yes, beautifully. I'm glad it's over, though. I'm exhausted.'

The birth of our first child was rather eventful. For a start, I was determined to be present, which in those days was not the done thing. It took a while to persuade the powers that be, but I became one of the first fathers ever to be allowed to witness a birth at Queen Charlotte's Maternity Hospital, which is a source of enormous pride. It very nearly didn't happen, though. After arriving at the hospital Pru got into bed and I set about trying to make her feel as comfortable as possible.

'Would you like me to read to you, darling?' I enquired.

'Oh, yes please.'

'All right. What would you prefer, *2001: A Space Odyssey* by Arthur C. Clarke, or *Only When I Larf* by Len Deighton?'

'Start with the latter.'

I read from both, after which we did *The Times* crossword together and then chatted about the issues of the day. After about twenty-four hours (I was allowed to stay in the room with Pru overnight) nothing much had happened, and on realizing that I was in fact quite hungry, I decided to go and get myself something to eat. Pru was fast asleep so it seemed like perfect timing.

I did try to inform a member of staff about my plans but there was no one in the vicinity and so, with my stomach now making all manner of strange noises, I went foraging. As I left the entrance to the hospital it suddenly struck me that Richard Briers and his wife, Annie, lived literally around the corner. Perfect, I thought. A couple of friendly faces and a sandwich, that's what I need, and so off I set.

'Hello, love!' said Richard on opening his front door. 'Come on in. What news, dear fellow? What news?'

Me and Pru had got to know Richard and Annie very well since *Marriage Lines* had started and as I filled Richard in about what had been happening at the hospital (or should I say, what hadn't been happening) he made me a cheese sandwich and poured us a large scotch each.

'Isn't it terrible,' I observed to him some time later, not worse for wear, exactly, but lightly refreshed, 'that in these days of advanced medical research nothing has really been discovered that can relieve the pain – nay, the trauma – of childbirth to any great degree? It's ridiculous. Don't you think so?'

'Terrible!' he agreed, pouring us another scotch.

'I mean,' I went on, sinking back into the armchair, 'there's Pru lying there in hospital. She's been there for the best part of thirty hours; I've gone through all the heavy breathing with her, I've read to her, we've done the crossword together, she keeps having contractions, but nothing happens.'

'Terrible, old chap,' sympathized Richard. 'Must be hellishly frustrating.'

'It is,' I agreed. 'It's just that to keep thinking that it's going to come, you know, and then it doesn't . . . I'm going to be there, though. At the birth.'

'Really? Is that allowed?'

'Well, not if the matron has anything to do with it. She believes a father's place is in the waiting room. Pru's gynaecologist, who is also the registrar, agrees with me, though, and has overruled her. She's not very happy. Pru is, though, which is obviously all I care about.'

'Good for you!' said Richard, raising his glass. 'I'm not sure I'd want to be there at the business end of the proceedings myself, but if it's what you two want, you go for it. I tell you what, I've just bought a couple of new Al Jolson records. Would you like to hear them?'

'What a good idea!'

While all this was going on, Pru was being wheeled towards the delivery suite, while at the same time frantically handing a list of telephone numbers to the nurse.

'Try not to worry,' the nurse said to Pru. 'We'll find him. He can't be far away.'

'Please hurry, though. I don't think we've got long.'

The first number the nurse called was our home in Barnes, where Pru's parents were waiting for news.

'Mr West hasn't been back there, has he?' enquired the nurse.

'No,' replied Bim. 'Why, isn't he at the hospital? He should be. Oh, good lord. John, Tim's gone missing!'

'No, Mrs Illingworth. Please calm down. He hasn't gone missing, exactly. We just can't find him.'

'What?!'

I'm not quite sure how many telephone numbers the nurse called or who she spoke to, but after relaying the news to Pru that she hadn't been able to track me down she was given one final lead.

'Try Richard Briers, will you?' Pru said, writing down his number. 'He only lives across the road.'

'Isn't that the telephone?' I said to Richard a few minutes later.

'I think you could be right. 'Scuse me, old chap,' he said, pushing himself upwards. 'Shan't be a tick.'

When Richard left the room, I drained my glass of the last few drops of whisky and started thinking about negotiating the Goldhawk Road and getting to the hospital. Not for long, though, as just a few seconds later Richard's instantly recognizable voice broke my train of thought.

'Erm, Tim old chap,' he shouted. 'Would you like to come to the telephone, please? It's the hospital. Apparently, your presence is required.'

Within about three minutes I was at Pru's side in the delivery suite voicing a series of apologies and reassurances. A nurse had met me in reception, and while we were in the lift she'd thrown a gown over me and handed me a cap and mask. 'You can't go in until you've put these on,' she said. 'And your wife's fine, by the way. She'll be so glad to see you.'

The nurse was right. Pru wasn't at all interested in my apologies.

'Never mind all that. You're here and that's the main thing.'

A few minutes later a purple object emerged and after being unrolled it became clear that Pru had given birth to a baby boy who we later named Samuel Alexander Joseph. It was miraculous and I was ecstatic.

'Very good,' I said. 'No retakes.'

Night is for Delight

S uch is the lot of a brace of jobbing actors that I went back to work almost immediately after Sam was born and Pru did likewise within a few weeks. When Sam arrived, I had just started rehearsing a play about Samuel Johnson in which I played the lead role alongside Julian Glover (of 2B, Bristol Grammar School) who was playing James Boswell. In actual fact, I wasn't supposed to be playing Dr Johnson at all. My original role had been Sir John Hawkins, one of Johnson's biographers, but when we started rehearsals, the actor playing Johnson didn't turn up. Indeed, there seemed to be some secrecy as to the identity of this actor and all such enquiries were met with a grim face and stony silence.

When it became clear that the actor wasn't arriving, I was asked to stand in and read for him on the first day. He still wasn't there the next day, or the next. By the end of the week, we were all becoming a little bit tetchy. The part was significant, with Johnson being on stage practically from start to finish. Finally, the director turned to me one morning and said, 'Well, I suppose you'd better do it.'

'Fine,' I replied. 'I'd be delighted.' There was no improvement financially, but the role was far more substantial and would be a welcome addition to my CV.

At one point during the play, Julian and I were required to dance. A chap called Ben Pearce Higgins had written some beautiful music and a choreographer named Bill Drysdale was called in for the occasion.

'Have you ever danced before, Tim?' Bill enquired cheerily on his first day.

'Well, yes,' I replied. 'Although never very well. I'm afraid I have . . .'

'Don't tell me,' he interrupted. 'Two left feet?'

'I'm afraid so.'

'We'll see,' he said, showing off a wide smile. 'I'm sure you'll be fine.'

Bill had obviously heard this line a thousand times before and by the somewhat confident nature of his reply he had a decent record of turning two left feet into one of each.

'Now, Tim,' he began at the start of his choreography. 'This is very simple – just like walking really. Sway back on the first beat, and on the third, step forward with your left foot – no, left foot . . . All right, we'll do something even simpler.'

At this point Bill was still cheerfully confident but soon enough my inability to comprehend and repeat even the most rudimentary steps had started to wear him down.

'You've been smoking rather heavily this afternoon, Bill?' I said towards the end of the day.

'Have I?' he snapped.

He stopped short of blaming me directly, but I could tell that I had become his nemesis.

Pru was sympathetic. 'That poor man,' she said. 'What an awful thing to have to do. I bet he doesn't last the course.'

'What do you mean?' I said.

'He won't be able to teach you. Some things just aren't possible.'

At the time I didn't agree with Pru's assessment but by the end of the third day I was beginning to see her point of view. Bill had been smoking constantly and looked like he hadn't slept a wink. What's more, his proteges had made next to no progress.

He put another cigarette on the ashtray ready to take the place of the one he was smoking. 'Places, please,' he said, clapping his hands. 'Come on, we've a lot to do.'

That day was by far the worst of the three as in conclusion Bill claimed that, far from having made any progress since his arrival, we had actually got worse.

'Never mind,' I mumbled in desperation. 'We still have one more day.'

Roughly fifteen hours later Julian and I stood in the centre of the rehearsal room staring at our watches. 'He's not coming, is he?' I surmised.

'Nope,' agreed Julian. 'Pru was obviously right.'

With regards to the actual routine we'd been meant to learn we just had to try our best and it became a source of light relief. A kind of comedic interlude.

Roughly five years later, while I was staying at Mrs McKay's celebrated Astra House (the Home of the Stars) in Manchester, I came down to breakfast one morning to find Bill Drysdale sitting at a table buttering a slice of toast.

'Hello, Bill,' I said. 'Remember me? Timothy West? Dr Johnson?'

The knife dropped from his pale, nerveless fingers. 'Oh my God,' he whispered faintly. 'You're not in *Ragtime* for the BBC?'

'No, I'm doing a series for Granada.'

His fearful face suddenly broke into a smile, and he stood up and gleefully shook my hand.

It's different now, I'm happy to say, but in our younger years Pru in particular feared penury more than anything else on earth and so when jobs came along, providing they wouldn't damage our careers, we'd take them.

In order to facilitate this, childcare had to be arranged, and so when working out our budget as a family of three we had to factor in the cost of a fulltime nanny. We had many over the years, but our first nanny was a young lady called Rosie, who hailed from Aberdeen. I forget how they knew each other, but she came highly recommended by Pru's own childhood nanny, Nan Patterson, and sure enough Rosie was marvellous. When Pru was working away from home, Rosie would travel with her and look after Sam while Pru was either rehearsing or performing.

The first job Pru accepted after Sam was born was a part in a revue at the Yvonne Arnaud Theatre in Guildford called *Night is for Delight*. As well as not being too far from home, the engagement only lasted a couple of weeks and was a perfect opportunity for Pru and Rosie to get to know each other, and to work out how on earth you're supposed to manage day-to-day while on tour with a baby. Fortunately, Pru and Rosie got along famously.

'She's not really a theatregoer,' Pru said, during a rare telephone conversation one day.

'You'll have to educate her then,' I suggested.

'What, with this show? She'd never forgive me.'

Pru set about furthering Rosie's education and one

matinee she asked the wardrobe mistress to look after Sam while Rosie went out and watched the show. I was appearing in something at the Arts Theatre in Cambridge at the time and the following day I received a letter from Pru telling me how it had gone.

'I think she was dazed,' wrote Pru. 'Everyone was very sweet to her and sent up her accent and told her what lovely hair she had and she hardly stopped giggling.'

No sooner had *Night is for Delight* come to an end than Pru, Rosie and Sam were on the road again, this time in a production of Noël Coward's *Hay Fever* starring Celia Johnson and Roland Culver. The only potential problem with this show was the fact that Noël Coward's own legendary production, which had taken place at the National Theatre and had starred the likes of Maggie Smith, Derek Jacobi, Robert Stephens and my own former co-star, Dame Edith Evans, had appeared just a few years previously. Comparisons would undoubtedly be made. Pru wasn't worried, exactly, although when word got out that Noël Coward himself would be attending one of the run-throughs, she got an attack of the jitters.

'I do wish they hadn't told us he was coming,' she complained. 'I shall be ever so nervous now.'

'Look,' I said. 'Who was it who played your role in his production originally? Lynn Redgrave?'

'Yes, that's right.'

'Well, as long as you don't mention her, you'll be fine.'

The rehearsal took place in the afternoon and when Pru returned home early that evening she looked crestfallen.

'What happened?' I asked.

'He wanted to shake hands with everyone afterwards and when he got to me, I couldn't think of anything to say.'

'You should have let him speak first.'

'I know that now.'

'What happened then?'

'He said some awfully nice things to Roland and Celia, then to Richard Vernon, and when he got to me, he just shook my hand and smiled rather glibly. I muttered something about Lynn Redgrave being a very hard act to follow and as he continued down the line he said, "Oh yes, *wasn't she good."'*

'Oh dear,' I said putting my arms around her. 'Would you like a drink?'

'Yes, please. Actually, I'll have two. One for me and one for Lynn.'

The play was due to run at the Duke of York's Theatre on St Martin's Lane, but not before a lengthy tour of the provinces, hence Pru, Rosie and Sam going straight back on the road. One of the early dates was in Brighton and the day after opening a tired and exasperated Pru wrote me a letter explaining that she'd had rather a day of it.

I had to sleep with Sam, who wakes at six and sings and makes plughole noises for an hour, and Rosie, who snores very gently all through it, and what with that and a really appalling hangover, I didn't think I'd be able to open at all. But caught up just in time, and it was OK I think, though will be better and I haven't seen any notices yet.

Her next letter arrived two days later, on a Friday, offering me a vivid description of the digs they were sharing.

We're living a very 'Look Back in Anger' existence, with the clotheshorse the salient feature in the room, and in a way thank God you missed it. But Sam is being pretty ravishing and has settled down very well. He sings rather loudly from 7 a.m. on, which is not very engaging, and I swear has woken me up every morning by sheer hypnotism through the bars in his cot.

The thing that perturbed Pru the most during the first few months of Sam's existence was the constant lack of sleep. This was compounded further by the fact that Pru's worrying had gone into overdrive, so even if she wasn't awakened by a baby or an au pair, the chances are an anxiety of some kind would do it instead. I must have at least a hundred letters from Pru that were written between the hours of three and four in the morning.

'You really will have to do something about this,' I said to her over the telephone one day.

'I shall just have to see if I can nap before the show,' she said. 'If I can grab an hour and a half or even just an hour, I'll be fine.'

And so, it came to pass. Pru arrived at the theatre in good time for the show, lay down on the sofa, closed her eyes and succumbed to the sandman.

'I did it,' she said the following day. 'I slept for almost two hours before the show last night and woke up feeling marvellous. I was awakened at the crack of dawn this morning, of course, but I don't care anymore. Anyway, how are you, my love?'

I later found out that Pru had form in this department. When I say form, what I mean is that she had a history of falling asleep in theatres, except that instead of confining this to a sofa in a dressing room or a seat in the stalls even, she had actually managed to achieve it not only on a stage, but during a performance of *Othello* while playing Desdemona with Salisbury Rep. Pru informed me that the actor playing Othello was quite a large fellow and for some reason he used to take an awfully long time over the final scene, in which he commits suicide after killing Desdemona.

'It was a matinee, and I must have been out the night before,' she told me. 'Anyway, halfway through being murdered I started to feel ever so sleepy. At first, I tried to fight it but then I realized that in a few moments I would have to play dead anyway, so I just succumbed to it.'

'Let me get this straight,' I said scratching my head. 'You mean you consciously decided to nod off in the middle of the afternoon on a stage in Salisbury during a performance of *Othello*?'

'That's right. It was right at the end of the performance, though, and I was about to die. I'd have woken up for the curtain call.'

I don't know how long it took Othello to do away with himself but sometime in between him doing so and then Cassio saying, 'This did I fear, but thought he had no weapon,' Pru woke up with a loud shriek, which resulted in several even louder shrieks from the audience.

'Good God,' I said. 'What on earth did you do?'

'Well, it took me a few seconds to come around, but after I did, I realized our predicament.'

'What, that Desdemona had come back to life suddenly in front of a live audience after having been murdered by somebody who had now killed themselves?'

'That's right. You should have seen the looks on the actor's faces. They were as white as sheets.'

'And what of Othello?'

'At first, he didn't move so I gave him a nudge.'

'You nudged a dead Othello?'

'That's right. Eventually he began to stir, and I whispered, "Sorry, but you're going to have to kill me again."'

'And what did he say?'

'Nothing. He was so shocked, I think, that at first, he just lay there staring at me, but only out of one eye.'

'Then what happened?'

'I gave him another nudge, which seemed to bring him round, and eventually he started murdering me again – a bit more hurriedly this time – and then killed himself, again, in next to no time. The applause was rather muted at the end.'

'I can't say I'm surprised. Do you know, Pru,' I said, taking her in my arms. 'I think that might be my new favourite anecdote.'

The next date of the tour was up in Edinburgh (a mere 464 miles) and although I advised against it Pru insisted on driving the three of them up there.

'It's going to take you at least ten hours,' I said. 'Why don't you just go by train like everyone else?'

'We'll be fine,' said Pru. 'As long as we set off at the right time.'

I dislike the phrase 'I told you so', and so I kept my mouth shut even when I learned that, due to a constant and extremely powerful headwind, the journey from Brighton to Edinburgh had taken Pru, Sam and Rosie the best part of thirteen hours.

'We were going so slowly I thought we'd broken down,' said Pru. 'And poor Rosie. It's a wonder she hasn't taken the opportunity to abandon us in Edinburgh and catch a train back to Aberdeen.'

Instead of staying in another John Osborne-esque boarding house, Pru, Rosie and Sam had been invited to go and stay with an ex-boyfriend of Pru's called Bill Black-wood. Pru and Bill had first met back in 1959, so a couple of years before I arrived on the scene. An engineer by trade, Bill was a wildly eccentric man who lived in a large house with his bedridden mother, her nurse and a cook. He had decided many years previously not to become involved in the family business and had put all his efforts into building ski-lifts on the Cairngorms near Aviemore. It was a ridiculously impractical plan as he had no money and was having to work in London. Moreover, the ski-lifts he'd designed were little more than ropes attached to tractors. That said, the three tractors that he'd managed to purchase had been named PS1, PS2 and PS3 after Pru.

'Do you miss him?' I asked.

'Sometimes,' she said. 'But only because he's so entertaining.'

They were at Bill's bleak house for five or six nights and by the time they left for Glasgow, Pru had turned to drowning her sorrows and Rosie had committed to memory the entire train timetable from Glasgow to Aberdeen for the entire year. Fortunately, their experience in Scotland improved on every level, and not just with regards to the accommodation. The notices for the show, for instance, had been polite at best until now but in Glasgow they were positively fawning. Despite the upturn in fortunes, Pru had decided that it might be better for both nanny and baby if Rosie took Sam to visit her family for a few days. After all, she'd memorized the timetable. Pru wrote to me shortly after.

> *Sam and Rosie went off safely yesterday. Sam distressingly jovial, I was nearly in tears . . . Spent yesterday in bed mostly asleep and felt alarmingly fresh and normal for the show, makes one realize how 'sub' one is generally: is this to continue until Sam is grown up? Will I never be able to bring full energy and concentration to a part? Perhaps marriage/babies are incompatible with work, am I giving less than full value, I seem to have felt tired for months, it's all so unfair.*

I should make the point here that Pru playing three roles at once – mother, wife and actress – was both exhausting and incredibly rare. Mothers, regardless of age, were expected to stay at home in the 1960s and those who rallied against this were frowned upon by a great many. Not that it troubled Pru at all. She's always been able to rise above that kind of nonsense and chose to have her cake and eat it.

'Sam's perfectly happy and so am I,' she said to me at the time. 'I grant you, it's damned hard work sometimes, but we manage.'

Pru's resolve and fortitude were put to the ultimate test in January 1968 when the producers of *Hay Fever* announced that they would be taking the show to Canada for two weeks. 'Are you sure you want to take Sam?' I asked. 'We could easily make alternative arrangements here. You know, grandparents and nannies. It'd be a break for you. And a well-deserved one at that.'

'Absolutely not,' said Pru. 'As long as I have Jutta with me [Rosie's successor] I'll be fine, as will Sam.'

'Fair enough,' I said. 'It's your decision.'

Before anyone starts accusing me of being a chauvinist for standing back, as well as pleading the 1960s (different attitudes etc), I did and still do believe that this was Pru's decision to make and Pru's alone.

'We'll be absolutely fine,' she said, while holding Sam at the airport. 'Won't we, Sam? Anyway, darling, you take care and I'll write to you as soon as we get to the hotel.'

The post was rather more reliable and regular in those days than it is today and despite her being on a different continent and many thousands of miles away, Pru's first letter arrived just two days later.

'Oh goodness dearie me,' it started.

Well, we were eight hours on that plane, and I hardly stopped being frightened for one minute. In fact, it was a very good flight and a good landing, but we took off at two and didn't arrive until HALF PAST THREE, by which time Sam, who had remained remarkably cheerful and winsome, was so crazed with hunger that he couldn't eat and had to be forcibly fed between screams. The prescribed teaspoon of sedative failed to have any effect at all but Sam eventually slept for about three-quarters of an hour. Otherwise, constant yell. Everyone very nice about it. Even Roland Culver only said, 'This aeroplane is more like a school bus.'

A few days later I received another letter from Pru informing me that our son had learned some new words. 'One of which I'm afraid is "elevator",' she wrote . . .

> *Weather has been very dramatic here. On Sunday it was cold, and the cars were all wrapped in frozen rain like polythene – when you open the door it shattered like the toffee on a toffee apple. Then on Monday it snowed heavily in the morning and stopped magically for the dress rehearsal, leaving all the little cherry trees on the sidewalks encrusted with ice, and looking incredibly valuable. Fantastically efficient clearance of the main streets, and now you'd hardly know, and it's not much colder than at home.*

I'm pleased to report that both the play and the experience of having Sam with her in Canada were a success, and when Pru returned home she was adamant that her decision to combine work with motherhood had been the right one. What's more, I agreed with her.

A few days later the three of us were at home together one evening enjoying each other's company (it must have been a Sunday) when we inadvertently presented a scene to our neighbours and to passers-by that resulted in a series of very strange looks and, I'd imagine, not an inconsiderable amount of trauma. We'd never really bothered closing the curtains before in our living room (I don't think it had ever occurred to us) because on the rare occasions we were in there, we'd just be splayed out on the sofa reading books or talking. On this particular night, however, I was trying on a costume for a play in which I had to cross dress (it was a rather fetching off-the-shoulder number with yards of net at the back) and as Pru advised me how to put it on she was stripped to the waste feeding Sam.

'Hang on,' she said suddenly. 'Somebody's looking in through the window. There's two or three of them! Tim, look.'

'Really? Good God, you're right. Nothing to see here, sorry,' I said, closing the curtains while attempting to tame my errant bosom.

Wandsworth

In 1968 Pru was asked by Peter Ustinov to appear alongside him, Michael Aldridge and Simon Ward in his new play, *The Unknown Soldier and His Wife*. It had already had a successful run in New York and was opening that year's Chichester Festival. I was appearing in a play called *The Italian Girl* in the West End at the time, and each night after the show ended I'd jump in the car and drive down to West Sussex. Pru had rented a cottage in Chichester for the duration of the run and had Sam and the nanny for company. The drive down there took at least a couple of hours but as neither of us had to be at our respective theatres especially early (even on matinee days) and had every Sunday off, it made sense. We spent little enough time together as it was so an opportunity like this was not to be missed.

Two things of note happened in Chichester, apart from the show being a success and everyone involved receiving splendid notices. After having arrived at the cottage about 1 a.m. one Sunday morning I was allowed a lie-in, and when I awoke nine hours later, Pru had some news.

'Peter's coming to dinner tonight,' she said.

'What, as in Ustinov?'

'Yes, that's right.'

'Oh, splendid.'

Despite having met Peter on several occasions, unlike

Pru I'd never spent much time with him socially and, as one of the world's great raconteurs, not to mention intellects, I was thoroughly looking forward to catching up. He arrived early and after walking through the back door into the kitchen he immediately banged his head on one of the beams. I realized then not only how tall Peter Ustinov actually was, but just how low the ceilings were in the cottage.

'Blast!' said Peter. 'I'm always doing that.'

'We never have to worry,' joked Pru. 'Are you all right?'

'Yes, I'll be fine,' he said, rubbing his head. 'Are we in here?'

After fixing Peter's drink I joined him in the living room and when I opened the door, I got the shock of my life. In the corner of the room there was a standard lamp that had a large red shade with black tassels like a fez. Peter had removed said shade from the lamp and having placed it on top of his head he was standing in the middle of the room.

'I wish to apply for Turkish rights,' he boomed authoritatively.

He didn't leave the cottage until almost 3 a.m. Eight hours of Ustinov. A privilege.

The second Chichester happening took place in my absence, although I was involved to some extent. When approaching the edge of the twelve-inch-high Chichester stage one afternoon during a photocall, Pru experienced an absurd feeling of vertigo.

'The photographer beckoned me forward even further,' she said. 'But I refused. I knew at once that I was pregnant again.'

And, indeed, she was. They obviously took great care

of her at the theatre and Pru finished the run. We also enjoyed Mr Ustinov's company on one or two more occasions.

When Pru and Sam arrived back in London we realized very quickly that our current abode would not be big enough for four (or five, if you included the nanny) and without any further ado we set about finding a bigger house. Toby Robertson and his wife had recently bought a place in Wandsworth near the common and they suggested we look there. We didn't think for a moment we'd be able to afford it but, on our way back from visiting them one day we saw For Sale notices outside a tall, rather forbidding-looking four-storey Victorian house on the South Circular.

'That could be promising,' I said to Pru. 'Shall we have a look?'

'Don't be silly, darling. We shan't be able to afford it. And besides, it's enormous.'

I completely ignored my expectant wife and the following day I called the estate agent and requested a viewing.

It turned out that the house had been split into four flats and was owned by a retiring greengrocer who informed us that it had been in his family for two generations.

'We couldn't possibly buy it,' Pru said, as we left the building. 'For a start it's far too big and imagine how much it would cost to convert it back to a house again. I'm sorry, darling, I know you've fallen in love with the house, but we just can't.'

The following week we put in an offer that was immediately accepted by the owner.

'I do hope you're right about this,' said Pru.

'I am, my love. Trust me. This place is perfect for us.'

We sold the house in Barnes for a profit, which pleased Bim and John, but when we informed them that in order to pay for the house in Wandsworth we'd had to take out an even bigger mortgage and arrange a loan with Pru's cousin, Stephen, they very nearly passed out.

'You're going to be in debt for the rest of your lives if you're not careful,' warned Bim. 'You do know that?'

'It has potential, though, don't you think?' I said.

'Yes, but at what cost?'

The only people who protested more than Pru's parents about the fact that we were moving to a large house that we could barely afford and needed a heck of a lot of work doing to it were our friends and neighbours – soon to be former neighbours – in Barnes. They were horrified when we told them, but for wholly different reasons.

'Wandsworth?' they said disapprovingly. 'Really? It's a bit, you know.'

'A bit what?'

'Well, you know.'

'No, I genuinely don't.'

'Well, it's just . . .'

'Not *Barnes*?'

Joe, our second son, was born at King's College Hospital, Denmark Hill, on the evening of 1 January 1969. Our doctor, having anticipated that again there would be some delay, went home for supper and almost immediately had to speed back across South London, arriving just too late to witness the birth, and with quite a lot of curry on his chin.

It is a good plan, if possible, to organize things so as not to have your baby on New Year's Day. The hospital seems rather depleted, and the few staff who are there look exhausted. Then for many years you will have to hold noisy children's parties whilst you and the other parents are nursing hangovers. Later on, you may find it advisable to book into a hotel for the night while your offspring takes over your house for a party of their own, and you will return to find your marital bed full of earrings, if nothing worse.

Following Sam's birth at the Queen Charlotte Maternity Hospital, we found a very sophisticated-looking man wearing striped trousers and a dark jacket had entered Pru's room.

'Good morning, Mrs, er . . .' he looked at his list. 'West. Congratulations on the birth of your son. When you and your husband – good morning, sir – have decided on a name, would you mind coming down to the office and registering him? There's no rush, by the way. Thank you so much. Once again, may I offer you my heartfelt congratulations.'

We duly did as requested, and we were handed an extremely posh-looking birth certificate. Pru was extremely impressed by the gentleman. In fact, had she had the resources, I think she might have offered him a job.

Registering Joe's birth was a wholly different affair. A typed slip was sent to Pru at home that read: *Please register your child by such and such a date. Failure to do so will be frowned upon, etc.* Being an Olympic-standard worrier, Pru did as she was told and travelled down to King's College Hospital as soon as she could and was pointed in the direction of a Nissen hut beside the main building. A queue of about ten people were standing outside the hut so Pru joined the end.

'I was in that queue for at least forty-five minutes,' she told me that evening. 'And when I reached the front of it I realized why.'

The registrar, Pru said, appeared not to be from the same planet as her. 'It was one of the oddest encounters I've ever had,' she said. I'll recount it as she told it to me.

'First of all he asked me when my baby was born.

"New Year's Day," I said proudly.

"Oh yes," said the registrar. "That would be January the . . . ?"

"First," I said. "He was born on January the first."

"Right then," said the registrar, "next question. Are you married to the baby's father?"

"Yes, I am."

"Are you *now*?"

"Yes," I repeated. "I am, still."

"Right then, next question. What are you going to call your baby exactly."

"Exactly?"

"Yes, exactly."

"Joseph John Lancaster."

"But your surname is West."

"Yes, they're just his Christian names. His full name is Joseph John Lancaster West."

"Exactly?"

"What? Oh dear."

"Would you mind spelling the names, please," he then asked. "The Christian ones, that is. I can spell West."

So I dictated all the names as requested.

"And it's a little . . . ?"

"Boy!"

At this point I started giggling and I didn't stop for about ten minutes. I so wanted the registrar to giggle too but he didn't. He just sat there playing with his pencil and tutting. He thought *I* was strange.'

The house we bought in Wandsworth had been converted into a number of individual bed-sitting rooms, with other facilities dotted haphazardly around, so that original bedrooms had become kitchens, intended kitchens had been put to use as bathrooms, and obvious bathrooms were doing service as broom cupboards. All the plumbing and all the wiring had been contorted to suit, and we laid out £3,000 – a vast sum – for a comprehensive firm of builders to put things in order. This meant that for the first three months Sam and his nanny lived up on the second floor while me, Pru and baby Joe camped in the basement. Meanwhile, the builders lived in luxury on the ground floor. The first thing they built was a very solid tea-bar for their own use; they had their post delivered to the house, and they brought in quite a number of their own personal effects, including their wives and girlfriends.

A few weeks after Joe was born, I had to wrest myself from this apogee of domestic comfort and put up with the hardship of a five-star hotel in Manchester for several months while making a new series for Granada entitled *Big Breadwinner Hog*. Still preferring the pen to the telephone, Pru and me continued to communicate via letter generally and it soon became clear that, now the builders had moved out, a green-eyed monster had taken their place.

'Joseph is coming along splendidly as far as one can tell,' she wrote . . .

I'm doing the night feed as well now, as he doesn't seem to fancy bottles. Sam is very jealous, as expected, but very sweet with him. I asked Sam if he would like to hold Joseph and for thirty seconds, he was magic. Then Sam got bored and said, 'Here you go,' and then threw him back. He says, 'Joseph will go away very soon,' quite often; also, 'When is he going back inside your tummy?' But it is all so manifest that I think it should settle eventually.

Pru's prediction did eventually come to pass, of course, but the intervening period was not at all easy. She still insisted, however, on taking both children on tour with her. Sam admitted later that he found this rather unsettling as he'd had two and a half years alone with Pru and they had established a working pattern. 'Then Joe came along and got in the way rather,' he once joked.

Having two children in tow limited the kind of jobs that Pru was able to take on, which frustrated her. Even so, her desire to spend as much time with the boys as possible while they were small outweighed this. 'Being an actress and being a mother is a strain,' she once said. 'Especially if you think that being a mother is as important as I do. It was all right with one baby, but with two, that was when the guilt started. In a play you have to hold something back of yourself for that play. It's like carrying a baby; it takes some of your strength; you have to give it as well as your family. Of course, you could say that you shouldn't take on a play like that, but if it's offered, and it's good enough, you have to take it.'

With me having to take every job offered in order to guarantee a steady income, the only other option when it came to childcare or help for Pru continued to be nannies. We did explore other possibilities but each of them came to naught. My own parents, for instance, were both still working at the time; moreover, their house was far too small. Pru's parents, although extremely bright mentally, were physically rather frail. Bim had suffered a heart attack in 1965 and since then her mobility had suffered somewhat. They were fine coping for short periods, as were my parents, but we're talking a matter of just a few hours, so one of us could never be far away.

One of the most significant and immediate advantages of our new home in Wandsworth, at least for Pru, was that it had a garden. To this day gardening gives Pru unlimited hours of pleasure. 'It gives me a sense of continuity,' she once said. 'And also, a sense of time.' In a long marriage or relationship, I think it's very important for each person to have something in their lives that the other isn't as interested in, and in Pru's case it's gardening. In fact, the only time I can remember having anything to do with our garden is when Pru had asked Sam, who was only about eight at the time, to excavate about a ton of earth from the side of the summerhouse. Why she wanted it doing I have absolutely no idea, but it was bob-a-job week, I remember, and when Sam, as a good Boy Scout, asked Pru if she had any jobs that needed doing, instead of asking him to do some housework or something, she handed him a spade and put him to work in the garden.

My interest was piqued when I heard Pru say to Sam, 'You'll need to go down about a metre and a half, darling, all right?' Fortunately, I just about knew my way from the kitchen to the garden and when I arrived there, I asked Pru what was happening.

'Oh, Sam's just doing a job for me,' she said casually. 'It's bob-a-job week.'

'All right, but what's this about him going down a metre and a half?'

'That's roughly how far I need him to dig down.'

I remember looking at Sam holding the spade. It was bigger than he was.

'You mean, half his height again? This is a job for a navvy, Pru, not an eight-year-old.'

'Perhaps you're right,' said Pru eventually. 'Sam, darling, why don't you wash the car?'

I've no idea where Pru's obsession with gardening came from but it first became apparent to me shortly after we started living together. As our abode in Battersea was situated on the top floor of the building, we didn't have a garden, so Pru decided to liberate several window boxes from a garden centre instead. Apart from having to water them when I was around and Pru wasn't, that was my only input. This began to change slightly in 1968 while we were living in Barnes. Pru was on tour in Toronto with Sam and a nanny, and I was at the Theatre Royal in Bristol appearing in Iris Murdoch's *The Italian Girl*. The fact that neither of us had been at home for some time bothered Pru enormously, not least because the garden had not been tended to or even checked on. After several letters begging me to do so, I finally agreed to take a train up to London one Sunday to walk our estate and check on things, with a further instruction to report back via letter the following day.

How are you in Toronto? Is it still very cold? I went home at the weekend so here is your report on the garden: Ah, well now. Umm. Yes. Right you are. Well, here goes then. RIGHT. From the beginning. My general impression is that there are more leaves than flowers. Just so. Quite a lot more, in fact. The next thing that strikes the intelligent observer is that what flowers there are, are to be found on the left, as you look out of the window. None on the right. No. What are these flowers, you will wish to ask. Well, they are mostly those pink ones, you know several to a stem, also available in blue. And white too. Oh, and purple. Or are those different? Anyway, there are about ten in all. Now I don't want to stick my neck out here, but I believe I may be right in saying there are some daffodils on the same side of the garden, and one thing I'm pretty sure of is that there were a lot more of them at this time last year. At the end of the garden, we seem to have a lot of tall green stuff with small yellow bits on top. A considerable amount. Probably more than anyone else in the road. Well, that's about it. Yes, I believe that just about wraps it up. Anything else you want to know about the garden, you only have to ask.

Soon after we moved to Wandsworth, Pru's aunt Freda died, and she left Pru £500.

'What are you going to spend it on?' I asked her.

'What do you think?' she said.

'Sorry, how silly of me. The garden.'

'I'm going to pay some bills but if there's anything left over, I'm going to have the garden landscaped.'

'Good for you.'

She really was most excited.

The garden itself is oval-shaped, with a lawn in the middle, a border featuring flowerbeds and shrubs mainly, a few trees here and there, and a summerhouse at the back. In size, it's nothing very special, but it's Pru's pride and joy and she's always taken very great care of it. Outside the front of the house is a small patch of earth where Pru used to grow vegetables. 'If you lead a creative life and you're not working,' she once said, 'then to grow things is a relief and satisfaction. A sort of substitute for creative work.' Despite this, her endeavours with the front-garden vegetable patch came to an end when certain people who were waiting for a bus just outside the house started helping themselves to her produce.

'Where on earth are all my green beans?' she asked one morning.

'Oh dear,' I said. 'Have the commuters been at them again?'

As ever, Pru's ability to fret has always enjoyed a starring role in the life and survival of our garden and plays a big part in Pru's gardening persona. Indeed, one day, she came out with a line that has become immortal in our family. Sam and Joe were playing in the garden one afternoon and Pru was watching them keenly from an upstairs window.

'Come and sit down,' I said to her. 'They can't do any harm.'

Completely ignoring me, she carried on watching them like a hawk for several more minutes before suddenly shouting the immortal words: 'Darlings, please don't jump over the lavender until its established.'

I sat there in a state of complete shock. 'Please don't jump over the lavender until it's established?' I repeated. 'My word.'

She wasn't at all embarrassed and I do believe that Sam's partner, Laura, who is a playwright and who has always found it hilarious, has managed to include it in her latest script.

Even today, when Pru meets somebody for the first time she will invariably ask them one or more of the following questions: 'Where do you live?', 'Do you have children?' and 'Do you have a garden?' An exchange will take place regardless of the answers, but if you answer in the affirmative re the garden, Pru's eyes will immediately light up and she'll enquire as to what the layout is and what you grow. The length of the conversation is rather dependent on the answers thereafter, but if she's talking to somebody with green fingers and they're in the mood for a chat, Pru will happily talk for hours. Also, when the weather allows, Pru will spend the majority of her days in the garden deadheading and such like. Apart from spending time with her family, it's what she looks forward to most.

Letters from the Homestead

Much has already been made in our book about letters that are written home when an actor is away on tour, but what of those that are written to the actor from the homestead? The aforementioned subject of financial woes was prevalent in our early days as a married couple but over the years we have reported on hundreds of subjects including (having recently had a good look through some of the letters) pets, gardens, self-confidence, daytime television, school reports, calcium deficiency, adagio dances and even fascists. Whatever's happening in our worlds, basically. Where to begin then? I think fascists is as good a start as any.

This is one of my favourite letters from Pru and there are many to choose from. It was written in 1965 while she was at home making *Marriage Lines* and I was away on tour in something or another.

18th April 1965
Darling Love,

Do hope you didn't ring last night and think I was being unfaithful, I was next door having dinner with Martin, Willow and THREE FASCISTS. Father, wife and 25(?)-year-old son, fat with beard, dark suit, gold-rimmed glasses and beautiful French! I played it very intelligent and upper class and the father fell flat and tried to

recruit me. 'Our movement has sent representatives to seventeen
university debating societies in the last two years and won every
time.' I got awfully drunk and said it was disgraceful and he
LOVED it . . . 'You speak French, my dear, I thought so,
I could tell you were a highly civilised woman, just the sort we want
in the movement.' Gosh, it was funny. Change a word here and
there and they might have been Moral Reasoners. I do think
rich upper-class movements are the most frightening of all. Both
father and son were wearing navy blue white-spotted ties by
COINCIDENCE. The father was a hard rider, and I was
sorely tempted to say that I was anti bloody sports as well, but I
was afraid he might have an orgasm at the table. Ho, ho. WISH
you had been there. Martin and Willow behaved beautifully
throughout, I believe they're friends of the sort of people Martin is
working for in Spain. Really stinking rich, so rich the wife's hair
looked as if she'd just got out of bed.

Great Love,
Your Pruey xx

I arrived home roughly two weeks later and although we
hadn't seen each other for well over two months that was
the first thing we talked about.

'Tell me more about these fascists you encountered,' I
asked hungrily.

'Oh, darling, they were awful! The son was completely
repugnant. I do wish you'd been there.'

I can't recall a time when either of us was out of work
for more than a few days during the late 1960s and early
1970s. Even so, money remained scarce after we bought
the house in Wandsworth and, due to her being rather

good at it, Pru did the majority of the worrying. In addition to repairs to the house and everyday living expenses we were paying £5 a week towards her parents' rent, and we were paying almost £10 a week for the nanny. It did get to a point in 1970 when we thought that we might have to sell the car, which would have had a material effect on our earning power, not to mention our domestic life. The following letter is the earliest I can find from Pru after moving in.

Darling

Herewith gas bill, which though not as much as you thought, is still pretty staggering: I promise the next one won't be as bad. I've got everything off most of the time now, and this covers the installation time when it was roaring away full blast each day. BUT, I'm afraid I can't pay it, nor Harvey's, which I also enclose. They have agreed to allow us £21 for the decoration etc, so it's only £71:17:0. I will send them Alf's statements when I get them.

Don't know what we're going to do for money. Have heard nothing about Tetley's. Still, we're luckier than most. Bob and Patti have not been out for MONTHS. Both working again now. Bob dropped in this morning.

URGENT: did you complete that form about the rates? We'll go to prison or something if it's not in before 21 days.

Much love,
Pruey xx

Like Pru, I did worry about our situation, although not nearly as much as she did. This began to change, however, when in the early 1970s Pru claimed to feel like a failure in one of her letters.

Would welcome suggestions on how to cut down. Shall stay in digs in Cheltenham, not buy any more plants for the garden, etc. etc., but short of sacking the au pair and selling the children I don't know what else I can do. I feel a frightful failure . . . very depressed about it all. It seems so easy to get into debt, and so cripplingly hard to climb out of it.

This letter had a profound effect on me and although I continued writing to Pru as often as I could, I also began telephoning her regularly.

'Look, darling,' I said after reading the letter. 'This financial thing is just temporary, you have to believe that. It's more to do with cashflow than anything else. We just need to get paid a bit quicker, that's all. If it hadn't been for your efforts in economising, by the way, we'd have been in the workhouse. Failure, my foot!'

Although my words had an effect of sorts, they were fortified by way of some timely well-paid work – namely, a television advert. Pru had already made several of these, most notably for Tetley Tea a year or two before *Marriage Lines* first started and it had paid handsomely.

'Tetley Tea want me for a second time,' she said excitedly, after putting down the phone.

'Oh, that's a relief. We'll be able to pay some bills now.'

The company had enquired about Pru some three months previously and knowing full well that the money would put us back on an even keel again had made the wait almost unbearable. Not just for Pru, but for both of us.

The first advert Pru made for Tetley Tea was basically a thirty-second infomercial telling the great British public how to make tea using tea bags. It sounds rather ridiculous now, but back then teabags were a new thing and, regardless of their convenience, the general public were mistrusting of them. Pru and me actually watched the advert a few days ago and her performance is a real *tour de force*. 'Hello, I'm just making a cup of tea,' she says. 'And I'm using Tetley Tea bags. Look, here's what you do. You put one tea bag per person into a nice warm pot,' etc. etc. etc.

'Good lord, how long ago was that?' Pru asked me.

'I'm not telling you,' I replied. 'It'll make you sick.'

'As long ago as that then? Oh dear.'

As part of her deal for the advert in 1970, which we haven't seen since, Pru was given what was supposed to be a year's supply of tea. This was an added extra, by the way. Had they tried to swap cash for tea bags they'd have received short shrift. The tea bags arrived in a very large box and, because I was at home alone at the time, I decided to open it. Inside were lots of smaller boxes and after finding the individual tea bags I proceeded to hide them all over the house, or wherever Pru might venture – drawers, wardrobes, cupboards and so on. I even hid them in her clothes. It was 1974 by the time she found them all.

'Are you sure there aren't any more?' she asked me.

'Fairly,' I confessed.

Pru remained in demand with advertising companies until fairly recently, whereas my own career in commercials never really took off. The most memorable one I ever made was for Pilkington Glass in 1987. One or two readers might even remember it. Literally, one or two. While I stand in a studio extolling the many virtues of Pilkington Glass a marksman prepares to fire a gun at my head and when he finally pulls the trigger my life is saved by what else but a large pane of Pilkington bulletproof glass. Instantly forgettable, but the money was great.

Ten years earlier, I'd really thought I'd made it in the advertising world when I was asked by Cadbury, no less, to play Henry VIII in an advert for a new product called Cadbury's Plain Six. It was part of a series of commercials directed by Richard Lester featuring Shakespearean characters such as Hamlet, Henry VIII and Richard III, extolling the virtues of this exciting new confection.

As Bluff King Hal, I was to be discovered lying on a couch beside a comely wench and, after growing tired of her charms, would reach beneath a cushion and retrieve a Cadbury's Plain Six. It was quite a funny idea, I thought, and after the first morning's rehearsal Richard Lester informed me that he was happy with the progress we had made thus far.

Less happy was the worried-looking gentleman in the canvas chair with 'Client' written on the back of it. He asked if he could have a word with me, so I pulled up my own canvas chair and invited him to go ahead. 'Look, he said, before drawing a long breath. 'What we're trying to sell here is plain chocolate. Right?'

I agreed.

'In fact, this is a plain chocolate campaign, right?'

'Right,' I said with less certainty.

'What you are doing would be fine if we were selling milk chocolate. Do you see what I mean?'

Try as I might, my brain would not play ball. 'No,' I said. 'I'm afraid I don't.'

'At the end of the war,' he began, 'when chocolate reappeared in the shops, it was almost all milk chocolate, which is easier to produce. Our parents bought us milk chocolate, and we in turn passed on the habit.' He was already losing me. 'Consequently, the only indigenous plain chocolate consumers tend now to be in their seventies, and it's our business to try to enlarge the market.' He then looked at me intently. 'Look at the After Eight adverts,' he said. 'Dinner parties, black tie, expensive dresses, candelabra. Silver! That's the impression we're trying to create. The world of plain chocolate is something to aspire to.'

'You mean –' I said cannily – 'you want a soft sell?' I forget where I'd heard the phrase, but it was in context and impressed him greatly.

'Exactly,' he beamed. 'Do you think you can help?'

'I will do my best,' I said solemnly. 'You have my word.'

When it came to shooting the advert, I merely lowered my voice slightly, but the client seemed delighted. 'That's it,' he said, after Richard had shouted 'cut'.

The product flopped, of course, and I was later told by a marketing expert that the number six had been its downfall. 'If the buyer wants to share it with someone, how do they break it? With eight pieces, or twelve, or sixteen, it's easy. Not with six. You have to end up with an even number each.' I didn't quite see what he was getting at but it was better than blaming the advertising.

I obviously can't prove it but I think Pru must have been one of the first people in history to report on outsized knitted sweaters, calcium deficiency, a macabre adagio dance, insubordination, tax and lettuces in the same letter. It was written in August 1970.

Darling Love,

Here, at last is your sweater. Sorry it's so long and wide.

Boys are well, Sam does a macabre adagio dance ending up under the bed, very impressive, and Joseph eats a good deal of eggshells, like an old hen, I suppose it's calcium deficiency.

Yesterday I asked Sam to get me something and he said, 'Fetch it yourself, I'm doing this.' So I protested sharply and he said, 'Mummy, could you possibly manage it yourself because I'm rather busy at the moment.'

Do you think you could possibly start saving a fiver a week towards tax? It should be ten really, but I know your running costs are high. We still owe £262, and you are, at the moment, earning more than I am, and it looks as if that's going to go on for a bit.

The potatoes have succeeded triumphantly, and we should have some lettuces soon, so the garden isn't all that of a self-indulgence.

All my love,
Pruey xx

One thing we have never been in short supply of since moving to Wandsworth is pets, which is the subject of perhaps my second favourite letter from Pru. These days we have one cat, Hannah, who you might say is at the top of the food chain. In the 1970s, however, it was sometimes like a menagerie.

Before meeting Pru, I had always been a dog person, whereas she had always preferred the company of cats.

Soon after getting married, Pru informed me that she intended to bring home a cat and at first I was in two minds. After all, I had married Pru, not Pru plus feline companion. I eventually gave her my blessing and so she acquired one – a ginger cat she called Lion – from a farm belonging to some friends of my parents.

'Why did you name him Lion?' I asked her one day.

'Watch this,' said Pru.

'LION!' she shouted. 'COME HERE, LION!' A few seconds later the small and very un-lion-like cat trotted into the room looking a bit bemused. 'There,' said Pru smiling. 'Isn't that fun?'

At first I was indifferent to Lion's presence and just ignored him. He was Pru's cat, not mine. Then, while we were staying at the cottage that we had rented just outside Stratford while I was appearing with the RSC and Pru was working in Birmingham, Lion, who hadn't taken to War-wickshire at all and clearly missed Barnes, started acting strangely. He seemed to adapt very poorly to touring and we were nervous that he would try to walk back to London. One morning I was in the bath and Pru was at the wash basin and a towel suddenly slipped off the rail behind my head and into the water. I immediately leapt out of the bath and shouted, 'Christ!'

'What on earth's the matter?' asked Pru.

'Oh, thank God,' I said. 'I thought it was the kitten com-mitting suicide.'

That, according to Pru, was confirmation that I had become a cat convert.

A few years later after Lion had passed away, we got two Burmese cats. One was already called Lilly and nominations to name the second cat came in thick and fast. Sam, who was a big cricket fan, wanted to call him Thomson, as in Dennis Lillee and Jeff Thomson.

'I don't like cricket,' said Pru. 'How about Skinner, as in Lilley & Skinner?'

'I am very much against cruelty to animals,' I interjected, 'and if you decide to name these two cats after a shoe shop, I will inform the RSPCA.'

'How about Gish?' said Joe. 'Mummy loves Lillian Gish.'

'Lilly and Gish. Mmm, maybe,' said Pru.

At the time of the cat's arrival, I was working at the Old Vic Theatre, so I suggested the theatre's one-time licensee, Lilian Baylis. 'That's the one,' said Pru. 'Lilly and Baylis it is. It's the perfect pun.'

Lilly and Baylis became the cats of Sam and Joe's childhood and fortunately they have many memories of them, as do we. Sam thinks that his mother has always been a little bit cat-like, but especially these days. Because of her condition, she'll quietly enter a room without purpose and without knowing quite why she's there. When I meet people in the street the first thing they ask me is, 'How's Pru?' and I always say that, actually, she's quite jolly. We'll come onto that later, though.

Lilly and Baylis used to sleep on the wooden radiator covers in the living room and the boys worked out that if you stroked Baylis between his back and his shoulders, and not too hard, he would arch his hind legs and then push them up. Positioned correctly, he would push the picture above him off the wall. Sam and Joe used to find this most amusing. Pru and me, less so.

Anyway, on to this letter from Pru. In addition to cats,

reptiles and, later, rats, we also kept a variety of fish in the house. The demise of one such gill-bearing aquatic animal caused a great deal of worry for Pru, not surprisingly, and robbed me of a trusted friend and confidant.

Darling Love,

I'm sorry to say, – Hector the goldfish has died entirely through my fault: I finally got around to cleaning and moving the tank, cleaning the gravel etc., yesterday, and I put Hector and Silver in a bowl while I was doing it and Hector jumped out while I was out of the room and was dead when Sam and Kelly [the nanny] found him. They've gone to get another one this morning although Sam was very upset at first I'm afraid he and Joseph now discuss it with extreme enthusiasm and cheerfulness. The tank I must say is better in the dining room and I've fixed the light so I hope Silver will adjust to new chum but I'm most terribly sorry for being so careless.

Took Kelly to see Sunday Bloody Sunday last night. Very enjoyable. She's doing quite well now, I've got her L-plates and she should really pass next time.

Sam in cap and blazer is deeply moving and obvious Scoutmaster fodder I'm afraid. School seems to be going OK.

Sorry!

All my love
Pru xx

On receiving Pru's letter I sank into a mini-depression. I can't tell you how or why it started, but before his pal Silver arrived on the scene (or should I say, in the tank) I was alone with Hector in the conservatory one day and I just started talking to him. He seemed like quite an amiable sort of chap and was always interested in what I had to say and so it became a regular thing. Some people talk to plants, so why not a goldfish?

'How could you, Pru?' I said after deciding to call her on the telephone. 'My one true friend and confidant, gone forever.'

'Oh, I'm sorry, darling,' she said feigning contrition. 'Would it help if we named the new one Hector?'

'I suppose it might soften the blow a bit,' I said gloomily.

I still miss him.

Australia

The first trip of note that we made together as a family was to Australia in 1972. The Prospect Theatre Company, which I was now heavily involved in, had been invited to perform *King Lear* and *Love's Labour's Lost* at the Adelaide Festival followed by a ten-week tour. Happily, due to some cast changes, Pru was able to join the company playing the Princess of France, which meant the boys would have to come too. And their nanny, of course. She was called Kelly (you might recognize the name from one of Pru's letters) and she'd been with us for some time.

The only holiday of note that Pru and me had taken prior to leaving for Australia had been to the island of Majorca for a few days. Sam had just finished weaning and Pru was exhausted, so I booked it as a surprise. Pru was initially reluctant as she didn't want to leave Sam, but as I began to recount the list of friends and family who I knew would be only too happy to look after our firstborn for a few days, the concern began to lift from Pru's face. 'Actually, I think that might be rather lovely,' she said.

We visited the town of Deià, situated on the northwest coast of the island, and one day we were invited by the celebrated poet and author, Robert Graves – he of *I, Claudius* fame – to have dinner with him and some friends of his in his garden. Robert had arrived in Deià in the late

1920s and after deciding to make it his home he built a handsome two-storey house made from locally quarried stone and mortar. These days La Casa de Robert Graves is shrine to the great man and receives thousands of visitors each year.

Robert told us that Deià had served as a police observation post during and after the Second World War, when locals did a brisk business smuggling cigarettes and other goods across the Mediterranean from Tangiers. Sometime during the 1960s the smugglers turned to hashish, which had made the area popular with the police once again. Having lived through it all, Robert decided to write a play about the smugglers and, thanks to an assembled cast consisting mainly of villagers, he was presenting it for an invited audience of which Pru and me were part.

It quickly became clear that every single member of Robert's cast was stoned, as were the majority of the invited audience, and in no time at all we were both in a similar state. Subsequently, neither of us remember a damn thing about the play, except for the fact that there was very little movement and not a great deal of text.

The flight we took to Australia was something of a marathon (Heathrow–Zurich–Dubai–Calcutta–Singapore–Perth–Melbourne, with a connecting flight to Adelaide) and in total took something like thirty-six hours, during which time I managed to procure a very painful throat infection that felt steadily worse as the hours wore on. With festival appearances and a ten-week tour on the horizon this caused a not inconsiderable amount of concern within the company, and so when we got to Melbourne a doctor in North Adelaide was contacted who said he would see me

as soon as we landed. When we did so there was a car waiting to take me to his surgery.

I'd hardly slept a wink on the plane and so after Pru and
the boys had waved me off on my journey I dozed grog-
gily. The door to the surgery was opened by a beautiful
nurse who appeared to be slightly flustered and rather
taken aback by my arrival.

'Oh gosh, we didn't expect you quite so soon,' she apologized, pushing a stray lock of hair back from her forehead.
She glanced behind her, and a young man appeared at the
end of the hall. He was buttoning up his white coat but
beneath that he appeared to be without trousers.

'I have clearly interrupted a very important meeting,' I
said earnestly. 'Would you like me to go for a quick walk?'

'No, no, no,' said the nurse, quickly adopting a professional tone. 'Please, do come in. The doctor will be with
you in a moment. Can I get you a glass of water, Mr West?'

'That would be very nice, thank you.'

The doctor, who appeared to be anything but flustered,
was politeness itself and after inviting me into his surgery
he examined my throat, sprayed it with something and
then wrote out a prescription.

As I got up to leave, I thanked him for seeing me at such
short notice and apologized if I had, erm, disturbed him at
an inopportune moment.

'No worries,' he assured me cheerfully, 'my wife –' indi-
cating the nurse – 'was just fixing some lunch.'

I thought, *Is that what you call it?* Thereupon the doctor
stood up and on taking off his white coat he revealed a pair
of knee-length khaki shorts.

I relayed all this to Pru when I eventually arrived at the

hotel but when she asked me the obvious question – 'Well,' she said absorbedly. 'Were they, or weren't they?' – I couldn't tell her.

'Let it be another of life's great mysteries,' I conceded.

'Really?' she said. 'Well, that's no fun.'

We were very impressed by Adelaide. The square mile of the city proper is indeed a square, bound by four broad avenues simply named the North, South, East and West Terraces. Beyond each of these lies another mile of open parkland, giving space for golf courses, tennis courts, a racecourse and even a zoo. Beyond Adelaide's green belt lie its suburbs – single-storey houses with their own little gardens, accommodating all together a population of just over a million, but covering an area about as large as Greater London.

By the time the Adelaide Festival of Arts began my throat was no longer infected and the entire affair was really most impressive. In addition to Prospect's two Shakespeare plays, the Melbourne Theatre Company were presenting the mighty Leo McKern in Ray Lawler's *The Man Who Shot the Albatross* while the celebrated Irish actress, Siobhán McKenna, made several appearances with her one-woman show, *Here Are Ladies*. Over on the musical side they had secured the services of Neville Marriner (not yet a Sir) directing the Academy of St Martin in the Fields with a repertoire featuring Purcell, Mozart, Elgar, Bach and Handel, and The Australian Opera performing Benjamin Britten's *The Rape of Lucretia*. We really were in terrific company and our own performances were well attended and well received.

From Adelaide we moved on to Sydney, playing at the

fine old Theatre Royal in Castlereagh Street. Our tenure here proved to be a bittersweet experience for the entire company as the theatre-going public of Sydney had been in a years-long battle to save the theatre from developers who had bought the freehold and wanted to pull it down and build an enormous office block on the land. The plans had been met with fierce opposition, of course, and ultimately instead of managing to save the theatre from demolition the committee in charge had persuaded the developers to build a new one in its place. Given the theatre's history (it had been built way back in 1875) this was a great, great shame; worse still, our performances were to be the last ever put on there.

'You should make a speech,' Pru suggested.

'Really? Do you think it's my place?'

'You're leading the company, so of course it's your place.'

So, on Saturday 29 April 1972, at the end of the performance of *Love's Labour's Lost*, I delivered a valedictory speech before the curtain fell on the old Theatre Royal for the very last time. The 'sweet' part of our experience was that our run had been a success in Sydney (it would have been an awful end to the theatre's history if we'd been a flop) and that final night was extraordinary. People stayed in the auditorium until dawn, singing and crying. When I cleared out my dressing room, I helped myself to an old notice from the previous century that sternly forbade the bringing backstage of cooked food, alcohol, fruit, animals or visitors, on pain of dismissal.

After Sydney, we did a quick dash up to Brisbane, where we stayed with some cousins of Pru's in the Queensland backwoods. 'You deserve a bit of peace and quiet after

Sydney,' they told us, and my word, were we ready for it. It hadn't been all work, however. We'd spent quite a lot of time on the beach in a place called Nielsen Park and it's fair to say that our nanny, Kelly, had caused quite a stir there.

'Why is everybody staring so intently at her?' I asked Pru.

'What, you mean all those young men? Why do you think? Have you seen what she's wearing?'

'You mean what she's not wearing.'

The peace and quiet that we had been hoping for in Queensland, and indeed had been assured of by Pru's cousins, alas did not materialize. The kookaburras started 'laughing', as I believe their call is called, at roughly five o'clock each morning and they set off the cows, which also had bells tied around their necks. Shortly after that, all six of the children would jump out of their beds, leap on their individual ponies and ride around the gardens, whooping and shouting to one another. While at the Sheraton Hotel overlooking Sydney Harbour, we had enjoyed perfect tranquillity (and had not been required to inspect the underside of the 'dunny' just in case a snake had paid us a visit).

After bidding an altogether fond farewell to Queensland we moved on to Melbourne, where we played for two weeks before flying home. Or should I say, before sitting on the runway opposite the airport's observation gallery while our hosts waved and laughed for an hour and a half before they eventually shrugged good humouredly and slid away.

'The boys are starting to get a bit crabby,' Pru said worriedly. 'Shall I speak to somebody?'

'No,' I replied. 'Leave it to me.'

As is so often the way in situations like these, after

making several enquiries it quickly became clear that nobody had a clue as to what on earth was going on.

'I'm afraid we've drawn a blank,' I said. 'Here, pass Joe over. I'll keep him company for a while.'

After a couple of hours, the plane turned back to the terminal and we were instructed to alight. There'd been some kind of technical fault, apparently, and after waiting around for another couple of hours we were eventually put on a coach and taken to a nearby hotel. The next morning, having lost twelve hours, we took off for Hong Kong, Bangkok and Tehran. At Tehran there was another delay on the ground and after a good hour we were informed by the captain that we were going to be offered free drinks from a trolley. Now if you're travelling Economy Class, an announcement for free drinks always signifies bad news and, sure enough, just a few seconds later Pru called me over.

'Have a look at this, darling,' she said, pointing out of the window. 'It looks like they're taking the engine to pieces.'

'What? Good God, they are!'

The entire port-side engine had been laid out in pieces on a large tarpaulin and was being stared at by what I hoped were mechanics.

Once again, we were turned off the plane and taken to another hotel, this time at gunpoint, and having had to surrender our passports.

'I'm not sure I quite believe what's happening to us,' said a somewhat bewildered Pru as we boarded the coach. 'Still, at least the boys are enjoying themselves. To them it's just an adventure.'

At some ungodly hour we were herded from the hotel

back to the airport and this time made it to Frankfurt before one of our toilets sprang a leak. It was at this juncture that the cabin crew came around with the questionnaires asking for passenger's comments.

'Has this been done in an attempt to lighten the mood?' I asked one of the attendants.

'I beg your pardon, sir?' She appeared to have no idea what I was talking about.

'The questionnaires,' I persevered. 'Bearing in mind the issues we have encountered thus far – little things like being herded at gunpoint from the plane to a hotel and then back again – one might have surmised that questions regarding satisfaction might be somewhat untimely.'

Again, the young lady who had handed me the form appeared not to be on the same page. 'I'm sorry if you're not completely satisfied, sir.'

'Do you have a pen, please?'

I'm sure that most of the questionnaires were filled in on that flight (there was nothing else to do) and in all cases they must have made for interesting reading.

We finally landed at Heathrow airport on Wednesday afternoon. 'Look at that,' I said to Pru, pointing at my watch. 'Thirty-six hours almost to the minute. Quite impressive.' All joking aside, the financial consequences of the entire company landing a day and a half late were potentially dire for Prospect. Each of us had lost two days holiday entitlement, which would have to be paid by the company as travelling days. A lengthy legal battle ensued, at the end of which the airline finally coughed up. There was one condition, however.

'They asked for a photo from *King Lear* to use for

promotional purposes. Apparently, they want to display it in their window underneath the slogan, "BOAC Takes Care of You".'

'So what did you choose?'

'Gloucester having his eyes gouged out.'

Family Matters

The following passages concern our children, Juliet, Sam and Joe.

Juliet

The words you are about to read have not come easily to me. Indeed, at the last count I have attempted to begin this chapter four times and on each attempt I have failed. Perhaps this is appropriate, however, as my own failures are at the crux of the story you are about to read.

I claimed much earlier in the book that when my first wife Jacqueline and I began to drift apart, our daughter Juliet became my priority. This remained the case for all too short a period, as over time I began to drift apart from her too. Jacqueline had suffered her first major breakdown when Juliet was about two years old, and after time, it had made both of us realize that we were very different people. There had been no vehement demonstrations of this, and I dare say that, had we been inclined to, we might have rubbed along OK together. It wasn't to be, however, and with me working away from home most of the time, a separation became inevitable. What happened next, you already know.

Over the next four or five years I saw Juliet perhaps four or five times a year. I am completely to blame for this and having thought about it a great deal over the years I have concluded that I must have put up some kind of barrier between us in order to draw a line under everything. A similar thing had happened with the divorce, of course, whereby I offered to act as the guilty party as a means to everyone being able to move on. I did keep in touch with Juliet, but I only ever saw her at birthday parties and such like. I was not being a father to her.

The catalyst for change was certainly Pru. She had always been anxious about my daughter and the barrier I had put in place did not sit well with her. 'You should really try to see more of Juliet,' she used to say to me. 'Why not invite her for tea?' Juliet was living in Putney at the time with her mother and grandmother and so gradually, after taking Pru's advice, we began purposely to see more of each other. 'Are you my new mummy?' she used to ask Pru at the very beginning. 'No darling, I'm your new step-mummy,' Pru would tell her.

For a not inconsiderable amount of time, Juliet's relationship with Pru was far stronger than her relationship with me. In Pru's opinion, this was partly down to them both being female and so having certain related things in common. A degree of shame on my part, however, was also undoubtedly to blame. I simply did not know what to say or what to do about it.

Some small amount of progress was made in 1968 when Juliet confided in Pru that she was dreadfully unhappy at her new school, a huge comprehensive just down the road from us in Wandsworth.

'Can't she go to Moira House?' suggested Pru. 'Both mum and I were blissfully happy there.'

'But what would Jacqueline say?' I countered. 'It will seem like we are interfering.'

'We can only ask her,' said Pru. 'Shall I speak to Juliet first?'

Fortunately, Jacqueline had also been made aware of Juliet's problems at her current school and so after telling her and Juliet all about Moira House, Pru and I took Juliet down there for a look around. There had been well over two thousand pupils at the comprehensive she attended, and when Juliet asked how many were at Moira House, the answer went down rather well. 'About a hundred and eighty in all,' said Pru. The tour was a resounding success. Juliet adored the school and she and the headmistress seemed to get along famously.

'So, darling, do you think you'd be happy here?' Pru asked.

'Yes, definitely,' she said. 'I really do.'

Jacqueline's mother had already insisted on paying her granddaughter's fees for Moira House, so it was all systems go.

Despite her initial enthusiasm, it took Juliet several months to get used to boarding away from home and she informed me recently that her early letters to her mother and to Pru featured 'circled tears', no less. Fortunately, her grief was only temporary and not only did she become extremely happy at Moira House but she has since admitted that from the age of about thirteen she would happily have stayed on during the holidays.

Rather ironically, during the years that Juliet attended Moira House she and I probably saw even less of each other, as during the holidays she felt obliged to spend time with her mother and grandmother. She was happy, though, and me having been a part of something positive in her life for once was undoubtedly a source of comfort.

In the early 1970s, Jacqueline and the man who had

become her new husband decided to move to South Wales. Having been born and bred in London, Juliet was unhappy at the idea of having to go with them. She once again confided in Pru. 'Then you must come and live with us,' Pru suggested. And so, she did. The boys, who had always adored Juliet, were thrilled when we told them.

Far from using this as an opportunity to get to know my daughter, I'm afraid I cocooned myself in the comforting notion that Juliet, Pru and the boys were all happy. I was also incredibly busy, and was still at a loss as to how best forge any kind of meaningful relationship. The longer this went on, the easier it became for me to hide behind the realization that Juliet was turning into a happy, beautiful and well-adjusted young lady, which is where I remained into her adult life.

One great blessing is that Pru and the boys were never encumbered by my own emotional issues regarding Juliet, which meant they were free to treat her as one of our own, and they did. I asked Joe a little while ago if he remembered Juliet arriving at the house. 'Not really,' he said. 'Jules has always been a part of my life. She's always been there.' Sam too has little recollection of life without his big sister being around. And as for Pru, well, in addition to her always having been a stepmother, strictly of the non-evil variety, as time went by her relationship with Juliet grew stronger still. Pru always claimed that she wouldn't have liked a daughter of her own. 'Too much competition,' she once said. 'With Juliet, I didn't have to go through all that. It's been marvellous and I think we're good for each other.'

My own relationship with Juliet didn't really begin until

2001. I'm afraid that isn't a typing error. Two years previously I had written a volume of autobiography called *A Moment Towards the End of the Play* and in that featured a statement of regret that I had never been able to say to Juliet in person before.

The passage reads:

> I regret more than anything in the world the years of my daughter's life that I lost; that essential time between the ages of five and ten, when a father and daughter should be companions and discover all manner of things together. Those years are irreplaceable, and I feel them as a great hole into which even now I stare blankly, every time we meet.

Unbeknownst to me, when the book was first published in 2001, Juliet went out and acquired a copy. She'd long since moved out by then and I never thought for a moment that she might be interested in reading it. And therein lies part of the problem. It breaks my heart to write this, but Juliet assumed that I did not care about her and on reading the passage she realized that I did. And I do, enormously. In her letter she said that she loved me and always had and that she was proud of me. By return, I told her that I felt exactly the same.

'Isn't it funny,' I said, 'that we both find it easier to write what we mean than say what we mean. Very British.'

Juliet was having problems with a boyfriend at the time, and I reminded her in the letter that she was an attractive, intelligent, loving and thoroughly worthwhile object of such affection as our lamentably useless male sex might summon up the effort to offer when they feel like it, or something like that. Hearts were poured out, that's for sure.

A few weeks later Juliet came down from Winchester, where she was now living, to visit Pru and me, and when I answered the front door no words were spoken. There'd be time for that later. It had been forty-four years in the making but finally, thanks primarily to Juliet, we were able to embrace each other actually as father and daughter.

'She never gave up, did she?' Pru said to me later that evening when we were in bed. 'Never gave up on you and her. I'm so glad for you both.'

Sam and Joe

In a moment I'll tell you about our other two dependants, Sam and Joe. But before that, perhaps I should touch on what Pru and I were like as parents. On the whole, I think we were quite liberal and laid back, which I believe was a popular style of parenting in the 1970s and 80s. Allow me to give you an example. This is one of those famous family anecdotes that gets an airing at parties and such like, and as well as always guaranteeing a fair number of laughs, if somebody present hasn't heard the story before, the stock-in-trade response is usually shock, followed by incredulity, followed by laughter.

It all happened one sunny afternoon in the summer of 1977 on what must have been either a Saturday or a Sunday. Pru was away on tour at the time, and I was at home with Sam, Joe and one of their carers. I was reading a script in the living room when all of a sudden Joe made an appearance.

'Daddy,' he said. 'Can I have a bath?'

'But it's the middle of the afternoon. Are you sure you want to have one now? Why not wait until bedtime?'

'I want to play with my boat.'

Ever the amenable patriarch, I duly gave Joe permission to have a bath on the strict understanding that he keep an eye on it while the water was running.

'Yes, I promise,' he said, leaving the room and then bounding up the stairs.

I next saw Joe about half an hour later. He was playing happily in the garden, and I naively assumed that he must have had his bath and was in the process of getting dirty again, which he was always rather good at. After observing him for a few seconds I went back to my script and about five minutes later a colossal and worryingly prolonged crashing noise interrupted the afternoon's stillness. I remember thinking to myself very briefly that it sounded like a ceiling had collapsed. I went to investigate and quickly realized that unfortunately, my premonition had been accurate.

The scene that greeted me was incredible. For the first few moments my vision was impaired by a cloud of white dust that had completely filled the room and was endeavouring to permeate the rest of the floor. Watching it disperse and settle was like a nightmare unfolding. Debris was still falling so I decided against venturing any further and instead I went upstairs to assess the damage there. The first thing I did was turn off the taps in the bathroom, and realized that my feet were now soaking wet. Much of the water had journeyed south, of course, but there was still enough on the bathroom and landing floors to sink a small boat.

'What do you remember about that day?' I asked Joe recently.

'I remember you arriving at the back door,' he said. 'You were holding my toy boat and you were shaking your head. You were also a little bit dusty.' On seeing me standing there, it occurred to Joe what had happened. 'Uh-oh,' he said.

Despite all the chaos, damage, mess, expense and wet feet, there was no need for recriminations or histrionics. It was just one of those things that children do from time to time. And adults, I expect. Even so, Joe was reminded on several occasions thereafter about the importance of endeavouring not to destroy two rooms in one day.

I once regaled a friend of ours with this story and after delivering the punchline – Joe's 'Uh-oh' – Pru, who happened to be in the same room as us at the time but with her head buried in a script, suddenly piped up.

'My father shot my mother one day through a ceiling,' she said. 'It made a frightful mess.'

A moment of stunned silence followed. 'Really?' I said incredulously. 'You've never told me this before.'

'Haven't I?' she replied nonchalantly, as if half-heartedly trying to remember what she'd had for breakfast. 'It's all this talk of ceilings, I suppose.'

'Well, come on then,' I said impatiently as we turned around to face her. 'Enlighten us.'

'Oh, all right then. One morning when Dad was shaving in the kitchen, he saw a pigeon in the elderberry tree eating the berries, which we used for jam. He went into the sitting-room where his twelve-bore shotgun was hanging on meat hooks, loaded it, shot the pigeon through the open kitchen window, and went back to hang up the gun again. He must have forgotten to unload the second barrel, because when he hung it up again, his thumb, still covered in shaving soap, slipped on the hammer, and he inadvertently pulled the trigger.'

As Pru spoke our chum and I sat there completely agog. I couldn't believe it.

'The shot blew an enormous hole in the sitting-room ceiling. Ma's bedroom was above, and he thought he had shot her. The noise woke me up, and when I went into Ma's room there was powdered plaster coming through the floorboards and a white-faced Dad in the doorway saying, "Are you all right?"'

Getting back to parenthood for a moment, you can't allow your children to do everything, of course. Or should I say, you can't allow them to believe that they can do everything. The two are not the same. Sam once made the point that now he has children of his own he's come to appreciate what a difficult line this is to tread as a parent, as allowing your children to cross that line and make mistakes is an important part of them growing up and becoming who they are.

In hindsight, I don't think we got it quite right with Sam. He was rather shy as a child and could probably have done with some encouragement from me and Pru to rebel a bit more. 'You allowed me to do what I wanted,' he once said, 'but, on the whole, I didn't want to do it. I could have done with being made to feel naughty a bit more.'

Joe's first act of rebellion took place at the age of twelve when he completely fell off the rails by having one of his ears pierced. Although we weren't especially bothered, we knew our approval would not have gone down well and so, after making a few harrumphing noises, Joe was quite happy. The weekend following his revolt, we all went to visit Bim and John in Surrey and took Bim out for tea. In Joe's eyes, Bim – a genteel but strident elderly lady with a penchant for Pekinese – would have surely been considered an easy win in terms of disapproval. Outrage would be guaranteed. Sadly, despite making sure the earring was clearly visible to his grandmother, Bim failed to comment and, after stuffing an entire chocolate éclair into his mouth, Joe stomped off to the toilets.

'Mum, did you notice Joe's earring?' Pru asked.

'Yes, dear,' she said. 'I think it suits him, although I didn't want to embarrass him by saying so.'

'No, Mum, it's an act of rebellion! He wants you to be outraged.'

'Oh, I see. All right, dear,' said Bim. 'Leave it to me.'

When Joe returned his mood had not improved, but it was about to.

'Joseph,' began Bim, while leaning forward and staring intently in the direction of his appendage. 'What on earth is that? Good lord, it's an earring!'

Joe was absolutely delighted and so the job was done.

'Thanks, Mum,' Pru said before we left. 'You've made a very young rebel very happy.'

The relationship that children have with their parents these days is quite different to how it was when Pru and me were growing up. What's changed, I think, although I'm not quite sure when or why it happened, is that parents and their children now communicate a great deal more than they used to, and have discovered that, shock horror, they might actually have things in common and even rather like one another.

A consequence of this is that children can now inform their parents what's worrying them, which is, of course, exactly how it should be. This is something I wish I had been able to do with my parents, and especially when I was struggling at school. Alas, neither of them ever showed any interest, and so I didn't say anything. In fact, I can't remember ever having a conversation with either of my parents about anything when I was a child, although I'd have liked to. A bond existed between us, as I'm sure it did between the vast majority of parents and their children, but not a relationship. Adults were adults, children were children, and never the twain shall meet – except at mealtimes and at bedtime, or if an indiscretion was committed.

For Pru I believe it was different, at least with Bim. They were always very close, and communication had always been encouraged between them. Therefore, when the boys came along, Pru wanted to get to know her sons as soon as she was able. I did too, but I didn't find it quite as easy as she did. This was down to my upbringing, of course, but also my professional situation. As I have already stated, if my family seemed to be happy, I just carried on working and let them get on with it. That said, wherever I was in the world, Juliet and the boys were never far from my thoughts and had it not been for Pru's written updates, I wouldn't have managed nearly as well as I did.

Although I wasn't much good at pastoral care, I did manage to find other ways to show my children that I cared about them. One of these was when I started decorating cakes. Yes, really. One of the boys had a birthday coming up, I remember, and I was tasked by Pru with locating the birthday cake.

'How should it be decorated?' I enquired.

'I've no idea,' she said. 'Their name and age, I suppose. That's what they usually have on them.'

I'm ashamed to admit that I had never taken a great deal of notice of my children's birthday cakes before then (or any others, for that matter), but it seemed to me that 'name and age' on a child's birthday cake lacked imagination.

'Well, if you can produce something better, be my guest,' said Pru, after I'd voiced my concerns.

Unlike her, I had always been a stranger to the kitchen and the extent of my skills therein was opening bottles of wine. Even so, the challenge of creating a cake worthy of a child's birthday interested me and so I accepted.

'Really?' said Pru. 'You're going to make a cake and then decorate it?'

'I am indeed.'

'Well, I can't wait to see it.'

Having now given it some thought I'm fairly sure that the first cake I made was for Joe and featured a hamster playing a bassoon. The bassoon because Joe played it (rather well, it has to be said) and a hamster because he had one as a pet. I must have carried on making them for a good ten years or so, or until the boys had each flown the nest, and although I say so myself some of them weren't at all bad. I'd always been a keen amateur draftsman, you see, and had an interest in things like typography. One year I produced a cake with a full map of Manhattan on it, although I forget why, and another year it was a diesel locomotive. That one was for Sam's birthday and the locomotive in question was his favourite, D1048 Western Lady. As time went on, my designs became more and more elaborate, and I also began producing cakes for events other than just birthdays. For instance, when Joe passed his driving test, I made a prognostic cake featuring him, his car and a police car. Joe found it hilarious.

By far the most intricate cake I ever made was to celebrate Joe's finals. As part of his degree, he'd been studying the French writer Georges Perec, and after learning a bit more about this chap I came up with an idea. Perec wrote something called anagrammatic poetry, which is written using anagrams and is terribly complicated. How about an anagrammatic cake, I thought to myself. And so, that's what I created; a cake with an anagrammatic poem written on it. The average time it took me to make a cake was probably a day or two, whereas this one took me almost a week. Joe was mightily impressed, although when he learned how long it had taken me, he suggested that perhaps I might need to get out a little bit more.

To try and put into context just how out of character it was for me to even attempt to do something as domesticated as this, here's a quick story that Sam reminded me of a little while ago. On arriving home from school one day, he asked Pru where I was.

'He's upstairs doing the ironing, darling,' she said.

'I beg your pardon,' said Sam. 'Could you repeat that, please?'

'He's upstairs doing the ironing. Why don't you go and say hello?'

According to Sam, even the idea of me 'doing the ironing' had been difficult for him to comprehend. 'Difficult for anyone to comprehend,' he said.

On arriving in the 'ironing room', he found me pressing the pages of a script that I had been reading in the bath and had dropped accidentally. 'Oh, thank heaven for that,' he said to me. 'I thought Mum might have been drinking.'

While she would never describe herself as a domestic goddess, it won't surprise you to learn that Pru has always been far more adept at this sort of thing than I have. As well as being able to iron, mend, crochet and knit, she has an impressive repertoire of meals in her culinary arsenal, French onion soup and coq au vin being my own two favourites. Cooking isn't something Pru enjoys, however. It is a necessity that she approaches practically and, because she lived through the Second World War and abhors waste, with frugality. I remember her teaching Joe how to cook many years ago; as well as being able to feed himself, she believed that it would help him to respect certain processes and disciplines. 'Things should be done a certain way,' I remember her saying to him.

In order to promote the notion of frugality among her family, Pru once learned how to make a cheese sauce, the idea being that should there be any leftovers in the fridge, pouring some cheese sauce on them might make them more desirable. This has worked on a great many occasions, and over the years Pru's now legendary cheese sauce has probably saved at least a ton of food from ending up in the bin. It hasn't always been successful, though. About eight years ago Sam and his family came over to Wandsworth on Boxing Day to spend the day with us.

'What's for lunch, Ma?' he enquired.

'We're having goose,' she replied. 'Or rather, your father and I had goose yesterday so we're all having it again today.'

As I'm sure you're aware, goose is rather different to chicken or turkey and because it's quite greasy the last thing it needs before you eat it is more fat being poured on it. Even so, Pru presented at least a gallon of cheese sauce and then encouraged us all to pour it over the goose liberally.

'Come on, you lot, it'll make the goose lovely,' she promised. Then, 'Oh dear,' she said a few minutes later after having taken her own advice. 'Cheesy goose is absolutely disgusting, isn't it? Shall we have something else?'

'Cheesy goose' is still a phrase we use in our family, but usually by way of a threat.

I hesitantly broached the subject with Sam and Joe quite recently of what it was like growing up with two parents who are actors. I say hesitantly, as I am all too aware that our frequent absences from home were hard for them to take sometimes, and they often missed us terribly. In our defence, Pru and me were both jobbing actors when the children were young, with the majority of our work unavoidably comprised of long theatrical tours. It wasn't until the 1980s that television appearances and jobs in the West End became more prevalent than touring, but even so that didn't keep us in Wandsworth, necessarily. The majority of our West End endeavours would begin with a tour and television could take you anywhere.

When I spoke to them, Sam and Joe were predictably philosophical about the subject, and each made the point that, while Pru and me were indeed often away working for long periods of time, due to the fact that they were sometimes able to join us if a tour aligned with a school holiday, by the time they were teenagers they had each visited more countries and cities than the average sixty-year-old. We took them to America (which I'll come onto in a moment), Australia (twice), Egypt, where we had tea while watching the sun set in between two pyramids, which happens to be one of Pru's most cherished memories, and Jordan, to name but a few. We had so many adventures.

Joe mentioned another advantage to having two nomadic parents and that was the gifts that he and Sam would invariably receive on our return. 'You once brought me a Walkman back from Hong Kong,' Joe reminded me. 'Do you remember? It was the early 1980s when Walkmans were seriously coveted items. I was thrilled.'

As you are aware, some of the adventures we all had together while touring the world were exciting to say the least (being taken off an aeroplane at gunpoint being an obvious highlight), but there is one story that I'm afraid goes against Sam and Joe's strict instruction not to relay anything embarrassing. The reason I am at liberty to recall it for you, however, is because the embarrassment is all mine.

Allow me to set the scene.

I was on tour in a production of *Hedda Gabler* in 1975 – a world tour, no less – featuring the Oscar-winning Glenda Jackson as Hedda. Starting off in Melbourne, we played Sydney next and then made our way to Los Angeles. As Pru was busy doing a season at Greenwich, and with a school holiday on the horizon, I thought it might be a good idea if Juliet, Sam and Joe joined me for a week or two. The company was quite large, so there'd be no shortage of people to entertain them, and with the child-friendly tourist destinations of Disneyland and Universal Studios on our doorstep, not to mention a multitude of golden beaches, a good time should be had by all.

Working in a theatre in Los Angeles is rather like going to Lords Cricket Ground to play football. It's essentially a movie town, and while there are huge theatres for the multitude of touring musicals, the number of straight playhouses serving this enormous catchment area is limited. Even so, due primarily to the presence of Glenda Jackson, I should imagine, the play was sold out before we even opened there.

'Audiences in Los Angeles aren't too keen on plays in which there's much talking,' an American actor friend of mine had said to me after our arrival.

'But there's rather a lot of that in *Hedda Gabler*,' I replied.

'Oh, don't worry. They're a pretty polite bunch over here and because the tickets are expensive, they'll stick it out.'

'How incredibly reassuring,' I said to him. 'Thank you.'

From Los Angeles, Juliet and the boys flew with us to Washington, DC, where I immediately managed to lose six-year-old Joe at Dulles Airport. The trouble was that I didn't realize I'd lost him until our bus had completed its twenty-mile journey to the Sheraton Hotel in the centre of the city. 'You haven't seen Joe, have you?' I asked Juliet. She'd been suffering from tonsillitis and had spent the entire journey on the back seat under a blanket. 'No, not since the airport.' Sam had been in the company of one of the actors and I had foolishly assumed that if Joe wasn't with Juliet, which he had been for a time at the airport, he would be with them. 'No, we haven't seen him,' they said when I enquired.

On realizing what had happened my stomach hit the floor. 'OK,' I said, attempting to remain calm. 'I think I'll go and call the airport.' After doing so it appeared that nobody at Dulles Airport had seen hide nor hair of Joe and when I informed the hotel manager's wife what had happened, she immediately burst into tears.

'There, there,' I said attempting to comfort her. 'I'm

With Grandma West in Bristol, circa 1938.

H. LOCKWOOD WEST.

My father, Harry Lockwood West.

On the beach.

My mother, Olive.

HERE IS SIX-YEAR-OLD TIM WEST showing his father, Harry Lockwood West, of the Little Theatre, how he wants the tin actors moved in his miniature theatre. He'll have to carry on his performance without father's assistance, for shortly his father is leaving the theatre to join Bristol Police War Reserve. Tim's real interest is stage management. 'He's not only an actor and playwright, but a front of the house manager, who writes the programmes, takes tickets, and tells his patrons when the air-raid warning goes.

My first appearance in the newspapers.
From 1941, I think.

My sister and I (we're on the left)
with our neighbours and friends,
Julian and Susan Vinter.

One of my father's police pantomimes. *Peter Pan*, I think. I'm in bed next to my sister looking a bit nonplussed.

Pru looking quite angelic.

Bristol in the early 1950s.

Pru getting ready for a performance at the Theatre Royal, Bristol, right at the start of her career.

At Sam's christening. It looks like I'm wearing a wig, but I can assure you I'm not.

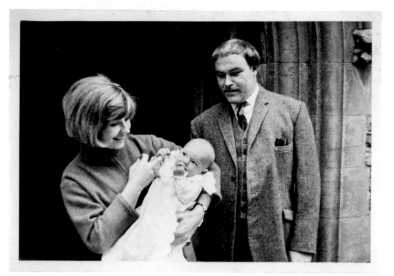

Proud Pru with a very young Sam.

Barnes 1967 with Sam and Juliet.

For as long as she was able, Pru insisted on taking Sam to work with her.

Relaxing in Salisbury.

The Wests on tour in Australia, 1972.

On tour with The Old Vic: Pru and me outside the Theatre Royal, Blackpool, in 1981 on the opening night of *The Merchant of Venice*.

Juliet with her new little brother, Joe.

The Wests out walking.

Joe and Sam.

Picnicking in a park somewhere in about 1972.

sure he'll be OK. Children are terribly resourceful these days.' As the tears cascaded down her face, she offered to drive me to the airport in her Oldsmobile and I accepted her offer gratefully. 'That's very kind of you,' I said.

'It's – it's – it's not – not – not a problem,' she replied, while reaching for a tissue. 'I just hope we're in time.'

I remember thinking, *What do you mean, I hope we're in time? I'm supposed to be the theatrical!*

It turned out that Joe had decided to take a leisurely tour around the airport before boredom struck, which is when he decided to tell somebody that he had been abandoned by his father. By the time we got there he had been placed in the care of the police. When we returned to the Sheraton, it was to the considerable relief of everyone there, not least my co-stars, Patrick Stewart and Peter Eyre, who had generously offered to sit with me while I made what might have been rather a tricky telephone call to Pru back in England.

'Darling, you know how irritated we get with the two boys when they quarrel and don't share things? Well, think I might have found a solution . . .'

Once I had put the boys to bed, I wrote Pru a letter detailing the escapade.

'I feel I should now give you a detailed account of how we lost Joe,' I began . . .

Both the boys were very sleepy on the flight, and Juliet was suffering with tonsillitis. The company's bus then arrived, and I called Joe, and we all got on the bus. I thought. Juliet lay on the back seat with a rug over herself and, I supposed, Joe. So, it wasn't until we reached the Sheraton, twenty miles away, that his

absence was discovered. I found the hotel manager's wife, who burst
into tears at the news, and together we rang Airport Security, the
Pan Am desk, the Duty Manager, everyone we could think of,
without eliciting any news of Joe's whereabouts; and finally, she
offered to drive me back to the airport. She was in a terrible state
and kept taking her hands off the wheel to find her tissues. 'Oh,
that poor little boy,' she kept sobbing, the car weaving across the
freeway as she blew her nose. 'It's all right,' I told her. 'He's only
six, but a sensible lad, he'll find someone and say he's lost and –
MIND THAT TRUCK!'

When we got there, I sat her down with a large bourbon and
went off in search of my son. I asked first at the sweet stall, and
they led me straight to him. Finding himself apparently
abandoned, he'd gone back to the stall, mentioned he was lost, and
they'd called the airport police. The police had taken him down to
their office, and by the time I caught up with him he'd learned the
form of arrest, how to use the phone intercom, and how to handcuff
the sergeant to the radiator. He was, in short, having a wonderful
time, and was very sorry to leave.

Throughout the drama, I was composing in my mind the phone
call I'd have to make to you. 'Yes, the show's going splendidly,
houses have been wonderful; fine, yes, we're fine, Patrick's fine,
Peter Eyre's fine, sends his love, weather's good, hotel's very nice,
yes; darling, what I'm really ringing about, you know we used to
have two sons . . . ?'

Believe it or not, we did actually lose Joe a second time,
although this was many years later and when he was an
adult. It was Easter 1988, and we were catching a train
from Bulawayo to Victoria Falls. We all thought that Joe
had already boarded the train we were travelling on and

when I realized what had happened, I was transported momentarily back to the Sheraton Hotel in Washington.

'It's happened again, hasn't it?' said Pru.

'I'm afraid so,' I replied with a sigh.

How does the saying go? To lose a child once is bad luck. To lose them twice is careless.

As many of you will know, our son Sam also joined what we call the 'family business' and made his professional stage debut in 1989. We can actually trace Sam's expectations – not aspirations – to having to become an actor all the way back to 1976 when he was eight years old.

He and Joe were having breakfast one day when all of a sudden, Sam said to Pru, 'Mummy, when I grow up do I have to become and actor like you and Daddy?'

'No, of course you don't, darling,' said Pru. 'You can become whatever you want. What would you like to do?'

'I'd like to become a professor of chemistry,' said Sam.

Incidentally, Sam claims that he still hasn't really decided to become an actor at all. Like me, it is something he is merely doing until he is asked to become a train driver, although time might be running out for at least one of us. We'll see.

Anyway, I've been trying to recall the moment when Pru and I suspected that Sam might actually be aspiring to become an actor after all, and after discussing it with him, he reminded us of the following.

In 1980 Sam, who was fourteen at the time, was asked to appear in an episode of a television series called *Nanny* alongside Wendy Craig. It must have been an approach from a contact either of mine or Pru's, and when we asked Sam, who had still expressed no ambitions whatsoever to become an actor, if he might be interested in having a go, he said yes.

Sam played a boy whose mother had become violent and after beating her son she would then smother him in love. As a consequence, the child had developed masochistic tendencies and would be deliberately naughty in the hope that his nanny would then punish him. It was quite a complex role for a fourteen-year-old but it was one that Sam appreciated doing and he was very good in it.

The story was set in the 1930s and in one scene Sam had to be seen reading alone in his bedroom. While setting up the scene the production design team handed Sam a comic from that period.

'I don't think he'd read a comic,' Sam said to them. 'Could I have a book instead?'

'Yes, of course,' said the production team, and so handed him a book.

When Sam came home after shooting the episode, he told us about this and Pru and me looked at each other, open-mouthed. 'Oh God,' she said. 'He's started making character-based decisions.'

Despite this early scare, after finishing his A levels, Sam was offered a place at Oxford University reading English Literature. This, alas, reminds me of another story that, when told, leaves me, at best embarrassed, and at worst mildly mortified, depending on how vivid the memory is.

I picked up the telephone one day and after articulating the usual words of greeting a stern female voice said, 'Good afternoon, this is Lady Margaret Hall.'

Oh my God! I thought. I was sure it was because of an

event I was supposed to be attending or some appeal to which I'd said I would respond and hadn't done so.

'Hello, Lady Margaret,' I gabbled. 'You'll have to forgive me. Your letter is on my desk, and I'm afraid I haven't had a moment to attend to it. If you could bear with me just a day or two more I –'

As I continued pleading, a tired but nevertheless audible sigh came down the phone. 'No, this is Lady Margaret Hall, Oxford,' said the caller. 'I am just ringing to tell you that your son, Samuel, has been accepted for a place at this college, starting next term in September.' Her tone suggested that, if his father's intellectual prowess was anything to go by, they might have made a mistake.

Although he didn't go to drama school, Sam did an enormous amount of acting while at Oxford and was president of the Experimental Theatre Club. He had been offered a place at the Bristol Old Vic Theatre School after he graduated, and shortly before he was due to sign his acceptance Harold Pinter telephoned, saying he'd written a screenplay from Fred Uhlman's book *Reunion*, about two schoolfriends growing up together in Vienna at the time of the Anschluss. Harold wanted to know if Sam might be interested in playing one of the two boys, which he most definitely was, and so that was that. Like me, Sam learned how to do it by doing it. If Pru and me helped him at all, it was by having quite a lot of books and records and playscripts in the house, by taking him to the theatre and concerts a good deal and subjecting him to our grumbling at the breakfast table about directors, critics and the state of the business generally. At least he went into it without the hindrance of rose-tinted spectacles.

In the latter part of the 1980s, our home in Wandsworth, in which we had all spent so many happy years, went from having at least four inhabitants, to just two. Juliet had been the first to fly the nest, but that had been in the late 1970s. Then Sam went to Oxford, and when Joe took a year out and flew to Africa in 1988 before going to study at Manchester, that was that. As a self-confessed homebird who obviously adores her children and is terrified of being on her own, this affected Pru far more than it affected me.

'It hasn't been just the two of us since 1966,' she complained. 'What on earth shall we do?'

This, I'm happy to say, was very easily remedied. 'Look at this,' I said, opening her diary. 'You've got more going on than the Lord Mayor of London. On top of which, you'll be seeing Sam, Joe and Juliet this coming weekend. They're coming to visit, remember?'

After perusing the pages of her diary for a moment, which was indeed packed with all manner of engagements, Pru smiled.

'And we have each other, of course,' she said. 'Let's not forget us.'

My Wife, the Agoraphobe

Although he appeared in several theatrical productions at school and at university, in which he was actually rather good, Joe made a conscious decision early on in his life not to become an actor. Writing and translating were, and still are, far more his thing, and he is also a more than capable musician. Before going to Manchester University, where he studied French and politics, Joe, as I mentioned, decided to take a year out and informed Pru and me that he was intent on spending at least part of that year teaching science and religious knowledge at St James's School in a town called Zongoro in Zambia. Although nervous about Joe taking such a step, Pru was thrilled. 'Oh, that's marvellous,' she said. 'Good for you.'

Now, there's been a myth circulating for decades that Pru suffers from agoraphobia. The genesis of the myth can no doubt be traced back to Pru herself, as she will have recounted the effect her journey with her brother Timmo from Buck's Mills to Windermere during the war had on her. Pru's assertion that she could be quite a nervous traveller when flying solo probably perpetuated the thing, together with the fact that she is ostensibly a homebird, which is true, but at one point the allegory gathered pace to such an extent that she was rumoured to have an aversion to taking out the milk bottles. Bearing in mind that

Pru has spent at least half her adult life away from the family home, I would like to make so bold as to declare the myth erroneous.

Pru's idea of heaven is being in our garden on a sunny afternoon with nothing at all to do, but with plenty of work in the diary. Despite my own nomadic tendencies, I would probably share her ideal, so long as some of the impending work involved a visit to a foreign country or three.

One of the most memorable and pleasurable journeys that Pru has made, *sans* me, was going to visit Joe in Zambia during his gap year. As always, her letters home were enormously entertaining and left little to the imagination. Subsequently, I thought it might be nice to share them with you. As you're about to find out, it was quite an adventure.

26 March 1988, Gatwick Airport, 6.30 p.m.

Gatwick a horrendous mess of litter and passengers – our flight delayed forty minutes by loaders' strike – but once aboard I feel guilty but relieved at having come business class and having room to stretch legs. I rate 'Ordinary' in the In Flight magazine trivia quiz. Disproportionately galled by this, SIX POINTS OFF EXCELLENT. Quite nervous about the whole expedition and cravenly choose champagne instead of orange juice when they come round. There's a lot of banging about on the tarmac underneath us – angry loaders throwing luggage out?

4 a.m.: (Having put watches on two hours, to Harare time). Lomé, in Togo. We made a detour to pick up some Euro MPs. Couldn't even find Togo on the map.

7 a.m.: Flying southeast, a staggering sunrise through the window, and a great grey-green greasy river below, which I think must be the Congo. We're going to be about forty minutes late in Harare.

28 March 1988, Manica Hotel, Mutare, 9 a.m.

Yesterday the longest day of my LIFE – my luggage the last off as usual. Waited half an hour by the carousel, thank God for crochet, then trundled through customs to find Joe, in a beard, holding a large card saying MA. Drove with Joe to Marondera. We sat round chatting until alarmingly late in the afternoon, Joe seems to be coping well. He likes the week best, but finds the weekends a bit lonely, and is ludicrously pleased to see me. Afraid I let him drive back to St James's, it's not exactly illegal, but if there were an accident he's not covered. Picked up several hitchhikers who were all utterly charming. Got to the house and unpacked all the goodies, which were greeted with whoops of joy. Joe and his friends still sleeping on the floor, which I find pretty disgraceful, but are coping with huge resource and cheerfulness. I got back here about 11.30 feeling I'd been awake a week.

29 March 1988, Manica Hotel, 6.24 a.m.

'I am Mr West's mother,' I say. I sit on the verandah with my tapestry and the children come and look at me and giggle and smile. One nubile girl said, 'I don't think so,' when I told her I was Mr West's Mother. I said that was very kind of her, which I hope it was. I wash up and cook and am treated with respect, well it makes a change. The boys are quite stern with the kids, like a lot of prep-school masters. It's sweet, you can practically tell exactly what the men who taught them were like. It seems to work, though

I haven't seen a class yet. New teacher turned up yesterday, Reuben, a Zimbabwean, to teach agriculture, science and English. He and Joe both had baths here yesterday evening and it's taken two sachets of shampoo and eight sheets of that brown Kleenex they give you to get the ring off the bath. Just as well I brought a nail brush.

7 a.m.: Room boy has just brought me tea which I didn't order, asked how I spent the night and if he can please call me again. Cheeky, but obviously cheering for Mr West's Mother. Incidentally, she leaves a fairly hefty ring round the bath too, the water is so absurdly soft here the boys have to leave their washing out in the rain all night to rinse it properly.

30 March 1988, St James's Secondary School, Boy's House, 1 p.m.

I've been up since 5.45 a.m. and I feel like a pioneer wife. The Africans call me Mummy. So, yesterday morning I bought chicken legs and onions at Omar's supermarket and drove out to Zongoro in time for the morning break. Went back to the school with them and sat in on two of Joe's classes. He's a wonderful teacher, I think, clear and rigorous and funny, but the schoolmaster acting is hilarious, he even cracks schoolmaster jokes. Some actual beds arrived in the afternoon, so I drove back into Mutare to buy mattresses and pillows, lovely lumpy cotton things, incredibly comfortable after concrete. Today we've been to the river to collect water in buckets to do the washing – school tap on the blink. They've now got a charcoal-burning tsotso stove in the wash house and can achieve constant hot water in an iron bucket on top of it. Afraid I bought them the bucket, also a primus lamp and small hurricane lantern, hope that wasn't overdoing it.

31 March 1988, Manica Hotel.

Yesterday not nearly so nice, drove Joe and Al up to Juliasdale where there's a horrible hotel, Godalming, by the swimming pool, cretonne everywhere and a casino. Absolutely delicious toasted sandwiches, however. Drove back to Mutare, met Lucy, Adam and Nick and everyone came back here for showers, then we went to the White House Inn out on the Vimba road and had a delicious dinner. I took Joe and Al back home. Had been going to doss them down and take them back early this morning, but we decided the deception and the drive not worth it, so lent them the car I'm afraid and prayed for the best. Joe is driving quite well now, and it has been nice to have a night alone to recover. For them too, I think, though at the house it's OK because one slips into the role of mother, bottle-washer and water-carrier, like Wendy with the Lost Boys.

1 April 1988, Zimbabwe Airport, 9.30 p.m.

The second longest day of my life. Yesterday nearly a disaster. Nick, Joe, Lucy and I set forth at 4.30 in a car for Masuingo, 297km to the south, to see the acclaimed ruins. One hour later on a delightful banana-lined road littered with baboon families ushering each other across, the tarmac gave out and I got a blast of setting sun in the driving-mirror — 'Why are we going EAST?' I enquired nervously — 'Not for long,' chirruped Joe, map-reading by my side. Twenty minutes after that Nick said, 'Could I have a look at that map, Joe?' by which time the sun had practically plopped and we were still climbing. 'Oh,' said Nick. 'Well, we're on the way back to Mutare. Quicker to go on and start again really.' Which we duly did, narrowly avoiding the Mozambique border and arriving back at the Manica at twenty-five to seven.

Everybody pretty good-tempered about it really, though Joe naturally rather subdued. We set out again at 7 p.m., Joe driving, had to stop for torrential rain and lightning, but I took a Pro-plus and the wheel at Thingy Bridge (once the longest suspension bridge in the world, v. impressive), and we hit the Griel Zimbabwe Hotel at 12.08 this morning. Sandwiches and beer, Joe, Lucy and I kipped down in the vast bed, Nick on the floor of our chalet, all slept like logs and ate huge breakfast at 8.00. The kids loved it and have stayed on for the Easter weekend. Bit touristy, I thought, but the ruins are wonderful, and I'm very glad we went. Melancholy and knackering drive back to Harare on my own, listening to Little Dorrit on Radio 1 and giving the odd lift. Hit the airport at 8-ish, where my knickers fell off. I stuffed them in my bag with huge dignity, changed in the Ladies, and here I am really.

Felt like an astronaut coming into Heathrow: the sun which I'd watched set on my left driving north to Harare, had swapped places with the moon (last seen rising on the right last night). And I'm still travelling north.

When Pru claims to be agoraphobic these days, which she still does from time to time, I fetch these letters and ask her to read them.

'If these are from an agoraphobe,' I declare, 'I am a monkey's uncle.'

Work, Work, Work

The following passages depict the ups and downs of life as a pair of busy jobbing actors.

Leading from the Front

When Pru and me eventually do fall off our perches, one or two obituaries might appear in some of the newspapers. In my own case, I'm not quite sure what they'll open with. 'Actor, best known for . . .' It could be a number of things, I suppose. '. . . his work on the stage', or *Brass* or *Edward the Seventh*. It could even be *Gentleman Jack* or *EastEnders*, if the obituary is being written either by, or for, a journalist or audience who have yet to reach middle age. Indeed, a friend called Mark was quizzed years ago by his daughter about what I had appeared in. After reeling off the traditional list of roles Mark eventually said, 'Hang on, he also played Stan Carter in *EastEnders*.'

'You're driving Stan Carter from *EastEnders*,' his daughter exclaimed. 'Mick Carter's dad? Wow, that's amazing!'

Fame at last.

In Pru's case, it is different. Although she too has appeared in a multitude of productions striding all of the major mediums, one role in particular, that she first interpreted for the small screen way back in 1975, gave her international recognition. I am referring, of course, to Sybil Fawlty from *Fawlty Towers*.

When I first informed Pru that I would soon be attempting to write something about Sybil and the series, she issued me with one simple instruction. 'You will do a good job, won't you, darling? Everybody loves Sybil.'

'I'll certainly try my best,' I said.

From a professional point of view, 1975 was a very special year for Pru and me. In fact, it's arguably been our best year to date, at least jointly. With regards to the theatre, we'd kind of cracked it, in that we'd each been gainfully employed within the medium on an almost constant basis for a good two decades or so and to this day it remains our professional home. Film appearances had remained sporadic at best but that didn't worry us too much. Neither of us has ever enjoyed making films very much but the odd job here and there, which is good for your profile and often pays good money, worked well enough for us. Prior to 1975, the only work that Pru and me would happily have accepted more of was in television. She had enjoyed the odd leading role, such as in *Marriage Lines*, but generally our skills had been called upon to play either supporting parts in a series, or major roles in one-off plays. When the initial scripts for *Fawlty Towers* first landed on our doorstep at the start of 1975, Pru didn't see that changing any time soon.

'I don't really know what to make of this thing,' she said after reading the scripts. 'Here, you have a look.'

'What's it called?'

'*Fawlty Towers.*'

'*Fawlty Towers*? What on earth is it about?'

'It's a sitcom set in a hotel in Torquay. They're interested in me playing the wife of the owner. She's called Sybil Fawlty.'

'Ah, hence the name *Fawlty Towers*. Who's behind it?'

'John Cleese.'

'John Cleese from Monty Python? The tall fellow?'

'That's right. He's written it with his wife, Connie Booth. I must say, it's quite funny. Very visual, though, I think.'

The scripts had been sent to Pru by a chap called John Howard Davies, who would be directing the show. He'd already worked with John Cleese on *Monty Python's Flying Circus*, and we later learned that it had been his idea to approach Pru about playing Sybil.

'I'm not sure either,' I said after reading the first script. 'I mean, how on earth did two people like that ever get married in the first place? They quite clearly hate each other.'

'That's what I thought,' said Pru. 'I'd like to find out, though, before I say yes or no.'

Later that day Pru called John Howard Davies and arranged to go and meet him at the BBC.

'What's your gut feeling?' I asked her before she left.

'Well, I like the scripts,' said Pru. 'It's the best TV I've been offered in a long time. It'll depend on the answers I get to my questions. I need to know more about her. And about him. I need to know more about everything really.'

This was nothing new, by the way. Whether it's an advert she's appearing in or a play, if Pru isn't able to achieve, either through herself or via somebody else, a rounded view of the character and their background, she will not take the job, and for the simple reason that in her mind, she will not be able to do it justice.

The meeting with John Howard Davies went well, in as much as he was able to explain to Pru why he had chosen her and how enthusiastic John Cleese had been about the idea.

'John Cleese is a big fan of *Marriage Lines*, apparently,' Pru said on her return.

'Really?' I replied. 'I'm surprised. It's not very surreal or subversive.'

'He likes the way Richard Briers and I play off each other, apparently. Anyway, he wants me to go and see him at his flat tomorrow. I wasn't keen at first as he's in bed with flu, but John Howard Davies persuaded me.'

By the time Pru arrived at John Cleese's abode the following afternoon she had all but decided to take the part if offered, providing he could answer one simple question: How on earth did Basil and Sybil ever get together?

'Oh God, I knew you were going to ask me that,' said John, putting a pillow over his head. 'To be honest with you, I don't really know. Do you have any ideas?'

'Well, sort of,' said Pru. 'In as much as I've come up with a theory as to how I think two people like that could get together and how they've come to own and run a hotel.'

'Fire away,' said Mr Cleese.

Pru's theory, which she told me later that day, was that Sybil's family had been in catering and had a pub on the south coast. 'Somewhere like Eastbourne,' she said. Sybil worked behind the bar in this pub and one day in walked a chap called Basil who had just been demobbed from National Service. What attracted her to him was the fact that he was posh, basically, and what attracted him to her was the fact that she was blowsy and flirtatious. Her theory about their current situation was that, because of Sybil's background in catering, after getting together they had decided to run a hotel together and the grim reality of the undertaking had now begun to catch up with them. 'She's been fooled by Basil's flannel,' supposed Pru, 'and too late, she realizes that she is landed with an upper-class twit. Whereupon the rot sets in because he has all these posh and potty ideas about how to run a hotel, and she has a great deal more practical experience and know-how. But behind all her apparent disenchantment with Basil, there is some real affection for him.'

It sounded plausible to me. More importantly, it sounded plausible to John, too.

The most exciting news Pru returned with that day, apart from the fact that she'd been offered the role officially by John Cleese and that she had accepted it, was that one of the other main characters, Manuel the waiter, was to be played by Andrew Sachs. 'Isn't that the most marvellous news?' Pru said. 'I really couldn't be happier.'

Andy Sachs had been the ASM at the Connaught Theatre in Worthing early on in Pru's career and in the early 1960s he'd appeared alongside me on tour in *Simple Spymen*. Knowing there's a former colleague or two in the cast of a new show you're appearing in is always good news. To have an old friend on hand is even better.

Because John had never managed to elucidate to Pru much about Sybil's character or background, she had been left pretty much to her own devices with regards to her creation and it's fair to say that after the first day of rehearsal Pru's interpretation was at odds slightly with what John and Connie Booth had in mind, however vague that might have been.

'I think they thought she was more on Basil's level socially,' said Pru. 'So, at the end of the first day, I got one or two funny looks.'

I later discussed this with John, and he agreed. 'We'd written Sybil differently from how Pru played her,' he said to me. 'Not too much, but enough to make Connie and I feel a bit uneasy after the first day's rehearsal.'

Fortunately, neither John nor Connie let on to Pru fully that they were harbouring any great concerns, and by the end of the second day they had begun to realize that Pru's blowsy and aspirational working-class interpretation of Sybil worked better than their own.

'Out of interest, what exactly did you and Connie have in mind when you wrote Sybil?' I remember asking him.

'I honestly can't remember now,' he said. 'I think we had an idea at the very beginning, but by the time it came to writing the scripts we'd forgotten. Anyway, it doesn't matter now. Pru's done it for us.'

Pru's characterization of Sybil Fawlty is based partly on somebody she used to know and it made her feel rather guilty.

'There was a woman who ran a hotel that my mum used to stay in from time to time,' she said. 'And although she was terribly nice to everyone, she had a habit of leaning over people while they were eating and saying, 'Do you find that tasty, sir?' or, 'Is that all right for you, madam?' She wasn't anywhere near as demonstrative or menacing as Sybil, but as soon as I started reading her, this poor woman came to mind. She's definitely in there somewhere.'

The story of how John created Basil, and how he came up with the idea for the show, is equally fascinating. He told me this first-hand many years ago, but I think I remember most of it.

Fawlty Towers is based on an establishment that is no longer in existence called the Gleneagles Hotel. Also situated in Torquay, it had been used by the cast and crew of *Monty Python's Flying Circus* in 1970 for a three-week stay while they were filming in nearby Paignton. Legend has it that the owner of the hotel, Lieutenant Commander Donald Sinclair, was dead against the 'Circus' staying, primarily because they were television types. His wife Betty, however, managed to persuade him simply because of the amount of money involved.

'He really was an absolute bloody nightmare,' John said to me. 'But I found him fascinating.'

Lieutenant Commander Sinclair bore no physical resemblance to John's later creation (apparently, he was rather short in stature), yet when it came to his behaviour there was little to tell between them. Donald Sinclair was an eccentric, and someone for whom everything to do with his guests was always too much trouble. The kind of man who, if a customer approached the bar wanting a drink, would slam the shutters down.

'He once removed Eric Idle's bag from his room and put it on a wall on the far side of the hotel grounds,' John told me.

'Whatever for?' I asked.

'He thought there was a bomb inside. Eric told him it was his alarm clock, but he refused to believe him.'

According to John, the member of the Monty Python team against whom Lieutenant Commander Sinclair took the most was Terry Gilliam. He did not care much for our American cousins and would look for excuses to berate Terry. 'He once bollocked him for cutting up his meat and then eating it only with his fork,' said John. 'He told him it was bad manners. I later learned that one of the waiters became so traumatized by Sinclair's behaviour that he fled the hotel one evening and ran away to London. It didn't at all surprise me.' Not surprisingly, by the time their three-week stay at the Gleneagles Hotel came to an end, only John remained from the Circus. 'Everybody else had scarpered,' he told me.

The inspiration for Manuel's character came from the influx of foreign workers in the early 1970s whose first language wasn't English. I remember this all too well as for a time ordering the right food in a restaurant became extremely difficult. This, I assume, is why John, who had also worked with Andy Sachs before on some of his management films, made Manuel Spanish. Andy later told me that, like Pru, he'd been in two minds about accepting the role initially, but for different reasons.

'I wasn't sure if I could do a Spanish accent,' he told me. 'And so I asked John if he'd object to him being German instead.'

'Why German?' John said.

'Because that's my first language,' replied Andy.

'Absolutely not,' John told him. 'Manuel is supposed to be inefficient and incompetent. Not very German, is it?'

The moustache, however, was Andy's idea. Not only did he think it right for the character, but he hoped it might help to disguise him from the general public. 'It didn't always work,' he told us. 'I was once accosted by an American woman outside a shop on Oxford Street and, assuming that I was actually a waiter, she asked me, very earnestly, how I'd managed to cope since the series had ended. "Oh, I get by," I said.'

Just like *Marriage Lines*, each episode of *Fawlty Towers* was rehearsed for just under a week before being recorded and sometime during the second week I asked Pru how it was going.

'I'm thoroughly enjoying it,' she said. 'It's very hard work, though. John has an enormous amount of energy and can be quite frightening at times. It's like working with a live machine-gun; you have to try and keep it pointing away from you.'

The other point Pru made was that John was extremely rigorous when it came to the script. 'I don't know anybody in the business who works harder,' she said. If the cast didn't know their lines by Wednesday (the show was recorded on a Sunday) John would be on the warpath. With two sons under ten in the house, not to mention a nanny, an eighteen-year-old stepdaughter and a forty-one-year-old husband, Pru really had her work cut out.

'I must admit I'm finding it a bit hard, darling,' she confided in me one day. 'There are just far too many distractions. John literally locks himself away for hours and hours on end.'

'Then why not do the same?' I suggested.

'How do you mean?'

'Check into a hotel for a couple of nights. That should do the trick.'

Ever the homebody, it took me an hour or so to persuade Pru that this was a necessary course of action, but I eventually prevailed.

'OK, I'll do it,' she said. 'You will be all right with the boys, won't you?'

'What – you mean me, Juliet and the nanny? Yes, I think we'll manage between the three of us. You go and learn your lines. Otherwise, you'll have Mr Cleese to contend with.'

Pru checked into the hotel on the Monday and by the Wednesday she was word perfect.

'I didn't enjoy it one bit,' she said. 'I kept waking up every couple of hours worrying. It was awful.'

'Yes, but you are word perfect, though, aren't you, darling?'

'Yes, of course I am.'

'Well then?'

It wasn't just the lines that Pru and the cast had to familiarize themselves with. In this case the devil was in the detail as, in addition to the script, John and Connie had gone to great pains in order to explain exactly what was happening in each scene and why. Indeed, a script for a thirty-minute episode of a sitcom would normally be around sixty pages long, but for *Fawlty Towers* they were something approaching 140.

The very first episode of *Fawlty Towers*, which was called 'A Touch of Class' and featured a conman posing as the non-existent Lord Melbury, was broadcast on BBC1 on 19 September 1975. The immediate reaction, not only from the press, but from our friends and family, was astonishing. Ordinarily, when one makes an appearance on television, one or two reviews might appear in the newspapers, and you might receive the odd telephone call. The majority of the calls will be congratulatory, which is nice, and generally it'll be forgotten about in a day or two. When *Fawlty Towers* went to air, not only did the press go bananas, but so did our telephone. And it wasn't just the first episode that got people talking. Exactly the same thing happened after the broadcast of all six, and by the time the first series was all over Pru, who dislikes attention enormously, was mightily relieved. 'I wasn't expecting anything like that,' she said. 'It seems to have gone down rather well.'

Understatement of the year.

Something I enjoyed was watching the opinions of the critics change as the series progressed. For instance, Peter Fiddick of the *Guardian* initially gave John Cleese the majority of the credit for the series being a success, but as the weeks went on, he began to see further than that. 'Miss Prunella Scales,' he wrote, 'a smashing actress at any time, having a ball as Mrs Fawlty, adopting a fine whine, somewhere in between Henry Cooper and Twiggy and attacking Cleese at the level she finds him, which is usually just below the nipples.'

Not everybody was impressed by the new series, however. Tony Pratt from the *Daily Mirror*, for example, when summing up episode two, wrote simply, 'Long John is short on jokes.' Indeed, had the show's legacy been carved from the overall reaction to the first three episodes then it wouldn't even be deemed an unqualified success. Fortunately though, it didn't take the sceptics or the naysayers long to come around and by the fourth or fifth episode it was already being hailed as one of the best.

My own favourite performance in the show, apart from Pru's, of course, is Andy Sachs' portrayal of Manuel. I once asked Andy whether or not he ever got hurt during the making of *Fawlty Towers*.

'Only a few times,' he said to me. 'Once, John had to hit me over the back of the head with a frying pan and instead of using the padded prop one he used a real one by mistake. In fact, I do believe he knocked me out.'

'Really?' I asked incredulously. 'He actually hit you over the head with a real frying pan?'

'Yes, that's right. It hurt a bit when I came to. He didn't mean to, though. John was devastated.'

I remember standing there completely agog. 'Then there was the time I suffered some rather painful burns,' Andy continued. 'There was a fire in the kitchen, and I had to leave the room quickly with my jacket smoking. The fire itself was managed with no mishaps, but the blend of chemicals that the props department used to create the smoking jacket was too strong. It soaked through to my skin and caused several burns. That was even worse than the frying pan.'

It has been suggested on several occasions that the general public's identification of Pru with Sybil Fawlty has perhaps limited some people's perception of her. We all know that if you're especially good in one role, the immediate reaction from some quarters is that you might not be very good in anything else. Quite often you'll have to prove yourself all over again, turning down roles that you would like to take but that fall into the same category. The parts Pru has been offered since *Fawlty Towers* have, on the whole, probably been more comedic, and what bothers her is the perception some people have of female actors in comedic roles.

'In French comedy you can be female, intelligent, attractive and young,' she once said. 'In American comedy, as a female, you can be pretty and dumb and funny – or intelligent and ugly and funny. But in English comedy you are not allowed to be female and funny unless you are post-menopausal, or so eccentric as not to be a sexual threat. Partly because of *Fawlty Towers*, I'm no longer asked to play women who are either very attractive or very intelligent. I think it's a shame.'

So do I.

King and Commoner

In comparison to Pru's 1975, my own pales into insignificance with regards to how iconic and influential the programme that eventually turned me into a leading actor on television became. That programme, which is called *Edward the Seventh*, has, for reasons which are unknown to me, never been repeated and has only quite recently been released on DVD. Each episode contains quite a lot of music, and music is expensive.

The initial approach about the series was made via my agent in 1974 and the reason I remember it is because me and Pru had finally figured out a way of stopping our two boys fighting and squabbling. Or rather, Pru had. They were at an age when it was beginning to happen a little too frequently, and sometimes interfered with our already erratic sleep patterns. If Pru and I were at home at the same time, which wasn't often, one or both of us might be performing in a play in the West End and, if that were the case, we wouldn't arrive back until the early hours. Being woken up just a few hours later by two boys fighting wasn't ideal, but no matter how many different threats we administered – and believe me, we tried everything – nothing seemed to work.

One morning – I believe it was a Thursday, as the previous day I'd played two shows of something – the hullabaloo started bright and early at 6.45 a.m. Due to reasons I forget, my head hadn't touched the pillow until about 2 a.m. I was just about to haul myself out of bed to remonstrate with the two miniature tyrants when I heard Pru's voice.

'Listen, you two. Daddy was up very late last night and has got to go to work later so here's what I'm going to do. I'm going to lock you in a room together and you can fight as much as you like. If you hurt each other of course I'll take you to hospital, but I want you to know that I am very bored of this. Right, in you go.' I then heard Pru marching the boys into a spare room and locking the door.

Should I try to go back to sleep? I asked myself. No, this was far too exciting.

The only sounds I heard coming from the room were a couple of squeals and when Pru went to open the door there was silence. 'Sit down and have your breakfast,' she said. 'I'm going to see Daddy.'

I was sitting up in bed by the time she entered the bedroom. 'All quiet on the western front?' I asked, as she perched herself on the end of the bed.

'At the moment. Let's listen.'

Silence.

'All I can hear is two boys eating cereal,' I said.

'Me too,' said Pru.

'How on earth did you do it?'

'Well, I read this book a while ago – I think I may have borrowed it from somebody – that suggested half the rows siblings have are for attention, so if you make them realize you're not interested, they won't bother.'

We learned very quickly that it's not an exact science, but it certainly made a big difference.

A second reason why I am able to pinpoint the date of

the approach about *Edward the Seventh*, which was made by ATV Television Company, is because I had also been asked to take charge for a second season of plays at the Billingham Forum on Teeside as their Artistic Director. I shan't attempt to burden you with the details of that particular appointment (which was a challenging but ultimately rewarding experience) but when the offer asking me if I would like to appear as Edward VII in a sumptuous new thirteen-part series about his life that would be sold the world over was made, all thoughts of Billingham and the Forum vanished in a trice. Had I not already completed a season there I might have thought differently, but as a jobbing actor who obviously wished to further his career and who (together with his jobbing actor wife, who spent a good deal of her life worrying about money) had certain financial responsibilities, it was an offer I could ill afford to refuse.

'It's incredibly exciting, Tim,' said Pru after we first discussed it. 'How long did you say you'd be filming?'

'I'm not sure. Front to back it'll take just over a year, but I won't be in the first few episodes.'

'Whyever not?'

'Because they cover Edward's childhood. As much as I like to believe that I am not aging quickly, the process is yet to go into reverse. A succession of younger actors will play him for the first four episodes, and I appear in episode five.'

If truth be known, Charles Sturridge, who played Edward in the pre-pubertal episodes and was in his mid-twenties, could have remained in the role for several more episodes as when I took over, Edward was just twenty-three and I was over forty. Also, the lovely actress playing Alexandra alongside me in my first few episodes, Deborah Grant, had played my daughter in a play called *The Italian Girl* and was thirteen years my junior. I felt a bit embarrassed in the first couple of episodes, but as the king got older, I got better, and towards the end I think I may have been OK.

The schedule for recording *Edward the Seventh* would be unthinkable today and wildly different to *Fawlty Towers*. Each hourly episode was given two weeks of rehearsal, with a full week allowed for recording because some of the palace sets were so huge (there was, for instance, always a ballroom) that they couldn't fit them all in the studio at one time. Consequently, some of the sets were erected on Sunday, and those scenes were rehearsed on Monday and shot on Tuesday. On Wednesday there was a changeover, on Thursday we rehearsed the scenes with the new sets and recorded them on a Friday. The cast had Saturday and Sunday off. Interspersed with this routine were batches of outside filming, according to season. Senior management threw their hands up in despair at what it was all costing, but in the end, the quality of the programme earned back at least four times its initial cost in immediate foreign sales.

All twelve episodes of *Fawlty Towers*, including rehearsals, took less than three months in total. It also cost next to nothing to make, had only four main characters, a small supporting cast and just the odd guest or two. *Edward the Seventh*, on the other hand, cost an absolute fortune and had no fewer than 187 speaking parts. For a television series at the time, that was almost unheard of.

One of the biggest differences for us between the two shows was that Pru had absolutely no idea that *Fawlty Towers* was going to be either popular or successful here in Britain, let alone overseas. In fact, because the style of humour was so different to anything that had been seen before in a British sitcom, she half expected it to fail. 'I think it's marvellous,' she once said. 'I just have an awful feeling that it might be a little too much for people. It's almost as exhausting to watch as it is to make.' With *Edward the Seventh* there were no guarantees in that department either. However, the format, which was tried and tested – historical British costume drama, yes please – the scripts, production values and cast and crew who had been assembled for the series guaranteed, at the very least, a sizeable initial audience, not to mention an inordinate amount of publicity.

I remember one day Pru asking me who else was starring in the series. We'd just started rehearsing in St John's Wood and it was all going swimmingly.

'Who's playing your mum?' Pru asked.

'Who, Queen Vic? Annette Crosbie.'

'Really? Oh, marvellous. I adore Annette. And your dad?'

'Robert Hardy.'

'Super! How's his German accent?'

'Faultless.'

'You haven't told me who's playing Disraeli?'

'John Gielgud.'

'Oh, you must be thrilled!'

'I am.'

Sir John Gielgud had been a hero of mine since childhood and when I was persuaded to play King Lear aged

Pru looking beautiful in the early 1980s.

At our home in Barnes in the mid-1960s. I'm afraid I've no idea who the other two people are.

Same kitchen, same home, just a few years later.

Pru backstage at The Old Vic.

From a magazine shoot when I became the Prospect Theatre Company's Artistic Director. The O'Toole debacle began shortly afterwards.

Juliet perming what little hair I had left for a role.

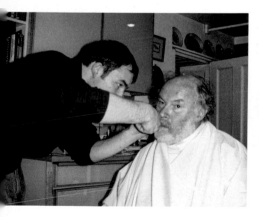

oe very kindly trimming my beard.

No idea what I'm doing but I rather like the hat.

Singing with our boys.

Enjoying ourselves with Juliet in 1989.

With Joe, Clem and Felix on the River Thames.

Celebrating our 40th wedding anniversary on board the *PS Waverley*, the world's last seagoing passenger-carrying paddle steamer.

Celebrating our 25th anniversary in Los Angeles.

This time, celebrating our golden wedding anniversary, again on board the *PS Waverley*. There's dear Andrew Sachs, bottom right.

The blessing of our marriage. Such a very special day.

Back on board the *Waverley* once again. It's one of our happy places.

Pru and me on a narrowboat. For a change.

More *Waverley*.

Pru and me out on the town.

In our garden in Wandsworth, June 2023.

just thirty-seven in 1971, he'd had several words of advice for me. 'Get a light Cordelia,' he said, referring to the final scene of the play where Lear has to carry his daughter's dead body.

'What else happened today?' Pru asked after I'd finished reeling off rest of the cast, which, while we're here, included Charles Dance, Michael Hordern, Helen Ryan, Felicity Kendal, Edward Hardwicke, Richard Vernon and Jane Lapotaire. Not bad.

'Well,' I began, 'I was stopped by two members of the public on my way to the rehearsal room this morning who each asked me what I was working on now.'

'That was kind of them. And what did they say when you told them? I hope they were impressed.'

'Not really. One of them commented, "Oh, I can't stand Shakespeare," before walking off, and the other asked, "Who's playing Mrs Simpson?"'

Funnily enough, those who still recollect the series are often convinced that it was about Henry VIII. 'I saw you as Henry VIII,' they say resolutely. I suppose there are certain superficial similarities between the two monarchs, but you'd think they'd notice that over the 294 years separating them the royal barge had been replaced by a motorcar. Or perhaps not?

Seven-year-old Sam and four-year-old Joe were in one episode of *Edward the Seventh* playing the two sons, Prince Albert Victor and Prince George.

'Where will we be filming, Daddy?' Sam asked me.

'Well, we'll be filming the exterior scenes at Sandringham House,' I informed him, 'which is where the Queen lives sometimes, and the interior scenes in a studio, where they'll be filming you and Joe having a tea party.' That went down rather well if I remember.

Other estimable locations we used for *Edward the Seventh* included Windsor Castle, St Paul's Cathedral, Wilton's Music Hall in East London and Osborne House on the Isle of Wight. The tea-party scene, which was by far the longest featuring the boys, took an absolute age to film, partly due to the fact that young Joe had three words of dialogue to deliver – 'So do I' – which took most of the afternoon to get him to say. We all had great fun, however, and one of my favourite photographs was of the boys and me, taken in costume on the steps outside Sandringham House during a break in filming.

As we'd hoped, *Edward the Seventh* was received very well on its release. In the United States, they changed the name of the series to simply *Edward the King*, as it was feared that *Edward the Seventh* would lead viewers to believe that they may have missed *Edward the Fifth* and *Edward the Sixth* a couple of weeks back. They don't like programmes with numbers in over there. It won four awards at the 1976 BAFTA Television Awards, including for Best Actress, which was won deservedly by Annette Crosbie.

I have nothing but fond memories of making the show and have always felt rather sorry for the somewhat marginalized monarch. He had a pretty awful life, really: disapproved of by his mother; an unhappy childhood leading to a furtive adolescence; a long period of frustration as the ageing heir to the throne, finally to become king at fifty-nine, when he had rather run out of energy. In the TV series we had hoped to perhaps rectify the popular image of him as simply a womanizing, race-going hedonist. But to some people, it seems, he will always be Henry VIII in different trousers.

One Sunday afternoon in the summer of 1982, Pru came into my study after she'd been pottering in the garden and caught me guffawing rather loudly.

'What's so funny?' she asked.

'It's this,' I said, waving the script I was holding. 'I haven't read anything so amusing in years.'

'Let me have a look.'

'No! I haven't finished yet.'

The script was for a new television series called *Brass* and had arrived the previous Friday, but because I'd been doing other things, my agent had had to prompt me to take a look at it.

'You'll love it,' he said. 'It's a pastiche, really, of soap operas and all those big expensive American TV dramas like *Dallas* and *Dynasty*.'

I must admit I was more bemused by his description than anything else and had no idea what to expect. But from the very first page of the script I was hooked, and while I totally understood my agent's references to *Dallas* and *Dynasty*, I saw it more as a pastiche of the north of England. J.B. Priestly, L.S. Lowry, *Love on the Dole*, *Coronation Street* – nothing was sacred. Indeed, just a few years previously I had had the pleasure of playing the successful but interminably uncouth northern factory owner Josiah Bounderby in a television adaptation of Charles Dickens' *Hard Times*. He and the super-capitalist mill owner Bradley Hardacre, the character I had been asked to play in *Brass*, were like two peas in a pod.

'Do you really like it?' I asked Pru after she'd read the first script.

'Oh, I do, Tim,' she said. 'You must do it.'

The series had been written by two men who couldn't have been less alike – an acerbic Mancunian called John Stevenson and an eccentric Shropshire landowner called Julian Roach – and after I had accepted the role we began to meet once a week in an abandoned office equidistant from their respective homes to plan Bradley Hardacre's next adventure.

The cast that Granada ended up assembling for *Brass* was top drawer and included Caroline Blakiston as my dipsomaniac wife, Barbara Ewing as my mistress, and Geoffrey Hinsliff as her husband, who also happened to be my faithful cap-doffing foreman.

I accepted the part of Bradley Hardacre on the understanding that the recordings would take place without a studio audience and that no laughter track would be used. 'A spoof,' I argued, as did John and Julian, 'must be as authentic as possible.' Granada didn't agree at first and fought back but the writers and I were resolute. 'If half the studio is taken up by an audience,' we argued, 'it will limit what we can do. Also, if people are laughing every two minutes we'll have to stop, which again will frustrate the realism.'

Fortunately, the director, Gareth Jones, and producer, Bill Podmore, agreed with us, although for quite some time Granada continued to argue their case. There was almost an unwritten law in television at the time that comedy shows should either have audiences and/or a laughter track, and if that wasn't the case they should be re-written if necessary and made as a drama. What we were suggesting, then, was the creation of a new production ethos. Unthinkable!

I don't know how we did it but in the end we managed to persuade our paymasters that this was the way to go and so without any further ado we decamped to the town of Ramsbottom in Lancashire and started filming.

Even God seemed to be delighted that *Brass* had gone into production. It rained appropriately when filming in and around the rows of terraced houses in Ramsbottom, which served well as the humble dwellings of my poor downtrodden workforce, whereas at nearby Holcombe House, which served as the opulent domain of the Hardacre family, the sun would shine almost constantly.

The reason I decided to mention *Brass* wasn't so I could give you chapter and verse about how we made it, which would no doubt send you to sleep. No, the reason I wanted to include it (in addition to being rather proud of it) is because it is one of the most enjoyable things I have ever had the pleasure of doing as an actor and I remember making it with great affection. Simple as that, really.

I asked Pru if she had her own version of this and at first she couldn't bring anything to mind.

'How about *Mapp & Lucia*,' I suggested. 'You had a marvellous time making that.'

Suddenly Pru's eyes lit up. 'Yes!' she said. 'With Nigel Hawthorne and dear Geraldine McEwan. Are they still with us?'

'I'm afraid they aren't.'

'Oh dear,' said Pru, sitting back in her chair. 'That is sad.'

Not everyone will agree with this, but I always tell Pru

the truth in these situations, out of respect more than anything. She may not have much of a short-term memory but although she needs protecting I don't hold with lying to her, not unless it's absolutely necessary.

We spent the next hour or so reminiscing about *Mapp & Lucia*, and to help jog Pru's memory I played her part of an episode. Just in case you aren't familiar with the show, *Mapp & Lucia* was based on a series of comic novels by E.F. Benson that were written in the 1920s about two women – Mrs Mapp, played by Pru, and Lucia, played by Geraldine – and their struggle for social dominance in their local community.

The show became enormously popular in America, apparently, and especially with the gay community. Indeed, I remember Geraldine McEwan once telling Pru and me that after its release in the United States the gay community of New York started holding gossipy English tea parties based on those that were given by Mrs Mapp.

I used to visit Pru a great deal while she was filming *Mapp & Lucia*, and for the very simple reason that I found the town in which it was filmed, which was Rye in East Sussex, absolutely fascinating. It appeared to be stuck in the 1920s. While obviously being an ideal location for the show, you couldn't actually tell the actors from the residents.

'I went to buy some crochet wool in full costume the other day,' Pru told me one day, 'and no one took a blind bit of notice!'

More Monarchs

In terms of portraying famous British monarchs, the scores are level between Pru and me at two apiece. My own efforts, Henry and Edward, each took place in the 1970s, whereas Pru's first portrayal began in 1979 and lasted the best part of three decades, and her second in 1988, which lasted about three years.

'Darling, I'm to play your mum,' Pru exclaimed to me one afternoon.

I was trying to learn a script at the time and hadn't wished to be disturbed. 'What on earth are you talking about?' I said, perhaps a little too brusquely.

'Queen Victoria. You remember I told you that a show was being written for me based on her diaries?'

'Yes, I seem to have some recollection.'

'Well, it's almost finished. We're to start rehearsing within the month.'

To cut what could become a rather protracted story short, after coming across and then reading the three volumes of diary that Queen Victoria had written, Katrina Hendrey, a friend of Pru's, had offered to write a show especially for her based on the words therein. 'I was absolutely knocked out by them,' Pru once said. 'They are so funny, intelligent and indiscreet.'

The show that Katrina devised and then wrote was called *An Evening with Queen Victoria*. It featured Pru as the

Queen, with Richard Burnett, a pianist who also happened to be Katrina's husband, and Ian Partridge, the famous lyric tenor. With the help of a costume, a prosthetic nose and a wig, Pru plays Queen Victoria from the age of thirteen to eighty-two, so we see her morph from being an impulsive young princess, desperately trying not to be too overwhelmed by her royal inheritance, through her joy at marrying Albert and then devastation at losing him, to her transformation into a formidable hard-hearted matriarch. Interspersed between these changes, music of the period (including some composed by Prince Albert) is provided by Richard and Ian.

The first two performances of the show took place in September 1979 at Richard and Katrina's house in Kent. This was followed up by a Sunday performance at the Old Vic Theatre in London, which is where it came to the attention of BBC2. They wanted to record the show live and so a performance was arranged at the Lyric Theatre in Hammersmith. Pru's performance in this show really is quite extraordinary and when the reviews appeared in the newspapers following the show's transmission it was quite clear that the critics agreed.

'We were considerably indebted to Prunella Scales,' said the *Newcastle Journal* in reviewing the previous evening's entertainment, 'who, in *An Evening with Queen Victoria*, delightfully portrayed the lady in all her moods.'

The *Daily Mail*, however, went one better. 'Prunella Scales shows just what a delightful, many-faceted artist she is. [With] movements lilting or laborious, and just the odd flick of a shawl, Miss Scales grows younger and older at will. You can imagine the magic working for a theatre audience, but to succeed in camera close-ups is a miracle of television that Miss Scales performs with consummate skill.'

Since the show was first televised in 1981, Pru, Richard and Ian have shown it globally well over 500 times and it became an intermittent source of work for the three of them. They've performed it in all kinds of different venues: concert halls, town halls, parish halls, arts centres, churches, cathedrals, hotels, nightclubs. They even performed it in the Library of Congress in Washington.

The first really lengthy overseas tour they undertook with *An Evening with Queen Victoria* was to Australia at the beginning of 1983 and I still have the first letter that Pru wrote to me from there. Come to think of it, I still have almost all the letters that Pru has written to me.

I have a punishing publicity programme tomorrow and Tuesday (when we open): they originally wanted me from 8.30 a.m. to 3.30 p.m. on Tuesday for TV and radio. Nick has said three hours only starting at 10.30 a.m. All this publicity effort means they haven't sold next week as well as they'd hoped. This week OK apparently. God, I hope we're going to be all right. Australia could easily hate it, I suppose.

Australia didn't hate it at all. They loved it, and every night during those first two weeks they had to put extra seats in the aisles.

'Well, we've opened,' she said in her next letter. 'The Victorian Arts Centre people amazed by the show, they've got awful posters up saying, "You will be amused" – but I don't think they expected it really.'

From Melbourne, where the tour had started, they travelled to Canberra for a week and then on to Perth. During one performance in Perth, Richard and Ian had to do battle with a local man who, despite the protestations of several of his fellow audience members, insisted on listening to some local election results on his transistor radio.

'Where to next?' I asked Pru during one of only two telephone conversations we had, I think, during the six-week tour.

'A ten-day tour of the outback,' she replied. 'Each venue will provide a piano (hopefully tuned) and the rest – me, Richard, Ian, our luggage, costumes and props et cetera will have to fit into a van that has been provided by the Arts Council.'

'Are you looking forward to it?'

'Performing, yes. Travelling, absolutely not.'

A few days later a letter arrived, and it appeared that everything was going rather well.

Posters in every window, newly tuned piano, laughter, breathless attention, rapturous applause and huge whiskies at the thrash afterwards. They couldn't believe we were there – farmers, teachers, housewives, dentists, schoolchildren, all saying it was the best thing they've ever seen or heard.

A week later another letter arrived informing me of an altogether different reception.

Full house, sat like stones for the first three-quarters of an hour except for applauding the songs. I worked heroically and got them

going by the interval, whereupon they produced a baby, two brilliant
coughers and a lady with a heart condition who had to be taken
out ten minutes before the end. Afterwards we were given a lot of
cold quiche and sandwiches and a choice of tea or milky coffee.
Bruce [the driver] had found a glass of vin rosé and I'm afraid
they thought I was the most frightful tart.

Something rather momentous but non-Queen Victoria related happened while Pru was in Australia. She discovered karaoke. I intimated earlier that our letters to each other cover all manner of subjects. This, I suppose, is one of the more surprising.

The manager of the entertainment centre is an alcoholic. Last
night he was judging the karaoke heats in the hotel lounge. Do you
know about this art form? The Japanese export pop videos <u>without</u>
<u>the vocal track</u>, and you have to sing it into a mic while they screen
the video behind you. It's quite wonderful in a horrifying way. Last
night a vast garage mechanic dressed as Ray Charles did a Presley
number, and a middle-aged schoolmaster did 'Pennies From
Heaven' beautifully. I could do without the videos, to be honest,
but there's something appealing about it. MUCH TOO
LOUD, of course.

In 1987 they toured the Far East and Pru's first letter told of a rather bumpy flight.

'Bumpiest I've ever known,' she wrote. 'Convinced last hours had come. Ian's hands blue with bruises from me clutching it, and a woman was sick all over Richard.'

By far my favourite letter from this tour was one Pru wrote in Brunei one day. With it being a very strict Muslim country, they had been asked to perform the show to a censorship committee before opening.

'The censorship preview was very funny,' Pru wrote . . .

There were five censors, four male, one female and we rather assumed that once they had seen me clad from head to toe in opaque white cotton, they'd OK it instantly – but they let us go on and on and ON: three-quarters of the way through the first half we were cutting CHUNKS of music and text and getting very giggly: I kept hands clamped to sides in quadrilles so not a smidgeon of ankle showed. I think perhaps they couldn't believe it was so boring and were waiting for some sort of dénouement. I resisted almost uncontrollable urge to rip Ian's trousers off at the end of 'Schmerz der Liebe' [a song written by Prince Albert], and we lumbered to the end of Act One. I then suggested that perhaps we shouldn't waste any more of their valuable time, as there was no further change in the costume; the two who were asleep woke up, the others put away their watches, and the main one came up to the front, shook our hands and said it was 'very great'.

A close second to this letter is one I received from Taipei where, while trying to clear customs, Pru had almost caused an incident after an officer mistook the contents of the wig box she was carrying for a severed head. 'The officer screamed for about a minute,' she told me. They had been booked to appear in Taipei at the discothèque in the Hilton Hotel, much to the bewilderment of many of the guests. Pru told me on the telephone that somebody had fallen asleep during one of the performances and a newspaper reporter had written, 'a kindly old sport must have found the erstwhile Mrs Basil Fawlty to be the woman of his dreams, because he spent the majority of the first act snoring in heart-felt appreciation of their efforts.'

The biggest problem they faced while playing the discothèque was avoiding meeting the audience while taking to the stage.

We were instructed by Mr Yu to make our way backstage via the kitchens of adjacent Golden China restaurant, so at 7.55 p.m. we duly proceeded in full costume and orderly British fashion through roomful of diners, only to be repulsed at the kitchen doors by restaurant manager and several waiters wielding trays of soup. We retraced our progress with as much dignity as we could muster to the door of the nightclub, where Mr Yu firmly propelled us back through the restaurant (inscrutable smiles of diners by this time giving way to undistinguished hilarity) and finally into the kitchen, to pick our way through hordes of steaming woks and emerge through the fire exit at the side of the stage in full view of the assembling audience. All thirty-six of them. After that the show was rather well received.

Pru's second monarchal interpretation was a dangerous one to accept, because the monarch in question was a living one. The year was 1988 and Pru had been approached about appearing in not one but two new plays by Alan Bennett. *An Englishman Abroad*, which is a dramatization of a meeting that took place in Moscow between the spy Guy Burgess and the actress Coral Browne, and *A Question of Attribution*, which records an imaginary encounter between Sir Anthony Blunt, Surveyor of the Queen's Pictures, and Queen Elizabeth II. The two plays were being performed together at the National Theatre under the combined title of *Single Spies*. Pru had been offered the role of Miss Browne in the first play, one that she was very much looking forward to, and, in the second play, Her Majesty Queen Elizabeth II.

'Haven't you had your fill of playing monarchs yet?' I asked her. 'I know I have.'

Pru had already appeared in a play by Alan Bennett called *Doris and Doreen* in the late 1970s alongside her friend Patricia Routledge and she'd been waiting for the telephone to ring with a chance to work with him again ever since.

This was actually the first time a reigning monarch had ever been portrayed on the British stage. The closer they came to opening, the more people speculated as to how things might unfold. Just in case you haven't seen either *Single Spies* or *A Question of Attribution*, and there's every good chance you might not have, as it all happened over thirty years ago, allow me to set the scene.

After one of her engagements is cancelled, the Queen meanders into the Long Gallery at Buckingham Palace, where she finds Sir Anthony Blunt up a ladder examining Titian's 'Allegory of Prudence', a painting of two men that unmasks up to three more when X-rayed. Hearing somebody approach, Blunt, without looking down, asks whoever it is to pass him a magnifying glass. On realizing he has just addressed the Queen he is mortified but a conversation then ensues about how to spot a fake from a genuine work of art. One of the subtexts of this scene is whether Her Majesty is aware that Blunt was a former Soviet spy and a member of the notorious Cambridge Five.

Pru's research while creating her portrayal of Her

Majesty the Queen was forensic. She produced her vowels perfectly, studied her walk and, after a conversation with one of Her Majesty's ladies-in-waiting, was even able to find out what kind of stockings the monarch wore. 'Research is absolutely crucial,' she once said. 'I'm fascinated by the way people behave and it's a great pleasure, as well as, I suppose, one's moral artistic duty, to get as near to the character as possible. It's more interesting, more fun – and more entertaining for the audience. I myself do not care a bit about how people behave, but as an actor it's a major concern for every part you play, and you have to find out as much as you possibly can.'

Pru's notices for both *A Question of Attribution* and *An Englishman Abroad* are among the best she's ever received, and deservedly so. There was, however, a different barometer for measuring her portrayal of the Queen.

'You'll never guess what happened yesterday,' she said to me after returning from the National Theatre one evening. 'I only found out today, but Princess Margaret was in the audience yesterday and when I walked on stage one of her security men stood up believing it to be the Queen.'

Clement Freud in *The Times* stated that, 'It must be very trying for a monarch to know that nightly and within totting distance there is a brilliant half-hour scene of herself with Sir Anthony Blunt. She misses an outstanding performance by her stand-in.' Michael Billington in *Country Life* was also rather impressed and seemed pleased that Pru went, 'neither for exact mimicry nor for revue sketch caricature, but somehow catches the essence while preserving the enigma.'

The late actor Frederick Treves, who was a great friend

of ours, was giving Pru a lift somewhere the day after the
television adaptation of *A Question of Attribution* had been
transmitted (which was actually some three years after
the stage show) when he was stopped by the police for
speeding.

'The policeman was writing me a ticket,' he said, 'when
he looked beyond me at the passenger. Pru had played
Elizabeth II on TV and suddenly he just stopped and waved
us away. He must have thought, my God, I've stopped the
Queen!'

We never found out if Her Majesty saw Pru's portrayal
of her on television in 1991, but when they met in 1992 at
Buckingham Palace when Pru was awarded a CBE, after
shaking hands, the Queen said to Pru very quietly, 'I suppose you think you should be doing this.'

Working Together

One of the most common questions Pru and me are asked by members of the public is whether or not we have ever acted alongside each other, and we always reply that we have, many times. I am not referring to our endeavours on the waterways. In that particular series, which I will come on to later, Pru and I appeared together as ourselves, and it was great fun.

The first time Pru and me appeared opposite each other in a play was way back in 1964. Given the fact that we knew so many of the same people within the industry, it had been only a matter of time, although I must confess that I hadn't expected it to happen quite so quickly. We'd been married for less than a year and in all the time we had been together we had barely spent more than a week or two in each other's company at any one time.

The play in question was an intriguing four-hander called *The Trigon* by James Broom Lynne. Pru had been attending a series of classes given by an American director called Charles Marowitz who was putting on the play and he thought Pru would be ideal for the female lead.

'And there's a part for you if you'd like it?' she said, after informing me of her good fortune.

'Oh, really. Who would I be playing?'

'A rather pathetic over-age Boy Scout. I think you'd be ideal.'

'It's kind of you to think of me.'

Although I eventually accepted the part of the pathetic over-age Boy Scout, I found Charles Marowitz rather annoying. His instructions, for instance, when directing Pru and me, seemed pretentious in the extreme. During a rehearsal one day he said to me, 'Tim, I think you need a physical reorientation here.'

'You mean you'd like me to move?' I said rather disdainfully.

Pru gave me one of her looks. She'd worked with Charles several times before and admired him enormously. This went on for a while and eventually we sort of met in the middle. He became more direct, I became less cantankerous, and in the end, we became friends.

I have a similar story regarding Sam. We were appearing on stage together in *Henry IV Parts I and II* – me as Falstaff and Sam as Hal. During a rehearsal one day we each picked up each other's script by mistake. Both had been opened at the scene we were rehearsing. Sam had written, 'Palliate the follies I can neither avoid nor deny,' which I believe is a quote from a book written by a rather eminent Shakespearean scholar. I, on the other hand, had written, 'Pick up boot.' My excuse for this is that acting is called acting because it is committing actions, and picking up the boot is what I intended to do.

Directors with slightly irritating habits notwithstanding, I do remember being a little bit worried about the effect that suddenly spending every waking hour together might have on mine and Pru's relationship. After all, she and I had spent many months moving heaven and earth in order to steal just a few precious hours together. What if absence really did make the heart grow fonder?

What saved us, I think — apart from the fact that the whole thing lasted just five weeks back-to-back — was the fact that, at least when we first started performing the play, we were each doing other things. I was working with the BBC Drama Repertory Company on radio and Pru was rehearsing *Marriage Lines* with Richard Briers.

The big test was when we first went on tour together. By that time, not only had we learned how best to avoid a confrontation, but we had realized that we actually enjoyed each other's company over prolonged periods of time. Hurrah!

I think the most fun we've ever had on a stage together — or in front of a camera, for that matter — was in J. B. Priestley's excellent comedy, *When We Are Married*. Set in Priestley's home county of West Yorkshire, it tells the story of three respectable nouveau riche married couples who discover on their joint silver wedding anniversary that, due to a technical oversight, they are not in fact married at all. Pru and me were one of said couples, and the cast also included Bill Fraser, Patricia Routledge, Patsy Rowlands, Brian Murphy and Elizabeth Spriggs.

The TV version followed a very successful stage production that took place at the Whitehall Theatre with virtually the same cast, all of whom had been born or brought up in the north. As you know, Pru had spent much of her childhood in West Yorkshire, so she was all right, while I kept very quiet about having left the city of Bradford aged three weeks. It was one of those blissful shows where everyone worked together wonderfully as a team, and we still watch it occasionally.

My character, Councillor Albert Parker, is a deluded misanthropic narcissist who, for the last twenty-five years, has endeavoured to make his quiet and long-suffering wife Annie appreciate just how lucky she is to be married to him. Fortunately, I hadn't long since finished playing a bombastic self-obsessed northerner, as from 1980 until 1983 I'd been appearing as the indomitable Bradley Hardacre in the comedy drama series *Brass*. If you have seen that particular show, you will undoubtedly recognize it as being a perfect platform from which to base a character like Albert.

On realizing that they are not in fact married, Albert sits Annie down to reassure her that, despite her failings as a wife and as a human being, and despite his elevation from being just plain Albert Parker to Councillor Albert Parker who has 'come to be a big man at chapel, vice-president o't'cricket league, an' so forth' he is still willing to do his duty and marry her.

'Y'know, Annie,' says Albert conceitedly, 'I've sometimes thought that right at first you didn't realize just what you'd picked out o't'lucky bag.'

When Annie finally gets a chance to speak and informs Albert that she actually might not wish to marry him he is, of course, somewhat perturbed.

'You talk about your duty,' says Annie. 'Well, for twenty-five years I've done my duty. I've washed and cooked and cleaned and mended for you. I've pinched and scrimped and saved for you. I've listened for hours and hours to all your dreary talk. I've never had any thanks for it. I've hardly ever had any fun. But I thought I was your wife and

I'd taken you for better or worse and that I ought to put up with you –'

'PUT UP WITH ME!'

Annie's final depiction of Albert, before the penny finally drops that he's being discarded by her, is sublime.

'Well, to begin with, you're very selfish. But then, I suppose most men are. You're idiotically conceited. But again, so are most men. But a lot of men at least are generous. And you're very stingy. And some men are amusing. But – except when you're being pompous and showing off – you're not at all amusing. You're just very dull and dreary.'

Key to the scene working is obviously the juxtaposition of Albert's arrogance and his dismissal of his thought-to-be wife, and her calm and measured but ultimately merciless annihilation of his character and of their relationship. It really is the best fun that two actors can have on a stage together and the fact that Pru and I were being paid to perform it eight times a week was rather wonderful.

In 1991 a new opportunity arose for Pru and me to act in a play together, this time in a co-production between the Bristol Old Vic and the National Theatre of *Long Day's Journey into Night* by Eugene O'Neill. Widely considered to be O'Neill's magnum opus, *Long Day's Journey into Night* had been awarded the 1957 Pulitzer Prize for Drama and concerns Connecticut-based James and Mary Tyrone and their sons, Jamie and Edmond. Me and Pru played James and Mary and the sons were played by Stephen Dillane, who is perhaps best known for playing Stannis Baratheon in *Game of Thrones*, and Sean McGinley, who, like me and Pru, has appeared in pretty much everything.

The entire play takes place in just one day and portrays a family who are struggling to come to terms with the realities and consequences of the failings of each family member in relation to their own. The mother, Mary, is a morphine addict who suffers from psychosis and the father, James, who is a Shakespearean actor by trade, is wealthy but miserly and despises himself for having given up a prestigious career in exchange for commercial success. The entire family are continually at war; rather tragically, the play was based on O'Neill's own upbringing.

'Are you sure you want to do this?' Pru asked me after the approach had been made. 'Four acts, Tim. And it won't be anything like *When We Are Married*. It'll be really hard going, and for fifteen weeks. Don't you think we ought to think about it?'

The choice of the play had not been ours, of course. There is a common misconception that when two reasonably well-known married people are cast in a play together, they have personally selected that play as a vehicle for themselves, possibly with an eye on saving money on hotels and taxis. They are perceived as the proprietors of the play, rather than performers in it. The knowledge that the couple on stage are partners in real life also conditions the audience's response: if the story is of two individuals who may or may not come together, or whose relationship is torn with strife, people can nevertheless sit back happily and think, 'Well, they're all right, really.' It's cosy. *Long Day's Journey into Professional Suicide*, as I began to call it, is anything but cosy and if it was going to work Pru and me would have to be at our very best.

'It'll be fine,' I said, attempting to reassure her. 'We'll be fine.'

If truth be known, I too was harbouring certain doubts and worries about what might come to pass over the next fifteen weeks, and some of these were realized as early as during the rehearsal period. Regardless of what we might be appearing in, when working independently of each other Pru and I are always able to switch off once we have shut our front door behind us. Indeed, I'd go so far as to say that it is an essential part of our wellbeing. This was never much of a requirement during *When We Are Married*, as after returning home from the theatre we would often quite happily regurgitate the evening's presentation. With *Long Day's Journey into Night*, this, alas, was all but impossible. In addition to it being, as Pru put it, 'really hard going', the play lasted just over three and a half hours and we found it difficult to switch off afterwards.

'I simply cannot relax,' I complained to Pru one evening after a day's rehearsal. 'And if it's like this now, what's it going to be like on tour or when we open at the National?'

Another worry was how the press might react to us appearing in something like this – and how we might react to them. Normally, if one of us is in a play and the other is doing something else, should things go badly for one, then the other can offer advice and consolation. But when you are both in it together every sort of feeling you have is doubled. So, if it is all going wonderfully you feel doubly delighted. However, if it is not . . .

Despite this, Pru and me went about our business of interpreting our characters in the usual fashion. As part of her research Pru talked to several doctors and psychiatrists, and she also spent time with some ex-addicts at Wandsworth Prison.

When we opened, the reaction from audiences was mixed. Like it or not, some people had undoubtedly bought tickets hoping to see either Sybil Fawlty or a happily married acting couple doing happily married things. What they got was a couple arguing all the time, and one's taking morphine and the other's getting drunk.

The production itself was physically all that could have been wished for. We had a superb set, wonderfully clever lighting, admirable direction and two fine performances from Stephen and Sean. Somehow, though, me and Pru failed to deliver, at least that was the verdict of the national press. Well, you can't win them all.

'Let's not do that again for a while?' I said, shutting our front door after the final performance.

'Let's not do what again?' said Pru.

'Exactly.'

Crises of Confidence

I fully admit that over the years I have found Pru's occasional lack of self-confidence to be quite maddening at times, but only because I am acutely aware of how capable and talented she is. That's not to say that Pru capitulates every time she is criticized or challenged, however. If Pru believes that somebody is in the wrong or is not doing something correctly, she will state her case politely but forcefully, whether that be to a director, a fellow actor or a member of the public.

One of my favourite examples of this took place in 1986, when Pru appeared in a television drama called *Home Cooking* in which she played a murderer. *Home Cooking* was part of a season of one-hour plays focusing on relationships that ended with a fatality.

'I'm to play the wife of a hotel owner,' she said to me after accepting the job.

'Sounds a bit familiar,' I replied. 'I take it there isn't much comedy, though?'

'Not exactly. My husband is a serial rapist and I end up doing him in by locking him in a sauna. After I've killed him, I seduce one of the hotel guests and then bump him off too. In one other scene, it is necessary that I appear nude. I'm expecting letters,' she said hopefully. 'Outraged of Purley will be up in arms!'

Joking aside, the chances of a scene such as this causing

consternation among certain members of the general public were very high indeed, not to mention the press. Sure enough, on the day of transmission, the papers had a field day, with Scotland's *Daily Record* declaring rather unimaginatively: *Sybil Fawlty appears on the box tonight – Nude! Who knows what Basil will say.* I'm afraid that was par for the course with regards to the pre-transmission headlines, although the reviews that appeared afterwards were, without exception, extremely favourable.

But it was the aforementioned 'Outraged of Purley' whose protestations really struck a chord.

'I thought I might receive the odd letter,' said Pru, 'but this is ridiculous.'

'How many?' I asked.

'Well, there were four letters yesterday, and a further five today. Some of them are quite rude, which is ironic.'

Each letter was a variation on a theme, expressing outrage that the actress who gave us Sybil Fawlty and Mrs Mapp in *Mapp & Lucia* was appearing nude on our television screens. Although the competition was extremely fierce, there was one clear winner in the indignation stakes.

'Good lord, take a look at this,' said Pru, after reading the letter in question. 'It's from a vicar and his wife.'

The vicar complained that the bedroom scene had left him and his wife so 'offended and nauseated' that they immediately turned off their set, and went on to say, 'We hope that you will take serious thought before you accept any further roles that involve similar scenes, as we believe they are not only letting yourself and your image down, but also provide the kind of so-called entertainment which is offensive to those who still maintain standards of decency and propriety.'

'Are you going to reply?' I asked.

'Absolutely,' said Pru. 'What a hideous man.'

'I find it curious,' she wrote, 'that while you apparently have absolutely no objection to my character killing her husband in the sauna, you object to scenes of romantic love. The nude scene wasn't gratuitous. It was necessary to the play.'

Needless to say, she received no reply.

Perhaps I should point out that Pru does not have a monopoly in our family when it comes to being deficient in confidence occasionally. Saying that, you'd hardly think she had a problem after what you've just read. Indeed, I myself have had to endure one or two crises over the years, most memorably while I was appearing with the Royal Shakespeare Company in the 1970s. I'd just finished a season with them up at Stratford-upon-Avon and all in all it had gone rather well. The critics had been most kind and had remarked on my versatility. Indeed, in the last eighteen months I had played a Worcestershire pear-picker, a Venetian Jew, a solid Windsor burgher, a disabled Maltese pimp, a lunatic, an elderly Syracusan merchant, a country parson and, would you believe it, a gorilla (in *The Governor's Lady* by David Mercer).

During one of the plays, I had a very long gap between entrances and to pass the time I would visit the company offices, searching for information about planning and such like. One evening while I was rooting around in the waste-paper basket, I made a rather dispiriting discovery. In the days before photocopiers (some of you might be old enough to remember), internal correspondence would be typed on stencil paper for the duplicating machine and then screwed up and thrown away. The stencil papers were still legible, though, and towards the end of the season when next year's plans were being hatched the bins would be overflowing with morsels of information.

Among one such crop I came across a chart, upon which were listed all the names of the present Stratford company divided into five columns, labelled A, B, C, D and E. The 'A' list was indeed just that and had under its heading the names of all our star performers: Glenda Jackson, Paul Scofield, Eric Porter, Janet Suzman and Ian Richardson. Not bad, eh? 'B' comprised the principal supporting players, 'C' the ones whose agents perhaps hadn't done a very good job at negotiating, 'D' was the bit-part players and 'E' the walk-on parts. Obviously not amongst the 'A's', I assumed I that would be towards the end of the 'B's, as they were listed alphabetically, or, if my agent had been having an off day, the 'C's.

I wasn't. I was in the 'D's.

'D?' I shouted incredulously while gawping wide-eyed at the list. 'Bloody D? Oh, for God's sake.'

'My darling, this really has upset you, hasn't it?' Pru said to me the following morning. Apart from telling her what I'd seen, I'd barely said a word since returning to our cottage from the theatre.

'I have to admit it has,' I said finally. 'I didn't really expect to be in "B", and "C" would have been fine. "D", though. Is that really what they think of me?'

I had already been asked by the company to play two

roles in Peter Hall's production of *The Government Inspector* at the Aldwych Theatre (the Aldwych was the RSC's London home for a number of years) but nothing else had been suggested so, for a while at least, I would just have to wait and see. By March no further roles had materialized and so I parted company with the RSC. All things considered it probably was time to move on. It turned out to be quite fortuitous in the end, as very soon afterwards Pru introduced me to Toby Robertson, the artistic director of the Prospect Theatre Company. Pru had appeared in Prospect's very first production and during lunch at our house in Barnes one day he asked me to join the company. The first part I played for Prospect wasn't especially interesting, but things very quickly improved, and I stayed with the company, on and off, for sixteen years. Thank you, Pru!

One of the most upsetting instances concerning self-confidence that I have ever witnessed as an actor was when the brilliant but tortured Kenneth Williams, who was so much more than just a comedian, was verbally abused by some fans of the *Carry On* films in the early 1960s while appearing in a play called *Gentle Jack* alongside myself, Michael Bryant and Dame Edith Evans.

Gentle Jack was a strange, allegorical piece and the fact that it didn't succeed when it opened was mainly due to the mistake of casting Dame Edith Evans in what was not actually the central role of the play. The true protagonist was the character played by Michael Bryant but Dame Edith's billing and status, not to mention some rather ostentatious costumes that had been created for her by Her Majesty Queen Elizabeth's personal fashion designer, Hardy Amies, distorted the audiences' attentions. Dame

Edith was undoubtedly aware of this but when she voiced her concerns to the producer, Binkie Beaumont, he was dismissive and complained that she wasn't doing the costumes justice.

Kenneth played Jacko in *Gentle Jack*, Michael Bryant's spontaneous alter-ego. As with Dame Edith, his casting had been questioned but he was brilliant in the role. Kenneth began playing him as a spirited, destructive androgyne, which was unnerving in the extreme and exactly what we needed for the play. Prior to coming to London, we had played two weeks in Brighton and during the run there Kenneth was accused by the aforementioned *Carry On* fans of cheating them. They hadn't understood the play and had been expecting to see him in *Carry On* mode. I remember being with Kenneth when one of these attacks took place and it cut him to the quick. We'd just finished a matinee performance and on leaving the stage door two women, who must have been in their sixties, I suppose, accosted Kenneth.

'What a load of rubbish,' one of them said. 'We were expecting something funny. We're here under false pretences.'

Poor Kenneth was clearly mortified and as the other woman began to have her two penn'orth he pulled up his collar, put his head down and made a run for it. At that moment I was torn between pursuing him and trying to comfort him and giving the two battleaxes a taste of their own medicine. In the end I plumped for the former and I'm very glad I did because when I finally caught up with Kenneth, he was almost inconsolable.

'You have to ignore these people, Kenneth,' I said. 'Your

performance as Jacko is a genuine *tour de force*. Do not, I repeat, do not, allow the ignorance of others to influence how you play the part.'

Alas, such was the effect that this attack had on Kenneth that his performance was completely destroyed. It's well documented that self-confidence had never been Kenneth's strong suit and so, in order to placate the *Carry On* crowd and prevent any further such attacks, he started camping up his performance and playing for laughs, which distorted the play even further. It was such a shame and absolutely dreadful to watch. Truly, it was heartbreaking.

The Price of Fame

The only time that Pru and I have been more recognizable to the general public, or more sought after by the press, than we were in the 1970s and 1980s was when *Great Canal Journeys* was at its most popular. More significantly, the celebrity that we achieved from appearing in that series was, and is, collective. Prior to that, we had always been Prunella Scales and Timothy West; a brace of jobbing actors who happened to be married. Now, post *Canal Journeys,* we have become, simply, Tim and Pru. Perhaps appropriately, this is how we have always been known to our friends.

On the whole (and if you care to discount any overly prudish clergymen), being either contacted by, or approached in person by members of the public has, over the years, bestowed on us a great deal more joy than anguish. It still happens from time to time but as Pru and me have never been what you'd call A-listers, and have also been quite prolific in our endeavours, the conversations are polite but often somewhat tentative.

'What was that show you were in back in the 1980s?' I was asked not very long ago. 'I used to love that. Oh, what was it now?'

'I was in quite a few,' I replied. 'Did I play a northern gentleman?'

'Yes.'

'Then could it be *Brass*?'

'No, it wasn't that. I wasn't keen on that.'

'I can't help then. Sorry.'

Pru and me were taking a stroll on Wandsworth Common a couple of years ago when all of a sudden, a smartly dressed elderly lady with a large black poodle in tow approached us.

'Excuse me, Mr West,' she began. 'I just wanted to say how much joy you have given me over the years through your work in classical theatre.'

'That's terribly kind of you,' I said, happily shaking her hand. 'Thank you very much indeed.'

'Oh, it's my pleasure,' said the lady. Then she turned to Pru. 'I've seen you in that comedy with that awful tall fellow. I've never liked him. It's a pity you don't do more theatre, you know. You're quite good.' Fortunately, just as she said this her dog began misbehaving so she made her excuses and left.

Now, before you start feeling sorry for Pru, a far more common exchange would go something like this: 'Excuse me, Miss Scales, can I just say how marvellous I thought you were in *Mapp & Lucia*, and *Fawlty Towers*, of course. It's still our favourite sitcom. Always has been. And this must be your husband. Nice to meet you. Are you still acting? I haven't seen you in anything for a while.'

To be fair, the balance of recognition probably shifted slightly while I was appearing in *EastEnders* and *Gentleman Jack*, but it's all good fun. The notion that our efforts, regardless of medium, might have given pleasure to some people has always been a source of great pride to Pru and me and for as long as we're drawing breath that will never change.

On to the members of the press. As with the public, we have always rubbed along quite well with the press and generally they have been kind to Pru and me, and especially recently. The only anomaly that we believe is worth including here is a disastrous interview I did with a local radio station in Leicester in the mid-1980s that resulted in a handwritten transcript of said interview being sent home to Pru, together with a rant concerning my severe dislike of well-known historical figures being mistaken for other well-known historical figures. Like this.

At the end of the first series of *Brass*, I was sent an interesting and quite brilliant play by David Pownall called *Master Class* that ended up playing in Leicester before eventually moving into the West End the following year. It's about an imaginary meeting between Joseph Stalin (played by myself) his cultural enforcer, Zhdanov, and the two composers Prokofiev and Shostakovich during the Russian Musicians' Conference of 1947. It sounds terribly serious but it's actually very funny. It explores the nature of art and power and was wonderful to perform as the characters desperately try to compose suitable Georgian music. A grand piano, which I later bought from the management and which to this day sits proudly in our drawing room in Wandsworth, stood at the centre of the stage and was played by each member of the cast throughout. As the infamous dictator, I only had the use of one hand to play with.

'I think we're in good shape,' I said to Pru in a letter

written from my dressing room at the Haymarket Theatre in Leicester shortly after we'd opened there . . .

And there is talk of a transfer. I can't do it until next year, of course, because of more Brass — don't know if it'll keep that long. Had a splendid interview on Friday with local radio, in the dressing room. It went like this:

INTERVIEWER: Look, before we start, I've got to confess, I'm supposed to have seen the play. I was meant to come on Tuesday, but you know how it is, Timothy, one of the lads had a birthday, and there we were in the pub, and I looked at my watch and I said, 'Christ, I'm supposed to be at the Leicester Haymarket!' So, I'm going to talk to you as if I'd seen the play, all right? Testing, testing. Mary had a little lamb. One two three four five. Good evening, Timothy West, and what brings you to Leicester in this powerful Socialist political drama, *Master Class*?

ME: It's not a Socialist political drama.

INTERVIEWER: What?

ME: It's not a political drama at all. It's a very funny play about music.

INTERVIEWER: Well, yes, yes! Yes, it is, a very funny play. In parts.

ME: At least, I think so.

INTERVIEWER: Yes, you're right, it is. I mean, it is a political drama; but there are, also, some funny – bits – in it. Right?

ME: Right.

INTERVIEWER: For instance . . .

217

ME: What?

INTERVIEWER: For instance?

ME: Mm? Oh! Yes, well, I think the 'composition' scene in Act II is a brilliant piece of comic writing.

INTERVIEWER: Yes! The composition scene! That really had me rolling in the aisles!

ME: And people seem to enjoy –

INTERVIEWER: The composition scene is hilarious!

ME: Yes? Good. What I was going to say –

INTERVIEWER: That composition scene is a hoot.

ME: Just because Stalin appears in the play, it doesn't mean –

INTERVIEWER: And?

ME: – that the play is necessarily to do with – what did you say?

INTERVIEWER: And?

ME: And what?

INTERVIEWER: And you ALL PLAY THE PIANO! [Terrible doubt.] Don't you?

ME: Well, yes, we do. I mean the other three play properly; I play like I think Stalin might have played.

INTERVIEWER: Ha ha! REALLY BADLY!

ME: [nettled] Well, the point is, he only had the use of one hand –

INTERVIEWER: You're a member of the Royal Shakespeare Company –

ME: No, I'm not.

INTERVIEWER: Aren't you? Well, you've done a lot of Shakespeare, anyway, haven't you, and heavy stuff generally, and we all remember you as Henry.

ME: Henry who?

INTERVIEWER: King Henry.

ME: King Edward.

INTERVIEWER: I meant Edward. Edward the Eighth.

ME: No, I'm sorry, the Seventh.

INTERVIEWER: [now tired and very bored] Timothy West, thank you very much.

Why does the whole Edward/Henry thing annoy me so much? It happens all the time. Last week it cropped up again, and I endeavoured to correct the man, but no, he corrected me. 'No, Henry the Eighth it was,' he said firmly. 'Have it your own way,' I told him.

It's disappointing that in thirteen episodes I failed to convey to viewers even the name of my character, but more importantly, it is disappointing in what it indicates about popular apprehension of history. Anything that isn't current is yesterday; as such, the Battle of the Somme might well have been fought with bows and arrows, King Alfred's cakes burned in the preparations for the Boston Tea Party, and it wouldn't be surprising to find Bluff King Hal driving to Epsom in a De Dion-Bouton or Bertie in doublet-and-hose attending executions on Tower Green.

An Upsetting Prospect

Whilst we have both been fortunate enough to have had lots of wonderful successes in our careers, which we have enjoyed looking back on, in the interests of balance, I think it only right that I include a few paragraphs about one of our more challenging epochs. Of course, I'd be delighted to report that our existence together has been one long run of performances, applause and adulation, but of course, life isn't like that. Even so, I think Pru and I have been extremely fortunate in this regard. Sure, we've had a few niggles here and there. Who on earth hasn't? But from a marital point of view, we firmly believe that spending plenty of time apart doing something that we each enjoy has helped to prevent any such unfortunate paroxysms.

Professionally, there has been just one period when our metal was truly tested. Or should I say, when my metal was tested. Pru's career was unaffected by this, I'm happy to say, although she certainly had her work cut out supporting me and ensuring I didn't suffer some kind of breakdown, which I very nearly did.

Some of you might already be familiar with this story but for those of you who aren't, allow me to set the scene. It's 1979 and the Prospect Theatre Company, who I had been working with for a number of years by that time, had taken up residency at the Old Vic Theatre in London. I had also recently become the Artistic Director of the company. Shortly before his departure, my predecessor as Artistic Director, Toby Robertson, had agreed with the actor Peter O'Toole that he should appear in a production of *Macbeth*.

A little while later I was offered a small part in a TV series called *Masada*, in which I was to play a Roman Emperor. The filming took place in California and starring as the Roman general was none other than Peter O'Toole. Having heard that I was now Artistic Director at Prospect he began filling me in on his ideas for *Macbeth*, which he had discussed, unbeknownst to me, with Toby Robertson. He was obviously full of enthusiasm, and I left the United States awash with excitement and anticipation. He even had a director in mind, who I was happy to consider, and said that he would be back in touch soon regarding further developments.

On my return to the Old Vic the first thing I did was catch up on my correspondence and the first letter I opened was from O'Toole's lawyers. It was their understanding, they said, as had been agreed by my predecessor, that Peter was to be given full artistic control of the production. This was obviously highly irregular and so I presented the letter to my board at Prospect. Although they all shared my concerns, it appeared there was little we could do.

'We're at the mercy of Mr O'Toole, I'm afraid,' said one board member, Anthony Quale.

'What on earth are you going to do?' Pru asked after pouring me a restorative glass of wine that evening.

'Our hands are tied,' I told her, after taking a larger than normal sip. 'We just have to hope that he's going to be reasonable and won't cause any trouble.'

'Fingers crossed. Poor you!'

The first note of doom was struck when the director Peter had hired, Jack Gold, came to my office and informed me that he would like to be released from his contract as a far more lucrative film had come his way. What on earth can one do in such a situation? I suppose I could have held him to his contract but really, what good would it have done?

'All right then,' I said. 'I'll release you.'

Finding a replacement was not going to be easy, as any director would need to accept having no control of the production, and although a fair number of people agreed to meet Peter, they all came away claiming that it simply wouldn't work. It was known that O'Toole had become extremely difficult to work with. We also had to find a designer and so I called a man called Bob Crowley, who was one of the best in the business. Bob duly designed a set, made a model of it, and then brought it in to show to Peter.

'It's rubbish,' Peter declared once Bob had left. I waited for an alternative to be suggested but nothing was forthcoming. Eventually, Peter implied that inflatable scenery was the way to go and that he would contact a friend of his who could help us.

'Inflatable scenery?' said Pru when I arrived home. 'He's taking the micky, surely to goodness?'

'Oh, I wish to God he was,' I said, pouring myself a whisky. 'It's already turning into a nightmare.'

The biggest problem we faced going forward – apart

from Peter being in full control of the production – was that he had surrounded himself with yes-men and syco-phants. Alternative suggestions or opposing views were not forthcoming. Peter could have proposed that we turn Shakespeare's great tragedy into a farce and call it *Carry On Macbeth* and I swear to you that the only person opposing it – openly at least – would have been me.

Peter's designer eventually arrived from Ireland and installed himself in one of the rehearsal rooms. Because Peter had already suggested that inflatable scenery might be integral to his backdrop we waited with bated breath.

'Is there anything you require from us?' I asked the designer on his arrival.

'Some black bin bags, some tins of adhesive, and a bottle of Powers whiskey left outside the rehearsal room door every morning,' he said.

'Fair enough.'

The designer had promised us a demonstration of his design within a week of arriving, but after three weeks nothing had happened.

'It's costing us a bloody fortune in Irish whiskey,' I said to Pru.

'Why not charge it to Peter?' she suggested. 'He's his man.'

After almost a month, Peter's genius designer declared that he was ready and so a few directors who hadn't already said no to the production were invited to join myself, Peter and several of my colleagues from Prospect. After taking our seats in the auditorium our ears were suddenly assaulted by the noise of what sounded like an industrial vacuum cleaner operating at full tilt.

'What on earth's that noise?' I asked, leaning over to Peter.

'Air compressor,' he replied tersely.

When the curtain rose a few seconds later I could hardly believe my eyes. At the rear of the stage, a collection of enormous black plastic phalluses were swaying to and fo, some having suffered the ignominy of having had scenery paint half-heartedly applied to them. Suddenly, from behind one of Peter's intermittently erect phalluses, stepped an actor wearing a black cloak. He immediately went into competition with the compressor. Unfortunately, I had absolutely no idea what the poor man was saying and so to spare him the humiliation of being drowned out by a wind machine on the stage of one of London's most prestigious theatres, I stood up and brought the proceedings to a halt.

'Enough!' I said. 'Peter, could I see you in my office please, and without your designer.'

I remember wondering how I was ever going to relay all this to Pru. She'd never believe me.

Peter's behaviour had been so completely unpredictable so far that when he sat down in my office a few minutes later I had no idea what he might say.

'Well?' I said to him.

'Awful, wasn't it?' he replied, smiling, and then he started to laugh. 'Genuinely quite terrible.'

'At last, something we agree on,' I said, joining in the merriment. We continued in this vein for twenty minutes or more. I considered it to be a breakthrough at last. Finally, Peter had realized the error of his ways and would start taking some advice.

'You seem a lot happier,' said Pru when I arrived home. 'Has Peter gone back to Hollywood?'

'No, but I think he's going to be all right,' I said. 'He had a bit of a realization earlier.'

'Sounds intriguing,' said Pro. 'Do tell.'

I forget how many glasses of wine I had to consume before I could bring myself to tell my attentive wife about the scenery debacle, but when I did she went into complete hysterics.

'I know,' I said, laughing along with her. 'Outrageous, isn't it! At least he's seen the error of his ways.'

'Thank God for that,' said Pru.

Unfortunately, the conversation I had with Peter earlier that day was the last happy occasion we ever spent together. Whilst I assumed that he'd seen the error of his ways, it seems that he had assumed that he'd recruited yet another yes-man. From then on, things deteriorated rapidly. A director was hired – by Peter – in the shape of Bryan Forbes: a brilliant film director, producer and screenwriter who had next to no experience working on stage. Peter then gave me his suggestions for the parts of Lady Macbeth and Duncan.

'Meryl Streep and John Gielgud,' he proclaimed.

When I remonstrated, he told me that had this been a film they would undoubtedly be at the top of the list.

'Yes, Peter, but this isn't a film, is it?' I replied. 'This is a theatrical production that will start in London and then tour around the United Kingdom.'

'Well, they wouldn't have to do the tour,' he said.

'Yes, they *would*, Peter.'

I suddenly realized that he had absolutely no idea how a theatrical company worked in this day and age.

'You must fight for your production,' Peter told me before leaving my office, 'and I will fight for mine.'

The next fiasco happened a few weeks later, after Peter and I had agreed verbally to cast Jane Lapotaire as Lady Macbeth. However, on his return from Hollywood where he'd been filming, he had other news. 'No, no, I want Frances Tomelty,' he said.

An Artistic Director who has to explain to an agent that he has offered their client something by mistake and doesn't really mean it does little for his own professional credibility.

'Tim, that's awful,' Pru said. 'What on earth's wrong with him?'

'I only wish I knew. The ceasefire's officially ended, though.'

Fortunately, Jane and her agent, Jeremy Conway, were extremely understanding and generous when I told them. Although I can't say for sure, I have a feeling that they appreciated the fact that they may have had a lucky escape.

Over the coming weeks Peter convinced himself that I and most of the organization were out to sabotage his production. Why he thought we should be so keen to commit theatrical *hari-kari* with the first production of the season I have no idea, but Peter firmly believed that we were there not to help but hinder him at every turn.

Finally press night arrived, by which time I had lost about a stone in weight and had been averaging three to four hours sleep a night for many months.

'Darling, you're going to have to see a doctor,' Pru had said a few days before.

'I don't need to see a doctor,' I snapped at her. 'I just need somebody to remove Peter O'Toole from my life.'

Pru sat on the arm of my chair and put her arms around my neck.

'You must always remember that whatever happens, you have me, the boys and Juliet, no matter what. One day soon, Peter O'Toole will be gone forever.'

The phrase 'There's light at the end of the tunnel' is obviously dependent on the light having been switched on. Alas, despite Pru's words of comfort, which were indeed incredibly welcome, I could not see beyond the abyss that lay ahead of me. It was interminable, and as far as I could see there was to be no happy ending.

The show, unsurprisingly, was a complete and utter disaster. The audience were at first bewildered, and then the giggles set in. When Peter appeared after the murder drenched in blood there was a burst of laughter. Ever the expert comedian, he waited for the laughter to subside before exclaiming, 'I have done the deed.' It brought the house down. *Carry On Macbeth* indeed.

Before the curtain call I went round briefly to thank everyone as they came off stage (apart from Peter, who I didn't see) and then I went home in despair.

'Oh Tim!' Pru exclaimed, on seeing me slumped in my chair, barely managing to hang on to my empty whisky tumbler. 'Was it that bad?'

'It was worse!' I bawled.

'Oh Lord,' she said, sitting on the arm of the chair. 'What are we going to do?'

The only thing I remember with any clarity from that conversation are Pru's words 'What are we going to do?' with the emphasis on the word *we*. I suddenly realized, although not for the first time, that Pru and me were far greater than the sum of our parts and that, whatever happened, I would always have her and she would always have me.

Unshakeable partnerships notwithstanding, the following day the aftermath of Peter's catastrophe began in earnest when at seven a.m. I was awakened by the telephone. It was a man from the *Evening Standard*. 'Have you actually disowned the production?' he asked me. Still half asleep, I informed the journalist that there had never been any question of me owning the production in the first place, as it had been understood from the outset that it was Peter's and Peter's alone.

'WEST DISOWNS MACBETH' read the front page of that morning's edition.

Many people assumed that I had read the notices, which were all terrible, and had attempted to distance myself from the debacle. If only it were that simple.

'Just let it go,' Pru suggested. 'There's no need to say anything else.'

That evening, during the curtain call, Bryan Forbes went on stage to make a speech. In reference to me he said, 'I have always thought that Judas was one of the least attractive characters in the whole of human history,' which I thought a bit unfair. As the author Nicholas Wapshott put it in his biography of O'Toole, the curse of *Macbeth* had split the Old Vic Company in two. The only consolation was that ticket sales were going through the roof. Even that was cold comfort, however, as the production costs had been astronomical.

Shortly after the debacle had finally come to an end, the Arts Council of Great Britain discontinued their grant to the Prospect Theatre Company and cited the controversy surrounding *Macbeth* as one of the main reasons. Anguished attempts by me and the board to try to save the company followed, but eventually we had to resign ourselves to liquidation. It was a sad end to what had been, for the main part, I think, a pleasurable and worthwhile endeavour and the company's demise was felt by everyone who had ever been employed by them, possibly including Peter O'Toole.

The Social Side

The social life of an actor can often be rather lively, it's fair to say. We are performers, after all, so whether we are in a pub surrounded by friends or at a party surrounded by strangers, our public will, and must, be entertained. Imagine then, if you will, what it must be like when actors socialize with other actors. Not easy, is it? I mean, how on earth does anyone manage to get a word in? While there's some truth in the public perception, Pru and me have been socializing with fellow actors all of our adult lives and I'm delighted to inform you that full conversations featuring anything up to four or five actors at a time have been known to take place. Amazing!

Truly, the friendships we have made since becoming actors have given Pru and me an immeasurable amount of pleasure and continue to do so. I was determined to work this aspect of our profession into the book somewhere and it was Joe who came up with a suggestion as to how I might go about it.

'How about the garden parties?' he said. 'The ones you and Ma used to host. They were always very joyous affairs.'

He didn't need to make any further suggestions. 'Perfect,' I said. 'Thanks, Joe.'

I forget when exactly, but sometime during the 1970s we

started hosting garden parties on summer afternoons at our home in Wandsworth and they became rather famous. As well as friends of old, we would always make a point of inviting the people we were working with at the time, so it could be actors, producers, stage managers, directors. Anyone and everyone we had befriended, basically. Numbers-wise, there'd normally be about a hundred to a hundred and twenty and we'd always try to have everyone out by 7 p.m., although we didn't always succeed.

As I have with so many subjects herein, I asked my three children what they remembered of these gatherings. Sam and Joe recall being asked to act as greeters, which they always did with great aplomb. 'Good afternoon, red or white?' they'd say brightly to our guests on opening the front door. This was the 1970s and 1980s when drinking alcohol at parties was almost obligatory, so it was best to get in early. Once the guests had arrived, the boys were free to socialize. Fortunately, they had always been comfortable in the company of adults (they'd had very little choice really) and there were always people wanting to make a fuss of them.

When I asked Juliet, who was quite often the instigator when it came to social gatherings at Wandsworth, she said that she would have to consult her diaries for her memories. A few days later she came back to me, informing me of an entry she had made consisting of just two words – 'Bryony streaked.'

'Good lord, I remember Bryony,' I said to her. 'What an afternoon that was.'

Now, before your imaginations begin to run away from

you, despite these gatherings of ours taking place in the 1970s and 1980s, our guests were not in the habit of removing all their clothes.

Bryony was not an actress, I should add. In fact, if memory serves me correctly, she worked in television production. Her reasons for deciding to streak across Wandsworth Common on a Sunday afternoon in broad daylight, however, are not known to me. I do remember it happening, though.

Until then, I had only ever witnessed streakers at cricket matches and such like, where they would eventually be apprehended by embarrassed-looking police constables who would cover up any offending items using a helmet. To have a streaker appear at one's garden party, then, was an honour. And I wasn't the only one to think so. Half the residents of Wandsworth (the male half, mainly) spent the best part of twenty minutes applauding Bryony as she circumnavigated the common. When she finally leapt up our steps again and came back into the house she received a standing ovation the like of which Pru and me would happily have died for at the end of a performance.

The only other story I have to offer you that features nudity in Wandsworth involves Sir John Betjeman, although not as the protagonist. I consulted Pru before including this story and when I reminded her of it and then asked if we should incorporate it into the manuscript, she said, quite earnestly, 'Oh, you must. John would love it.'

Fair enough.

It was in the 1960s that Pru and I first met Sir John Betjeman. It was, of course, a great honour to make his acquaintance and we were happy to learn that he knew we admired his work so much. Sometime in 1970, Pru received a telephone call from Sir John asking if she would like to join him on stage for a recital of his poetry and prose.

'What's it for?' I asked.

'It's for the BBC. Part of their Christmas schedule, apparently. *An Evening with Sir John Betjeman.* It's being filmed at the Collegiate Theatre in Bloomsbury.'

'And who else is taking part?' I must confess I was beginning to feel slightly jealous.

'Just me and Sir John,' said Pru.

'Right.'

As actors, I expect we always manage to derive at least some pleasure from every job we are lucky enough to be offered, but just occasionally, something comes along that makes you feel especially pleased to belong.

Unfortunately, I wasn't able to attend the recording as I was working, but at 10.05 p.m. on Christmas Eve in 1970, Pru and I sat down and watched the broadcast together. It has never been repeated on television since and could be lost, for all I know. It was marvellous, though. Highlight of the season.

Sir John visited us in Wandsworth from time to time. Very often he'd come for lunch and when it was time for him to go Pru and I would walk him to his car. One day, we were doing just that, after having had a protracted conversation about horticulture in one final attempt to impress our green-fingered guest. I informed him that one of our neighbours had a particularly impressive garden.

'They live in that mock-Tudor house over there,' I said, gesturing in its direction.

I was acutely aware that Sir John also had an interest in

Tudor and mock-Tudor architecture, so I was sure I was on to a winner.

'In fact, Sir John,' I said as we approached the house in question, 'why not take a look?'

The wall that ran along one side of the garden was just low enough for Sir John to see over it, but a few seconds after doing so he recoiled suddenly.

'I'm most terribly sorry, madam,' he called. 'Please forgive me.'

Curiosity got the better of me and while Sir John continued proffering words of apology, I took a look. Our elderly neighbour was happily sunbathing on her lawn in the almost all-together.

'Oh, please don't worry,' she shouted, after Sir John had offered yet another apology. 'Hi, Tim. How're you?'

'I'm fine, thanks,' I said, giving her a quick wave before retreating quickly. 'Enjoy the sun.'

'I'm most terribly sorry about that,' I told Sir John. 'I really had no idea.'

'Oh, that's quite all right, Tim,' he said. 'You were right. What an absolutely splendid garden.'

Growing Older

The following passages relate to Pru and me having to become grown-ups, and about Pru's dementia, the symptoms of which I first noticed in 2001, but was not officially diagnosed until 2013.

Moving Up a Generation

I dare say you'll have heard this many times before from people of our age, but one of the worst things about getting older is that people with whom you are acquainted start dying at a rate of knots. Having to purchase a new black tie heralded my own appreciation of this. As I was aware that, rather like London buses, departures could often be unexpectedly regular, I bought a second one, just to be on the safe side. It all sounds rather depressing but, as with our own mortality, it is something we must try to accept.

'There's nothing one can do about it,' Pru said to me, 'so why on earth worry?'

'If only it were that simple,' I replied.

Pru's comment surprised me as she had always been such a prolific worrier, but that's what age and experience does to you. The inevitability of death can cast a shadow over life if you permit it. Conversely, it can also help you find acceptance.

In March 1989 my father died. He was the last of our parents to go and I remember it had a profound effect on me, but also on Pru. The death of your last surviving parent moves you up a generation overnight. While you have a mother or a father living, you feel like you are in a sense still growing, that there's more to come. With their death you have to recognize that this is it, you've grown up; this is how you'll be from now on. How on earth do you prepare? The fact is, you can't.

Pru and me had been blessed that, right from the word go, we always enjoyed an above average relationship with each other's parents. Bim and my mother, Olive, were also quite close and for as long as I can remember they corresponded regularly by letter.

Pru's father John was the first of the four to go, aged eighty-two. It was 1978 and after a period of ill health he died after suffering a stroke. We had spent our first Christmas together as a married couple with Pru's parents at their cottage in Abinger near Dorking in Surrey. Her father was called John Illingworth (Pru had decided to use her mother's name professionally as she thought it made her sound less like a sportsperson). He was a kind and modest man who, unless he'd studied the matter comprehensively, would go to almost any lengths in order to avoid having to take sides in an argument. I remember a friend of ours once telling us all a story about someone they knew who had visited a Kenyan game reserve.

'On spotting an elephant he got out of his car and offered it a bun,' he said. 'The elephant wasn't impressed, however, and after picking him up bodily it threw him to the ground.'

'What happened?' I enquired.

'Killed him,' replied the friend. 'Cracked his skull.'

As we all began to express horror at the elephant's conduct and sympathy for the victim, John held up a hand in gentle remonstration. 'Yes, but, my darling, my darling, my darling, my darling – look at it from the elephant's point of view.'

John had fought in two world wars and had met a lot of elephants.

Unfortunately, John's final years were not especially happy. Whilst not being institutionalized, exactly, it was always clear to everyone who knew him that John undoubtedly missed the comradeship of his fellow soldiers and that civilian life post-World War II did not suit him, and this dissatisfaction with the world deepened over time as he aged. Conversations were often curtailed by way of curtly delivered one-word answers and when he wanted something, instead of requesting whatever it was formally or even politely, he would simply point and call its name. Try as we all might nobody was able to get through to him and it affected Pru deeply.

'I really am at a loss,' she said to me on more than one occasion. 'What am I to do? He's simply not interested in anything anymore.'

Although he and Bim remained married, the five years they spent apart during the Second World War all but finished their marital relationship, although things always remained cordial between them. Bim must have known that John was unhappy, but, as had been the case throughout the war, she had her own battles to fight and had become fiercely independent.

One small crumb of comfort with regards to her father, or should I say Pru's memory of him, is that because of her condition she now only remembers certain things and one of those is that he fought in both world wars. Quite rightly, Pru is extremely proud of this and when she meets somebody for the first time, she will invariably make them aware of it.

When John died, Pru asked Bim what she intended to do. 'Well, carry on as I am, of course,' her mother said resolutely. 'I'm surrounded by friends, and you and Timmo aren't too far away. I'll be absolutely fine, darling. Don't you worry about me.'

But Pru did worry. The reality of the situation was that Bim herself hadn't been well for a while and we all felt that it was only a matter of time before something went wrong. Even so, she continued to live happily in their rented cottage in Surrey for about eighteen months. Then, in 1980, she too suffered a serious stroke, which left her paralysed down her right side. Always a fighter, Bim immediately set about teaching herself to write with her left hand, which she mastered in next to no time. Unfortunately, Bim's power of speech was deeply affected, something that upset her enormously.

'She's still an actor,' Pru said to me. 'And if an actor can't speak, what do they have left?'

Pru did everything she could to help Bim, but in order to be able to support her financially, which she had been doing to some degree for the best part of four decades, Pru had to keep working. The upshot of this was Pru only being able to visit Bim when her schedule allowed. This resulted in a series of insensitive comments being made by some of Bim's friends and neighbours, which upset Pru and annoyed me a great deal. One especially odious family wrote Pru the most hurtful letter, accusing her of abandoning her mother for professional reasons, and leaving her to die. I was all for paying them a visit and furnishing them with a few facts, but Pru wouldn't allow it. 'We don't owe them an explanation,' she said. And she was right, of course.

When Bim suffered a further stroke in 1981, she was no longer able to cope on her own and so Pru and Timmo set about finding a local care home where Bim's friends, who were of a similar age and not all especially mobile, could visit her easily. On 5 November 1982, after having suffered another stroke ten days earlier, Bim eventually died. She'd been in a wheelchair for two years, in the care home for half that time, and by the time she died she was helpless and very nearly blind. 'One mustn't be too sad,' said Pru. 'But I shall miss her dreadfully.'

Roughly three years later, my parents' next-door neighbour rang to tell me that my own mother, Olive, had died quite suddenly in the middle of the night. It was heart failure, apparently brought on by food poisoning. A wartime housewife, my mother always had a horror of letting food go to waste – covering the remains of a meal with an upturned soup bowl and putting it away for future use was par for the course. 'There's some of that nice fish pie,' she would tell us, 'or would you like some of that nice lamb casserole?' By the phrase 'some of that nice' my sister Patsy and I came to understand that the dish described had spent a little more than its recommended lifespan in the fridge or, in earlier days, the meat-safe. My poor well-meaning mother – and such a good cook, really – had finally fallen tragic victim to her own lifelong habit of economizing.

The most upsetting thing about an unexpected death is the threads that are left hanging in the air. I was filming a sitcom for Anglia Television up in Norwich when it happened and unfortunately Pru was abroad in Australia playing Queen Victoria. Putting things in order, arranging the funeral and so on meant an awkward series of triangular journeys between Norwich, London and Brighton, where she and my father had a cottage. I informed Pru by telephone and, just like I'd been with the news of John and Bim's passing, she was very upset.

'Promise me you'll call me after the funeral,' she said.

'I'll probably write, if that's OK. I'm not sure I'll be in the mood for talking very much.'

Here's the letter I wrote to Pru on the evening after my mother's funeral had taken place.

The car wouldn't start this morning, so I decided to get the number 19 bus. Have you ever done that? It's quite an event. The news that a bus is expected travels like wildfire across South London, and the tension mounts. Shops put up their shutters, schools declare a half holiday, the children prettily strew flowers in the path of the coming vehicle, and there is a band. I waited a mere three-quarters of an hour at the bus stop, among a festive crowd carrying balloons and flinging streamers, and then round the corner came the triumphant bus, gleaming red, its indicator blind boldly proclaiming its intention to visit Battersea, Piccadilly Circus and Islington in the course of time. It was very exciting, and what's more, I got to Brighton in time to collect Harry and the others for the funeral. This went very much as we could wish. The local vicar, who had actually left the parish but came back for the occasion, read a letter from Ma in answer to an article he had written in the parish magazine about elderly people's conception of God – it was a splendid letter, and a total surprise to Harry, who was rather moved by it. Thank you for your lovely flowers, and indeed there were a vast number of very cheering messages. The crematorium service was clinical and seemed somehow irrelevant, and we all went to the Courtfield Hotel on the Drive for a drink or two, then back to the cottage for supper. The boys were splendid throughout. Left Harry with Patsy, then we had to come home, I feeling for the first time very empty and wishing I'd had all those conversations I'd meant to have with her. The most upsetting thing was seeing dozens of little messages dotted around the cottage, shopping lists, notes for the milkman, things to be put in the diary. It felt as if she had just gone down the road to change her library book.

The regret I experienced, which I must admit was unusual for me, did not begin to lift until Pru returned home. When it comes to counselling one another, we each know instinctively when to talk and when to listen and, in this instance, just like I had done when Bim and John passed away, I wished Pru to do the latter. At least initially. Had she not become an actor, it is my belief that Pru would have made an outstanding counsellor. She is caring, empathetic, experienced, intelligent, inquisitive, and very wise. In fact, just a few days ago I was talking to my daughter who reminded me that, in addition to Pru having helped her through several very difficult times when she was growing up, Pru would do the same for her friends.

'You remember my friend Lesley?' Juliet asked. 'Well, when she and I were sixteen she was going through some issues and Pru once sat up all night with her just listening. She really was amazing with her.'

I remember Pru answering a telephone call at home one day some time after she'd been diagnosed with vascular dementia and the ensuing conversation, which was both animated and quite detailed, must have lasted the best part of two hours.

'Who on earth was that?' I asked, when she finally put down the receiver.

'Oh, you know. Her from across the common. Whatshername.'

'Believe it or not, I don't think I know her.'

'Oh, come on, you do. I've known her for years.'

'No, it still doesn't ring any bells. Anyway, what did Mrs Whatshername want?'

'I don't know. Nothing, really. I think she just wanted to talk to somebody.'

I decided to call 1471. Back in the day when people used to use landlines, dialling it would often help you ascertain the number of the last caller. As suspected, I had never met the lady who answered the phone and after engaging her in conversation for a few moments it turned out that she had called Pru because she was lonely and knew that, if Pru were in, she'd be happy to talk.

I suppose this might sometimes be described as a skill, but it's not a skill at all: Pru really does empathize with people, and, if needed, she will happily share their sorrow. Her only failing as a counsellor would be an inability to not take work home with her and would probably result in her becoming an insomniac or an alcoholic. Or both. Perhaps best to stick with acting, then.

When my father died, I experienced regret as I had with my mother, except the conversations I wished I'd had with him were about our shared profession. I should have asked him about the many and profound ways in which our

business had changed since he threw in his job with Don-
caster Collieries and became an actor in 1927. There were
all sorts of things I never knew about him; for instance,
whenever we visited, he would excuse himself after dinner,
go into the other room and remain at his desk for half an
hour or so, and I used to assume he was studying a script,
perhaps learning his lines for the next day. Sometimes I
would see him jotting things down in a small Woolworths'
notebook. After his death, when we were clearing out his
belongings, I came across about thirty of these little red
books and opening one of them I saw that each evening
he had been meticulously noting down every single item
of expenditure for that day: newspaper, 15p; coffee, 12p;
bus fare, 20p; torch batteries, 88p. Though he and my
mother had for the last forty years lived quite comfortably
within their income, Syd apparently liked to imagine himself constantly on the verge of penury. If he had not
worked for a month, that signified the end of his career.
'The boycott has started,' he would tell us. 'I am in the
gutter!' If I ever complained about some aspect of a job I
was doing, I would be stopped with a sharp rebuke:
'Remember you're very lucky to be working.'

He loved arguing with the Inland Revenue, sometimes
over tiny sums, and would invent euphonious names for
commodities that he considered should be allowed against
tax. Incensed at being told toothpaste and mouthwash
were not regarded as professional expenses, my father
resubmitted them under the title 'Unguents and Pomades'
and got away with it. This made him very happy.

The only thing that affected me more than not having
had these conversations was that now that our parents had

all died, collectively, me and Pru had officially moved up a generation. We were now – grown-ups.

'I suppose we shall have to start behaving like grown-ups,' I said to Pru after my father's funeral.

'Oh, not yet, my darling,' she said. 'I'm not sure we're quite ready.'

Something's Not Right

The 1990s carried on pretty much the same for Pru and me, except that there were no more progenies left to fly the nest. Indeed, in 1996 a grandchild arrived, called Clement, and in 1998 another arrived called Felix and then finally one more called Matilda. While working as a translator after leaving university, Joe had fallen madly in love with a beautiful and very talented French woman named Hedwige. They would eventually move to France via a stay in Cornwall, but while still living in Manchester they had decided to start a family.

Strictly speaking, I was already two steps ahead of Pru in the grandparent stakes as Juliet had given birth to two beautiful children – Kate, who arrived in 1980, and Ben who came along in 1982. I doubt it will surprise you to learn, however, that the technicality of Pru not being a blood relative to Juliet's children made no difference whatsoever. She approached step-grandparenthood with exactly the same amount of enthusiasm, care and vitality as she had step-parenthood. So, by the time Joe happily informed us that he and Hedwige were expecting their first child, Pru and I were already quite well versed in the ways of grandparenting.

'Doesn't it make you feel old having so many grandchildren?' Pru asked me after Felix was born.

'Not in the slightest,' I said. 'In fact, if ever there was a time not to feel your age, this is it. That's four and counting. It's going to be exhausting.'

'Not as exhausting as it will be for Joe and Hedwige,' said Pru. 'I mean, they won't have a nanny like we did.'

'They also won't be performing eight shows a week the length and breadth of Great Britain and residing in a succession of boarding houses.'

'Good point.'

The start of the new millennium continued along much the same vein. Our diaries remained full to bursting with all manner of jobs and appointments, and on the very rare occasions when we weren't showing off on a stage somewhere in the world or in front of a television or film camera, we would either be holidaying on our narrowboat together or patronising a theatre or a concert hall. Then, in the spring of 2001, while Pru was touring a new play, something happened.

'We're in Greenwich next week,' said Pru.

'Yes indeed,' I replied. 'The prospect of spending a few nights in one's own bed while on tour is something you always relish.'

Despite us both being of pensionable age we still enjoyed going on tour, and especially Pru. In fact, I'd go so far as to say that her enthusiasm for touring at this stage in her life was keener than it had ever been. Or at least since I had known her.

The first night at Greenwich seemed to go splendidly. A performance in your home town, especially during a tour, usually sees the odd friend or loved one popping by to show their support and that night Pru had a few of each. As always, she gave a barnstorming performance and the notices the following day confirmed this. The following evening, the atmosphere at the theatre was slightly different. The previous night had been an undoubted success, yet Pru now seemed slightly on edge.

'Are you all right?' I asked. I was about to start rehearsing a new play at the time and, because I had a few days free, I was keeping Pru company at the theatre. 'You just seem a little quiet this evening.'

'I'm fine, darling, really. Sorry, mind elsewhere.'

As it was close to curtain up, I decided not to pursue my line of enquiry. I was concerned, though, as Pru only usually went this quiet when she was studying either a book or a play.

'Ready, my darling?' I said poking my head around her dressing room door. 'You've been called. Didn't you hear?'

'Yes, of course,' said Pru, springing to her feet. 'I'm ready.'

Pru's resurgence was only temporary as while sitting out front I could sense that she wasn't completely in character. This was most strange as Pru is always incredibly professional and will know the entire script back to front. For her not to be quite in character was unheard of in my experience. I was beginning to worry.

For the next few minutes, I studied Pru most carefully and it seemed to me that the reason she wasn't in character was because she was having to search for her lines. Again, this was so unlike her. Everything was always there with Pru, front and centre.

I must admit that the wave of emotion that began to engulf me when I considered what might be happening to her was almost overwhelming. One thought in particular almost floored me.

What if it's Alzheimer's?

I was hesitant to do so, but after the show I had to ask Pru again if there was anything the matter.

'This again? What on earth are you talking about?' she said rather abruptly. 'I'm fine.'

In the interests of not upsetting her, I immediately changed the subject. It had planted a seed of worry in my mind, however, and over the coming weeks and months I observed my wife slightly differently to how I had previously. Not always diagnostically, you understand, or even with concern. I was just aware that something might be the matter and so I paid her more attention. Whilst there was no other particularly troubling incident at this time, I was more tuned in to any episode of forgetfulness that I might otherwise have put down to tiredness or some other mitigating circumstance.

Life carried on pretty much as normal for us for the next four or five years. While not being quite as busy as I had been in the 1980s and 1990s (such is the lot of a jobbing actor over seventy), I still managed to remain gainfully employed for the majority of the time. Pru, on the other hand, had started battling a second issue, one that would become exacerbated by her loss of memory.

'We'll have to take you to see a doctor about your hearing,' I said one day for the umpteenth time.

'What, my darling?'

'YOUR HEARING! Oh, good heavens.'

I don't remember exactly when I first noticed that Pru's hearing was beginning to falter, but what I do remember is constantly having to repeat myself and becoming thoroughly fed up with it. After a visit to a doctor and then to a specialist, a pair of hearing aids were prescribed, and I naively believed that things would then improve. And they did, for a time. Alas, as Pru's memory steadily worsened she began to either forget to put her hearing aids in, which she would always strenuously deny at first, or forget where she had left them.

'Where are your ears?' I'd say to Pru, which is what we still call her hearing aids.

'What do you mean? I've got them in.'

'No, you haven't.'

'Yes, I have.'

'No, you haven't, Pru.'

'Haven't I? Oh dear, you're right. Where on earth are they?'

'I've no idea. When did you last have them?'

'Oh, God knows.'

I shudder to think how many times we have had that conversation over the last twenty-odd years. Almost as many times as Pru's lost her ears, I expect.

As far as I know, the first time that allowances had to be made for Pru's memory loss in a working environment was in 2003 for a production of Oscar Wilde's *A Woman of No Importance* at the Theatre Royal, Haymarket.

'What on earth am I going to do?' Pru asked, after the first week of rehearsal. 'I keep on forgetting my lines.'

'What, all of them?'

'No, just some of them. It comes and goes. I feel like such a damn fool, though.'

'Well, you mustn't. It happens to the best of us.'

'I bet it's never happened to you before.'

'Of course it has. I've lost count of the number of times I've dried.'

Although I said it to pacify Pru, I wasn't fooling anybody with that statement and we both knew that this was not temporary. Even so, Pru had a play to do, and somehow we had to try to make sure that she was able to fulfil the engagement. Dropping out would have devastated her, although it was something I considered privately. It was an awful thing to suggest, but I felt that I had to decide what would affect Pru the most – pulling out of the show before it had even started or failing in front of an audience.

'I'm sure they'll come up with something,' I assured her. 'What about using prompters?'

'What, idiot boards?' she said. 'Never.'

'Then what's the alternative? You can't rely on a human prompt as you won't be able to hear them. And please don't call them idiot boards.'

A few moments of silence followed.

'Laurence Olivier had to use them,' I said eventually.

'Did he?'

'Yes, most famously while he was filming *A Voyage Round My Father*. Remember, the John Mortimer play? It was adapted for television. Apparently, during a scene in an orchard, they had to write his lines on boards and then nail them to the trees. If it's good enough for him . . .'

Legend has it that while filming the aforementioned scene, the director asked Lord Olivier when he intended to start saying his lines.

'When I can see them,' he replied.

In the end, Pru relented and, based on her movements

during the play, a succession of boards were placed around the stage (out of sight of the audience) bearing the lines she was having trouble with. She was embarrassed at first, but there was little alternative. It was either use the boards and remain in the show or refuse them and . . . Well, that didn't even bear thinking about.

Domestically, things were going in much the same direction, except that at home Pru's prompter was indeed a human one – me. As is often the way in the early stages of dementia or Alzheimer's, the symptoms can come and go quite often and whenever it seemed like Pru was improving, I would pray that it had gone for good. This kind of seesaw situation kept on for a number of years, and although her decline has been mercifully gradual, as time went on Pru's periods of normality lessened and her symptoms became more pronounced and noticeable – although not always to me.

Due to the fact that we now spent more time in each other's company than we ever had, and because her decline was so gradual, I didn't always spot everything immediately. Sometimes I only became aware of these changes when either friends or members of our family pointed them out to me.

One weekend when Joe and Hedwige were with us – I think it was in 2006 – they noticed that Pru appeared to be very concerned about the dishwasher. After making me aware of this, I watched Pru; they were right. She seemed to be obsessed with either filling the dishwasher or emptying it, and regardless of what everyone else was either doing or talking about, Pru would be constantly drawn to the thing. It appeared to act as a kind security blanket; as in, this is what was on Pru's mind in that moment, so this is what she had to check, and in ever decreasing circles.

These days very little has changed in that department, except that Pru's domestic preoccupation when she's not in the garden is with our collection of serviettes and place-mats. It's her job to lay the table at mealtimes and she is extremely meticulous, about both making sure that the required amount of mats and serviettes have been depos-ited on the table before a meal, and that they have all been retrieved afterwards. If, by accident, one of the serviettes falls on the floor or is taken through to the kitchen, Pru might become mildly distressed, but is placated as soon as the item has been retrieved.

One of Pru's other early quirks again occurred at meal-times. 'How many people for lunch?' she'd ask. 'Four,' I'd reply. While remembering that she had asked the question, Pru would forget that I had answered. This frustrated her enormously and, because she fixated on it, it distressed her. This was the start of what has been one of the more difficult periods we've had to endure, and for probably a good year or so, Pru spent a great deal of time in a state of upset. Eventually, she learned to accept it and started using self-effacement as a tool by which to excuse herself, which is what she does to this day.

'Oh, my lord,' she says. 'Have I forgotten again? You must be thoroughly fed up with me. Are you going to divorce me?'

Before, Pru's Olympic-standard self-effacement used to irritate me somewhat, whereas now that it helps her, it's OK.

Although neither our domestic situation nor Pru's

professional situation were ideal, the thing I found most troubling and embarrassing prior to Pru's condition being diagnosed and us going public about it, were social situations. Every invitation used to fill me with dread. At a party, for instance, Pru would ask how somebody's mother was. After being informed that their mother had died, Pru would offer them her condolences, go and get another drink, and then ask the question again. Post us going public, everybody understood and so it wasn't really a problem. But the years preceding that were strewn with instances where people thought that Pru was either being impolite or that she simply hadn't bothered to take in the information. And then there were the jokes and the anecdotes. Like the dishwasher, if a particular joke or anecdote amused Pru she would tell everybody present, several times. With the benefit of hindsight, you obviously appreciate how unimportant things like that are, but not at the time.

Pru wasn't officially diagnosed with anything until 2013, such was the slow and gradual nature of her decline, not to mention the fact that we were still relatively busy. I know I said that I dreaded attending social events with Pru, but I never let those feelings stop us from going. Even now, we've always got things in the diary, and I expect that will only change when we can't physically move anymore, which will probably mean we're dead.

I first took Pru to see our GP in 2004 and he told us not to worry. The symptoms were still sporadic and quite mild, and he put it down to old age.

'Old age?' said Pru. 'But I'm only seventy-four.'

Then, a few years later, we decided to go to the GP

again, because things had got a little worse, and this time we took Joe with us. The GP informed me beforehand that he would be conducting the appointment with a certain amount of misdirection. 'It'll be pens falling off the desk and things,' he said, 'which will help me gauge how alert Pru is. It's a simple trick but quite effective.' After the interview the doctor was noncommittal as to a diagnosis, and he referred us to a consultant at the Chelsea and Westminster Hospital.

When I think back to when Pru's and my parents and grandparents were still alive, although conditions such as dementia obviously existed, people who were afflicted by them were often referred to rather dismissively. 'Oh, Granny's gone a bit gaga, hasn't she? Can't remember who she is these days.' The general term that is used these days for such conditions appears to be Alzheimer's, which is the most common form of dementia. This is what I feared Pru was suffering from. I freely admit, however, that at the time I was reluctant to dig any further.

When we went to see the consultant at Chelsea and Westminster Hospital, after conducting several tests he put Pru on a drug called Aricept, which, so he told us, might be of some benefit to Pru's mental function. The effect, alas, was minimal, and although he stepped up the dosage over several years, he eventually said that there was nothing more he could do. Then, in 2013, after more tests, Pru was finally diagnosed with having a condition called vascular dementia, a common form of dementia caused by reduced blood flow to the brain. The diagnosis itself made little or no difference, really. Whatever it was, Pru had already been suffering with it for over a decade. What interested me far more was the prognosis.

'Well, it isn't going to get any better,' said the consultant. 'The best you can hope for is that Pru's decline remains gradual. Then again, you must also learn to accept that one day she might not recognize you at all.'

Dealing With Dementia

I have never and would never profess to being an expert on either dementia or caring for somebody who has dementia. I have, however, through personal experience and a certain amount of study, managed to gain something of an insight into both. Consequently, I thought it might be beneficial to people who are perhaps in a similar situation to Pru and me to talk about how we have adjusted, while at the same time endeavouring to make it interesting to those who are not.

First of all, if there's one thing I have learned over the past two decades about dementia it is that no two cases are ever quite the same, and for the very simple reason that no two human beings are the same. Our very dear friend Andrew Sachs, for instance, was also diagnosed with vascular dementia back in 2012. Unlike Pru, his decline was relentlessly swift and he sadly passed away four years later in 2016. What a wonderful friend Andy was to us both. We miss him.

The point I am trying to make, I suppose, is that in our situation you have to be ready for pretty much anything, and you must also learn to accept the inevitable. It may sound a bit pessimistic but that's just the way of it. As the consultant said to me back in 2014, whatever happens it isn't going to get any better. With breakthroughs in research and treatment, that will hopefully change one day, but until then we must simply try our best and help each other as and when we can.

The part I have always found the most challenging as a carer is remaining patient. It's fair to say I have never been especially well-endowed in this department and I'm afraid that time has done little to change that. I do try and keep everything in check. Not just for Pru's sake, who these days forgets it all in a trice, but for my own, and for the sake of those around us. After all, the last thing our family and friends want to see is me losing my temper. I don't always get it right, of course. Who on earth does? I do always try, though. The thing I find especially frustrating is that Pru can actually understand perfectly everything I am saying. She just can't hear me very well. Like the dementia, her hearing problem is degenerative and even with her ears in, she can barely hear a thing. 'Sorry, my darling?' she'll say, then I'll repeat myself a few times and hope for the best. Sometimes she'll hear me, and sometimes she won't. I shall always keep trying. If I didn't it would mean just ignoring Pru, and I could never do that.

The other problem we have, of course, is that I am not getting any younger myself. I may not be suffering from dementia, but having to repeat oneself ad nauseum every day when you're in your late eighties can be a little exhausting at times. Fortunately, Pru is as keen at taking naps these days as she was when the boys were young (although she does it for different reasons now) and when she has one, which she does once or twice a day, I am able to have a rest for a few hours. Pru also has very little concept of time and when she joins me in the living room after she's woken up, we greet one another like a couple might after having been parted for several days. Familiarity no longer breeds contempt in Pru's world, which sometimes helps to neutralize any such feelings I might have at having to repeat myself.

I'm not sure if it was a conscious decision – I don't believe it was – but ever since Pru's dementia began to have a direct effect on our lives I have endeavoured to ensure that we keep on doing the things that make us happy as often as we possibly can. Very little has changed in that department in terms of what we enjoy doing. We still go to the theatre or to a concert at least three times a month, and we also go to see friends and family members quite a bit. Anything that piques our interest, basically. Indeed, this very evening we will be attending a recital of Bach's 'St John Passion' at St John's Smith Square in Westminster. We're very much looking forward to it. As well as keeping busy, which you may have already gathered is something that we have always been rather good at, it is important for us both to have something to look forward to, which in turn gives us something to talk about. And we do still talk to each other, by the way. Just because Pru can't hear me very well and might forget what I've said in a matter of a few moments doesn't mean I don't want to tell her things, and vice versa. The two of us not communicating with each other would be unimaginable. It's certainly important to Pru, I think, to maintain a semblance of normality, and it's vitally important to me. In fact, I'm sure we wouldn't cope anywhere near as well as we do if we didn't carry on trying to be who we are.

Pru has always taken great pride in her appearance and

whether she's coming downstairs after having had a nap or visiting a theatre, she will always look amazing.

'Good evening, my darling,' she says on entering the living room after her nap. 'Can I get you anything?'

'I'll have a cup of tea.'

'Tea? Oh dear. That won't do at all,' she says. 'Do you think we might have something alcoholic?'

'All right. Sit down and I'll fetch us something.'

We have exactly the same conversation every day of the week and it's something I never tire of. As I said earlier, repetition doesn't really exist in Pru's world and the look on her face when she enters the room and sees me sitting there on the sofa waiting for her makes me realize just how much I love her.

I think people are quite surprised when they see Pru and me taking our seats in a theatre or walking around an art gallery. A few months ago, when we were at the Criterion Theatre in Piccadilly Circus to see a new play called *The Unfriend*, Pru must have been approached by at least six or seven people all wishing her well and telling her how nice it was to see her out and about.

'What about me?' I said to one of them. 'Isn't it nice to see *me* out and about?'

'Don't listen to him,' said Pru. 'He's attention seeking. Typical actor.'

There's a common misconception among the general public that people who are suffering from dementia or Alzheimer's spend their days sitting in a high-seated chair and staring blankly at a wall. We have resolved to keep on moving as best we can and enjoy life to the full. After all, just because there's snow on the roof doesn't mean the fire has gone out. Pru and me are each of an Olympic-standard when it comes to making the most of life and I fancy we always will be. For as long as we all can then – and this goes for everybody, not just me and Pru and people in our position – remember three things: keep on moving, keep on communicating, and keep on doing the things that make you happy.

Great Canal Journeys

As you might have guessed, the following passages concern the television series Great Canal Journeys, *which Pru and me appeared in from 2014 until 2019.*

A New Lease of Life

By the time of Pru's diagnosis in 2013, apart from the odd cameo appearance here and there that didn't require much in the way of memory, she had been unable to work regularly for several years. Pru could still read from a script (she still can, in fact), but not being able to hear very well, and therefore take direction easily, precluded her from being considered for the vast majority of jobs. The only blessing, I suppose, was that the effect of this, which would have been truly devastating had she had to live with it every hour of every day, was disrupted by her loss of memory.

One of the upsides of what was happening – and you must always try to recognize the positives, no matter how small or insignificant they might seem – was the amount of leisure time we were now able to spend together. As you know, at least half of our first four decades had been spent apart, and because we still liked each other rather a lot, we decided that this could be the start of a new adventure for us. Also, Pru was becoming slightly more reliant on me these days and being away for long periods distressed her.

'Well,' I said to her one morning, 'if I still want to go travelling it looks like I'll have to take you with me.'

'Oh, that's marvellous,' she replied. 'Where are we going?'

'Fancy a few days on the boat?'

'Oh, yes please.'

'All right, let's pack a bag, shall we?'

Now, in order to bring you up to speed as to how Pru and me came to own a narrowboat in the first place, I must take you all the way back to the summer of 1976. It was a Saturday afternoon, I believe, and while me and Pru were both quietly reading in our drawing room, the telephone rang.

'Who was that?' Pru asked, after I'd put down the receiver.

'It was Lynn Farleigh. She's offered us the use of her narrowboat for a couple of weeks.'

'Her narrowboat? I hope you said yes please.'

'Of course I did.'

The reason that Lynn, who was an old friend of ours, had asked if we'd like to use her boat was because she knew I had a passion for our domestic waterways. Indeed, that particular fascination can be traced back a further twenty-one years to 1955, when a very good friend of ours, Peter Davy, and I attended the inaugural meeting of a society being formed to preserve the Kennet and Avon Canal. It took place at a lock in Bath and before the meeting came to order a farmer in a very smart suit climbed up onto the lock gates and shouted his fierce opposition to the scheme; apparently, he wanted to develop some of the land concerned. As you'd expect, the farmer found little support among the crowd and, just as he was coming to the crescendo of his diatribe, a young zealot with a bargepole pushed him backwards into the mud of the empty lock, drawing cheers from the hundreds of onlookers.

Despite my enthusiasm for the dear old K&A, as it's

affectionately known, in 1976 I'd done the majority of my sailing at sea and so Pru and me were both novices. The two-week holiday on the Oxford Canal turned out to be one of the best of our lives. The summer of that year was one of the hottest on record and as we leisurely wound our way through the enchanting Oxfordshire countryside we looked on as swans, ducks, moorhens and kingfishers all fed, frolicked and enjoyed life to the full.

Having informed Sam and Joe beforehand about the multitude of locks and bridges we would have to negotiate on our holiday, the boys, then twelve and ten, had been giddy with excitement prior to setting off. What came to pass, however, exceeded their expectations and by six o'clock each day, so blissfully exhausted from the day's exertions, they would collapse onto their bunks, leaving Pru and me to open a bottle of wine and talk, play Scrabble, or just sit on the deck and watch the evening light fade from the sky while listening to the plop of a water vole or the constant trickle of water from a lock-gate.

Sometime after that first holiday, Lynn suggested we buy a half share in her boat, which we did, and then sometime later again we bought it outright. I'm not quite sure how a pair of busy jobbing actors managed to find time to explore the canal network but find the time we did, and it quickly turned into a family obsession.

We eventually had a longer narrowboat built from scratch, which was launched at Banbury in the winter of 1988, and we christened her after our female accountant who was also a close friend. By giving our boat a female identity we were flying in the face of tradition as boatmen of old always referred to their craft as 'it', even if it had a female name. Likewise, 'port and starboard' were always frowned upon by boatmen: they preferred left and right; also, a boat had a front and a back. Pru and me found it hard to adjust, which in turn helped us to create the illusion that we are accomplished seafarers.

To this day we still keep a logbook of all our voyages. The launch of the new boat itself didn't get logged but here's an entry for the boat's first family trip, which was from Banbury up to Oxford and back again. The crew comprised of a captain, who always writes the log (me on this occasion), a first mate (Pru), two able seamen (my father and Aunt Joyce) and a mascot called Sally (Joyce's dog).

Sunday 18 December 1988

Everyone very impressed with the new boat, the cooking stove and, to a slightly lesser extent, the loo. Still discovering that a 60-foot narrowboat is at least 12-foot harder to navigate than a 48-foot one. Going round sharp bends you will have your rudder aground if you're not careful. Well, there's not much water in the Oxford Canal just now. Chief delight is how warm the boat gets, and how quickly. It was well nightfall by the time we got back to Tooley's and found there was no mooring available; while we were away, Barrie's new client had crept into our spot. We moored alongside, but it was clear that our senior passengers couldn't manage the plank, so we moved up to one of the staithes and put them ashore. It was then that the stern line got wound round the prop shaft, and I spent the best part of an hour on my face, with an arm in dark freezing water to unravel it. Never mind – I'm pleased to learn it can be done.

We had already covered a great deal of the national water-way system on our first boat and had sailed up as far as Ripon in North Yorkshire, which is the furthest point north in England that can be reached by canal. We had also explored the intricate waterways of Birmingham and the Black Country; and taken the Grand Union all the way back to London.

One route, though, which held some history for me, was not yet open to us. Since the day I saw that farmer shoved into the mud, the Kennet and Avon Canal had experienced a remarkable reversal of fortune. A petition with over 20,000 signatures had been addressed to Her Majesty Queen Elizabeth II, and it led to a truly aston-ishing restoration programme carried out by volunteers who included students, prisoners, pensioners, school-children and Boy Scouts. The entire length across the country – eighty-seven miles no less – was reopened in 1990.

We got two friends to accompany us on the journey and set out on our adventure, beginning at the start of the actual canal in Bath, just below Pulteney Bridge. Ner-vous but enthusiastic members of the K&A Canal Trust gave us a send-off and followed our progress at a dis-creet distance, while a considerable crowd turned out to watch us negotiate the momentous sixteen-lock staircase at Caen Hill.

We had to stop for a few days partway through our journey while the stretch of canal ahead of us was sup-plied with water. Then, a short time after that, we were asked to make an adjustment to our schedule to allow the Queen to perform the official reopening ceremony.

The Queen's impressive ceremonial barge had to be the first to pass down through the top lock at Devizes. All told it's a journey of just a few hundred yards, but in order to necessitate this our sixteen-ton narrowboat had to be craned out of the water, loaded onto a flatbed truck and then driven around Devizes before being winched back into the canal. So, when Pru and I boast of having sailed the whole eighty-seven miles of the Kennet and Avon Canal, it would be more accurate to say eighty-six and three-quarters.

After having observed the somewhat disquieting spectacle of our narrowboat being lowered back into the water, we were able to attend and enjoy the royal ceremony and talked briefly to Her Majesty. She seemed genuinely thrilled with the event and remarked on the distinctive variety of butterflies that she had witnessed on her trip.

Ten years later, in 2000, I was approached by Carlton Television about introducing a series of weekly half-hour programmes about canals and their history, entitled *Water World*. All I had to do was a short piece to camera to introduce each episode and the reason they asked me, I later learned, was because Pru and me had become quite well-known on the canal circuit.

Whether or not it was seeing *Water World* that motivated them I'm not sure, but one day in 2013 I received a telephone call from my agent informing me that Channel 4 had been in touch about the possibility of me and Pru making a new series about narrowboating. At first it seemed too good to be true. Voyages on our boat had become incredibly precious to us, and with Pru not being able to work very much and me not being able to work as much as I used to, it was potentially manna from heaven.

'What do you think?' I asked Pru, after first mentioning it to her.

'It sounds wonderful, darling. I mean, who wouldn't want to get paid for going on holiday?'

'I think there'll be slightly more to it than that. It'll be hard work, for one thing. And what's it going to be like filming on a narrowboat?'

'There's only one way to find out,' said Pru.

I hadn't seen her this animated or excited about anything since – well, the last time we went on our narrowboat.

'All right,' I said to my agent. 'If you could set up a meeting, we'll talk to them. I can't make any promises, but we're both keen.'

It turned out that the programme, should it be commissioned, would be made by a production company called Spun Gold. It took a while but eventually everything was agreed. A unit was assembled comprising a producer (who was also the director and screenwriter), two camera operators, a sound technician, a production assistant and a runner. The unit was later bolstered by my darling daughter Juliet who, as a professional hairdresser, took on the role of dresser and make-up artist, much to Pru's relief. She didn't have to bother with me too much in that department, but it was a joy spending so much precious time with Juliet.

The biggest decision we had to make once we had agreed to take part in the series was how open we should be about Pru's condition. While she had now been officially diagnosed with having vascular dementia, we still hadn't talked about it publicly, although because of her withdrawal from the professional arena, there had been several rumours circulating. Announcing it would essentially put those to bed.

'You do whatever you think is best,' said Pru. 'I just want to get started.'

'All right,' I said. 'Let me have a think about it.'

All Aboard

'Do I know where we're going or why we're going there?
Well, sometimes I do, and sometimes I just want to
watch the countryside slide by.'

After much deliberation, I came to the conclusion that we really couldn't ignore Pru's condition and that attempting to do so would be unfair, dishonest and rather senseless. So, with her agreement and that of our producers, I decided that I would make a clear statement about it on screen and revise it as and when necessary.

With this now out of the way, we were able to start planning the first series of our show, which was to be called *Great Canal Journeys*. It was natural, I think, to choose for our first subject the K&A. We knew it well, of course, and since the reopening it had become hugely popular.

We boarded the boat for the first episode in Bath. Alas, it would not have been practical to use our own boat, which would remain moored on the Oxford Canal, but the craft they had given us was extremely comfortable (and so no need for hotels for us) and was easy to cook in. It did have a television, though, which I found unnecessary, although Pru was terribly impressed.

'What about Scrabble and games?' I protested.

'Oh, don't be an old fuddy-duddy,' she said. 'We can enjoy both.'

It was the bank holiday weekend in August when we set off and there were a lot of other boaters using the canal, some of them not expertly. The senior cameraman, James, filmed me from the roof of the boat while Mike, the producer, sat beside him asking me questions. Thinking of things to say, while peering between the two of them to try to see where I was going and avoid the other boats was not easy, but we eventually found a rhythm. Sometimes I was criticized by onlookers for remaining at the tiller while Pru did all the work, but I'm afraid it is essential to have somebody in control of the boat. Again, it was something we just had to get used to.

One of the things we found most amusing during that first series, and during the subsequent ones, was being filmed from the towpath by the second cameraman. In order to make the audience believe that me and Pru were alone on the boat and not accompanied by seven or eight people, the unit all had to remain downstairs and out of the way while the filming took place. Due to the amount of equipment we had on board, they had to try to squeeze themselves into spaces that were most definitely not human-shaped. When they all finally emerged, grievances would be aired most audibly by various members of the unit about having had somebody's bum in their face for the last half an hour.

Attitudes towards the reopening of the Kennet and Avon Canal tended to differ a great deal and soon after the work had been completed all those years ago, I was approached by a very smart lady in a white hat while attending a wedding. 'Didn't you write something about canals in a newspaper somewhere?' she asked me abruptly.

I admitted that I had.

'Well, I live on the canal,' she said.

I asked her where.

'In Avoncliffe,' she said. 'Bradford on Avon.'

'Oh, yes, I know it,' I said. 'It's very pretty.'

'It was!' she admonished me. 'It *was* very pretty; and then they went and put water in it, and now I have to watch a lot of boats going by.'

After mumbling a short apology I went away to get a drink, but she kept following me with a resentful gaze. It was clear she held me directly responsible.

Fortunately, the vast majority of our experiences and interactions during the first *voyage avec le unit* were positive and friendly ones and I remember that we enjoyed it very much.

'How do you feel about having the unit around?' I asked Pru at the end of the first day's filming.

'It's not as if we're not used to being filmed,' she replied. 'I don't mind at all. They're a lovely bunch.'

Having watched the series back again quite recently, something we're both in agreement about with regards to what we like about it is the spontaneity of everything. As you know, Pru and me have worked together on several occasions over the years, but the words we have spoken have never been our own. Even though some of what you see and hear on *Great Canal Journeys* has been pre-planned or pre-written, such as the questions we're asked and the voiceovers we perform later on, much of what you hear us say on screen, at least while we're sailing, is off the cuff.

There's one scene in the first episode where we've just shared a lock with another boat and are extolling the virtues of doing so.

'It's like sharing a nice bath with somebody,' I remark, before realizing how it might appear. 'I mean, we don't do that,' I say, trying to backtrack quickly, 'but if we did, we'd save a lot of water.'

Who on earth would write something like that?

The statement I made about Pru's condition in that first episode was delivered from the tiller, and it was teed up by a voiceover from Pru that she wrote herself.

'Do I know where we're going or why we're going there?' she says. 'Well, sometimes I do, and sometimes I just want to watch the countryside slide by.'

I then made the point that because of her condition Pru can't always remember things, but that you don't always have to remember things on a canal. You can keep your mind vacant and just enjoy things as you see them, which is perfectly true as long as you're not the one driving. I also stated that, as opposed to mourning the person I was losing, I was trying hard to concentrate on what was still there, such as Pru's sense of humour, not to mention all the things that she was still able to do about the boat. Finally, I made the argument that we were both incredibly lucky. None of this was spontaneous, of course, but neither had I written it for effect. Everything you see and hear on that show is genuine – apart from the illusion that there are only ever two people on the boat at any one time, of course. There could be as many as eight!

For episode two of that first series, we explored the Rochdale Canal, which was new to us. Just as I felt a bonding with the Somerset countryside during episode one, the banks of the dales of West Yorkshire through which the Rochdale Canal passes found a resonance with Pru, as well as the people, how they spoke and how they lived their lives. Before we began recording, I managed to squeeze in a couple of days filming nearby for a programme called *Last Tango in Halifax,* alongside our old friend, Derek Jacobi. Having already played Derek's stepfather in *Hamlet,* and his gay hairdressing partner in a play called *Staircase,* I was to play his long-lost brother. Sam also came to join us on this Yorkshire trip, which was rather nice. He has always shared our love of canals, and he and his partner Laura still borrow our boat now and then. Now they were about to have their first child, so it was likely to be another few years before they would risk it *en famille.*

For episode three we explored the Llangollen Canal in Wales, which had been suggested by me as Llangollen had been the ultimate location of our long-delayed honeymoon – we never were altogether satisfied with our two nights at the Compleat Angler Hotel.

Although the weather was almost always against us, our Llangollen episode produced some stunning cinematography thanks to our two amazing cameramen, James and Gary. The only disappointment was that we never got to Plas Newydd, the home of Eleanor Butler and Sarah Ponsonby, the 'Ladies of Llangollen', two aristocratic spinsters whose relationship was the subject of much speculation in the late eighteenth century.

The occurrence of female couples sharing a romantic friendship was not uncommon in the eighteenth century so their union was not unique. Even so, in their little cottage just outside Llangollen, Eleanor and Sarah entertained Charles Darwin, William Wordsworth, Joshua Wedgwood, Lady Caroline Lamb and the Duke of Wellington. But why? Neither of the ladies was an artist, nor could they be classed as writers or academics. What they had was an incredible grasp of what was happening in the world and were great company.

They remind Pru of a pair of ladies who lived in a small cottage in Buck's Mills, where, as you know, Pru spent part of her childhood. The ladies were both artists of some distinction and, although they were quite reclusive in their rather Spartan circumstances, Pru says whenever she met them, she was much struck by their shared interests, their tenderness and sympathy. 'In another life,' Pru once said, 'I think I could have been like that.'

It was considered that for the fourth and final episode of our first series of *Great Canal Journeys* we should go abroad and, after deciding to remain in Europe somewhere, we eventually settled on France and the Canal Du Nivernais, which links the Loire with the Seine.

A few years previously, Pru and me had stayed on a hotel boat on the Canal du Midi travelling to Carcassonne and had enjoyed the experience. There were only eight guests on the hotel boat and the other six guests were all American. One of them was a somewhat ancient man from California, and I found him rather rude. At dinner on the first night, he loudly opened the conversation with the words, 'I consider it the inalienable right of every American citizen to keep and bear arms.' I immediately tried to change the subject, at which point the man took out a pack of visiting cards and passed them round the table.

'I need to solicit support for the Primaries,' he told us urgently, pressing a card into my hand.

Good God, I thought, *can this man be a senator? A congressman? A surprise presidential candidate, even?* It transpired that he was lobbying for election to the San Diego Water Board, but personally I wouldn't even have backed him for that. His daughter, with whom he shared a cabin and who must have been in her forties, came ashore with us one day, and we persuaded her to risk joining us for tea in a café, even though it was full of French people. A young couple next to us were enjoying a conversation, and she gazed at them mystified.

'I don't know how they understand each other,' she said.

The French attitude to living by a canal or a river seems quite different from ours. We like to make our abodes look attractive from the water, with nicely tended strips of garden if there's room, and perhaps a little boat tied up. The French perspective is quite different: they want to show their house to the road and the canal is round the back.

Joe and our granddaughter Matilda drove over to join us for part of this journey, which was marvellous. Bearing in mind Sam's recent appearance and also Juliet's involvement in the show (which happened later but was crucial to our continued involvement), this meant it had ultimately turned into a genuine family affair, something that pleased both Pru and me enormously.

With regards to how *Great Canal Journeys* might be received by the general public, it's safe to say that we kept our expectations fairly measured. For a start, instead of being part of Channel 4's schedule, the powers that be deemed the show better suited to More4, which specializes in documentaries. Although free to view, More4 is basically a subsidiary of Channel 4 and to be perfectly honest, as narrowboating is a fairly niche subject, we assumed the audience numbers would reflect that.

For actors of our generation, who have perhaps not yet fully embraced the joys of social media (and have absolutely no intention of doing so), you can often gauge the popularity of a show by the number of letters you receive. Yes, people do still write them from time to time! When the first series of *Great Canal Journeys* went to air, it quickly became apparent that, far from appealing only to fellow narrowboaters, its lure might be somewhat broader. In fact, I do actually have two fairly plausible benchmarks by which to measure this, as in 2013, while *Great Canal Journeys* was still in its embryonic stage, I appeared in *Coronation Street*, and by the time the show was transmitted, I was about to start a twelve-month stint in *EastEnders*.

By appearing in *Coronation Street*, which I did for six episodes, playing a character called Eric Babbage, I was merely following in Pru's footsteps as in 1962 she had appeared in two early episodes as a bus conductress named Eileen Hughes. But despite Pru having beaten me to Wetherfield by over half a century, it wasn't the first time I'd dropped by. That had taken place some sixteen years previously in 1987, while I was playing, of all people, Mikhail Gorbachev. I was making a television movie called *Breakthrough at Reykjavik* and it was being filmed at Granada Studios in Manchester. Knowing that the famous cobbled street was but a moment's walk away piqued my curiosity, and so during a break in filming one day I decided to pay it a visit. And in full costume and make-up, of course. Birthmark, glasses. It was all there.

When I eventually found the set, it was completely deserted and so I took advantage and began to look around. My first port of call, of course, was the Rovers Return, and after trying the front door of the pub, which unfortunately was locked (it must have been outside of opening hours), I stood back to admire the famous facade.

'Who the hell are you?' came a voice suddenly from behind.

I turned around and standing there, about twenty feet away, was a security guard.

'Do you work here?' he said, spotting and then staring at my bogus birthmark.

'No,' I said in character. 'I am the General Secretary of the Communist Party of the Soviet Union.'

Silence.

'Well, you'll have to ask at the main gate.'

Despite having been part of an ensemble of actors in both *Coronation Street* and *EastEnders*, which are still among the most watched television shows in the country, I can assure you that the reaction I received from the general public when *Great Canal Journeys* started, compared to the other two, was on a very different level. It was actually two-fold, really; when people stopped me in the street they either wanted to express their concern for Pru, which was terribly kind, or just tell me how much they enjoyed the show and, in many cases, confess that they had always wanted to take a narrowboat holiday. 'Then you must try,' I said.

The reaction from the press was also quite overwhelming and I can't remember a time when Pru and me had so many interviews in the diary.

'How many have we got today?' Pru asked one morning during the run of the first series.

'Five at the last count, and four more tomorrow.'

I certainly wasn't complaining. Being part of something popular is what every actor dreams of. We were just slightly at a loss as to how it had all happened.

It didn't take place immediately, but as I have already stated, the show eventually transformed us in the public's eyes, from being Prunella Scales and Timothy West, two busy jobbing actors who just so happen to be married, to Tim and Pru, a long-married and devoted couple who just so happen to be actors. The ironic thing is, of course, that that is basically what had happened to us in real life.

Once the first series had been transmitted, Channel 4 got in touch and asked if we might be interested in making a second and third series, which would air respectively (and on Channel 4, this time) in the spring and autumn of 2015. The only consideration was whether or not Pru felt well enough, and the answer from her was an emphatic yes. Although she was still deteriorating, both the making of the first series and the response from the general public had undoubtedly galvanized her.

'Let's carry on for as long as we can,' she said. 'I'm certainly good for a few more.'

And Around the Corner, Thrupp

For the second series of *Great Canal Journeys*, we once again made three voyages on our domestic waterways: on the Oxford Canal, during which we were joined by Sam for a time; on the London Ring, where we met up with Andy Sachs and Ian McKellen; and on the Forth and Clyde Union, during which we travelled through Scotland's longest canal tunnel and over its highest aqueduct. In addition, we also journeyed to France once more, this time on the Canal du Midi, where Joe and our grandchildren Clement and Felix came on board.

Our journey along the Oxford Canal was especially poignant, as that is where our waterways odyssey had begun almost forty years previously. We also stopped off at the world-famous Tooley's Boatyard in Banbury, where our own boat was constructed. Going back further still, while strolling past Oxford's famous playhouse and along the River Cherwell, we reminisced about the afternoon we had spent punting together in 1961, which is probably when I fell in love with Pru.

As we walked, I wondered how much she actually remembered about that special day, and a short time later I received my answer.

'We suddenly found ourselves outside this hotel,' I said to her, as we passed the Eastgate Hotel. It was where we had stayed when Pru visited me all those years ago. 'And the rest is history. Remember?'

'Yes, I do, of course I do,' said Pru, blushing deeply and staring at the ground. 'I'm just shy about it.'

When Sam joined us on this episode, in addition to helping with the locks (which Pru was very grateful for), he reminded me of a log I had written during that first momentous two-week family holiday, which he'd come to know by heart.

And around the corner, Thrupp, where we moored for the night, and to add to our evening on the boat, a group of morris dancers appeared and performed on the lawn. When, by popular demand, I stop acting and look for something better to do, I think morris dancing is an occupation that will claim my attention with less alacrity than most. We've all had the misery of having to perform in waywardly inappropriate costumes, but the morris costume does seem to me to embody the worst excesses of a Bavarian Sunday afternoon. Imagine coming out of the pub at eleven o'clock and realizing you still have bells around your knees and having to cycle home in the rain.

Sam went on to say, quite astutely, that the logs from that maiden voyage are like masterpieces of deliberate incompetence. 'It was so funny that we were so rubbish at it,' he said, and later described that first voyage, very astutely, as being like 'an elongated game of narrowboat pinball'.

I'm not sure who came up with the idea of exploring the group of canals that thread through the heart of London known to narrowboaters as the London Ring – it could have been me – but when it became part of our schedule for *Great Canal Journeys* I remember feeling rather excited about it. Pru and me had been living in London and working in its theatres for over half a century and we were looking forward to seeing the city from a new viewpoint, not to mention discovering a different part of its history.

We didn't really know much about the London Ring Canals until we sailed them, save for the fact that we'd crossed over the Regent's Canal by car many times on our way up to Swiss Cottage and Hampstead, and had driven past the picturesque Little Venice, and wrestled our way through the throngs around Camden Lock. We were also aware of Battlebridge Basin on the Regent's Canal, because long ago we thought we'd seek a permanent mooring for our boat that was easily accessible from home. But apart from these landmarks, the various bits of waterway that served the metropolis remained a mystery.

We began our journey at the back door of the Grand Union Canal, opposite Kew Gardens. In the Grand Union's early days, a lot of boatbuilding and repairing took place, as well as shipping goods from canal to barges situated on the Thames, and vice versa.

On this journey we travelled with a 'skipper', who was on hand to sort out any technical problems and, if needed, could reposition the boat to another site while we were filming ashore. A 'relief boat' was also chartered that could circumnavigate our own vessel and film us from various angles. On shore we had two vans, with two regular drivers, to carry us about and do the shopping.

I'm afraid I got impatient with Pru over the filling of our first rather deep lock. The lock in question was

Clitheroe's Lock, which is seven feet and seven inches deep, so the tide rushes in above water level and you have to control it. Pru's hearing, as you know, hasn't been what it should since the turn of the century, and I ended up becoming angry with myself for not taking this into account. I suppose it's natural that the longer you've known someone, the more you take it for granted that they can't change substantially; but of course, they can, and do. Pru was becoming a little less sure of herself by this time and I had to be constantly on the lookout. She still insisted on doing many of the tricky things, because she enjoyed them, so getting irritable with her was the worst thing I could do.

Luckily, at the six Hanwell Locks, we had two robust lock-keepers to assist us. At the highest point lies an aqueduct known as the Three Bridges, because it crosses over both a road and a railway track at the same time. The great Isambard Kingdom Brunel was responsible, and it's been suggested that this may have been the very last work he undertook. We enjoyed gazing down on the busy South Circular from our progress at four miles an hour. It was quite something.

While Pru and me had always known about Kensal Green Cemetery, with its impressive mausoleums housing all manner of deceased luminaries, including William Makepeace Thackeray, Anthony Trollope and the aforementioned Isambard Kingdom Brunel, and had indeed visited it once or twice, we had always travelled to it by road, so had never connected it geographically with the canal. But now here it was, on the port side, with a little overgrown gate leading onto it from the canal bank.

When we opened the gate to the cemetery it was just

like entering a Tardis. Just off the Harrow Road lies this peaceful seventy-two-acre space modelled on the cemetery of Père Lachaise in Paris. It is a haven of extraordinary ease and serenity. There was one person in particular whose grave we especially wanted to visit and that was Harold Pinter. We'd starred in many of his plays and, as well as directing both of us, he'd been our friend for over forty years. Despite Harold having been dead for some seven or eight years at the time it only seemed like yesterday and the experience was quite a sobering one.

'Would you like to be buried here?' Pru asked me.

'I wouldn't like to be buried anywhere, really,' I replied. 'I can see the attraction, though, of arriving by water and being laid to rest here among all these impressive people. You'd certainly be in good company.'

We wandered about reading the various inscriptions, before deciding that it was time to return to our boat for a glass of wine. As serene and picturesque as our environment was, we didn't want to waste any more time thinking about the end. As the poet G. K Chesterton wrote:

> For there is good news yet to hear and fine things
>   to be seen,
> before we go to paradise, by way of Kensal Green.

We returned to our boat shortly before dusk and as we searched for a comfortable mooring we quickly came to the conclusion that the city had taken on a strange and quite unfamiliar guise. We felt like outsiders and the behaviour of some of our fellow narrowboaters, not to mention some of the language they used, was not what we were used to. Alas, the moorings in charming Little Venice that had been recommended to us had been taken, so we ended up under the M40.

'Not the dawn chorus we're really used to, is it?' I said to Pru the following morning. 'Oh well, at least the sun's out.'

Our mooring was in what is called the Paddington Basin, which, with its proximity to the railway station was naturally once crowded with wharves and warehouses that gradually fell into disuse and decay. In 2000, in line with much top-class canalside evolution, the basin was drained and redeveloped.

In Little Venice, the stretch of the canal so christened by Robert Browning, we picked up Andy Sachs and his wife Melody. Andy's condition was probably at a similar stage to Pru's at this point, although his decline had been much quicker. This made our meeting rather poignant and as Melody joined me at the tiller, Andy and Pru sat at the front of the boat and talked about old times.

Shortly after this, Andy and I worked together on the last thing he ever did: our characters were in the same ward of a geriatric hospital in *EastEnders*, hurling insults at each other across the room. His character died, I'm afraid, and not so very long after, so did Andy himself. He was a man of many different talents, of which perhaps not enough people were aware.

For the rest of its length, the canal calls itself the Regent's Canal and skirts Regent's Park and London Zoo, which is where we dropped off Melody and Andy. It was here that we encountered our first, and I'm happy to say last, overtly abusive landlover. I later found out that our assailant was actually an actor, and after having smoked something rather exotic he had come to the unfortunate conclusion that our cameras and our presence offended him. Words were exchanged between him and our director and as the volume of the discourse gradually increased two police officers appeared. All of a sudden the actor began concealing certain substances about his person and went quickly on his way. I was actually slightly nervous for Pru as the quarrel reached its crescendo, but I think she rather enjoyed it. 'It's just like home really,' she said. That's my Pru. She may be only five feet two inches tall, but she's rarely intimidated by anything, least of all an actor with a big mouth.

A little while later we turned off to revisit Battlebridge Basin, which is a square stretch of water between four walls of sedate nineteenth-century converted warehouses, and now houses the London Canal Museum. It was all very tranquil, I remember, which reminded me of a canal's ability to exist in solitude within a stone's throw of bustling city life. In the museum we saw some photographs from the beginning of the twentieth century: boatmen and their families unloading cargoes of ice, shipped from Norway and brought up the canal from Limehouse.

'It's never occurred to me that ice was once an important commodity,' I said to Pru. 'But, of course, in hot weather food storage had to be surrounded by ice.'

'It says here that people excavated under their homes to create ice houses among the rocks,' she said. 'God bless whoever invented the refrigerator.'

We sailed through the Islington Tunnel next, or at least the cameraman and I did. Pru walked over the top of it with the director and his PA to do some shopping. Quite a few chocolates were sampled, I believe, including something called a Marmite truffle?

'I also had one called a cigar leaf,' Pru told me on her return. 'It was actually rather nice.'

The Islington tunnel was built in 1880 using over four million bricks. There's also no towpath, so when it opened the traffic must have been steam-powered. Slightly further on, we came to the short but perfectly formed Hertford Union Canal, that links to the River Lee. Due to it being a very narrow turn we weren't sure whether to venture onto the canal at first but decided to give it a go. As expected, we experienced a bump or two on entry and I remember saying the word 'bugger' quite a bit.

By the time we reached the Lee Navigation it was getting dark and all of a sudden I realized that I had no idea where we were planning to moor for the night. The director and his assistant started frantically ringing around (we'd had a mooring, but they'd double-booked), but had no luck. This was an area that I had never even heard of, let alone visited, but we sailed on regardless through dimly lit underpass after underpass, giving no hint of a location.

'Pull in here,' the director said suddenly. 'There's a landing stage ahead, with enough room to moor behind another boat.' I could hardly see a thing at the time but I had to trust him. The other boat turned out to be a mobile sixteen-seat cinema, which was rather fun. The two girls who owned it offered to run a film for us but we were all too tired. Pru and me went to bed, and after yet more ringing around the crew got hold of a taxi back to their hotel.

The girls and their cinema had gone by the time we woke up. It was a beautiful morning, though – perfectly still – and the scene that greeted me when I ventured on deck looked like a late-seventeenth-century painting. The crew arrived in their taxis about an hour later and we pressed on down the Limehouse Cut to the Limehouse Basin marina. Pru and me walked down to the river and turned into Narrow Street, where there's a pub called The Grapes that has been in existence for almost five hundred years. Not only is The Grapes a very fine pub, but it is owned by our friend, Sir Ian McKellen. Miraculously, Ian just happened to be there when we arrived (all right, it might have been pre-arranged) and after ordering a drink we sat down and discussed the pub and its history.

Ian had been living in the area for over thirty-five years and was incredibly knowledgeable. According to him the pub's most celebrated patron – even more celebrated than Ian – was Charles Dickens, who immortalized the pub in *Our Mutual Friend*. 'A tavern of dropsical appearance,' he called it, going on to describe the pub as 'long settled down into a state of hale infirmity. In its whole constitution it had not a straight floor, and hardly a straight line; but it had outlasted, and clearly would yet outlast . . . many a sprucer public house . . . Indeed the whole house . . . impended over the water, but seemed to have got into the condition of a faint-hearted diver who was paused so long on the brink that he will never go in at all.'

After saying goodbye to Ian we headed back to the boat but when we arrived we were in for a shock. A few days previously a narrowboat had ventured onto the Thames and had got into trouble: summarily, there were no more narrowboats allowed onto the Lower Thames. 'The whole point of the programme is to complete the circuit clockwise,' said the director. 'What on earth are we going to do?'

We sought the advice of the skipper of a nearby motor

launch, who offered to take us upriver to where we started. It was a bit choppy, and we were relieved not to be doing it in the narrowboat. As we sped along, we were given a surprise treat in passing the beautiful tall ship *Stavros S Niarchos*, making her way down the river Thames and out to sea.

Such had been Pru's inability to hear what any of us were saying, that at the end of the trip we immediately made what must then have been our sixth or seventh visit to a hearing specialist.

'It doesn't bother me,' Pru said. 'I don't know what all the fuss is about.'

'Well, it bothers me,' I countered. 'And it bothers other people.'

We settled on some state-of-the-art devices. The only trouble was that Pru still couldn't get used to having things in her ears and the morning after we collected them a rather familiar conversation took place.

PRU: Have you seen my hearing aids?

ME: No, I haven't, sorry. Where might you have put them?

PRU: Sorry?

ME: I said, where do you think you've put them?

PRU: I can't hear you.

ME: No, I know you can't, because you haven't got them in.

PRU: No, I'm so sorry. Where are they?

ME: Well, when they're not in your ears, where do you leave them?

PRU: In this box here.

ME: Well, they're not there now, are they?

PRU: Sorry?

ME: Why aren't they in your ears?

PRU: I take them out to wash my face.

ME: I see. So then where do you put them?

PRU: Sorry?

ME: Where do you put them when you're washing your face?

PRU: In the box. Oh, wait a minute. I think there's another box.

ME: Another box. What does it say?

PRU: Hairpins. Here it is, there they are. I'm putting them in.
   Hooray! Now I can hear you perfectly. What did you say?

ME: I didn't say anything.

PRU: Sorry?

Canal du Midi

The other journey worth mentioning from the second series is our voyage along the Canal du Midi. The Nivernais episode in the previous series had been very popular, so we thought we ought to go back to France. As you know, Pru and me had sailed on Canal du Midi on a hotel boat many years ago and had enjoyed ourselves immensely, so we were looking forward to going back.

The Canal du Midi was declared a UNESCO World Heritage site in 1996 and is generally accepted as being the *sine qua non* of the French canal system. Providing a route from the Atlantic at Bordeaux to Sète on the Mediterranean, it traverses the Languedoc-Roussillon region and earns its name 'Midi' from seeming to provide the warm sunlight of midday.

Before taking to the water we had to get to Montpellier, which is slightly to the east of the Mediterranean end of the canal. During the flight, however, the captain made an announcement that rainstorms had flooded the city and, while it was still possible to land, passengers would have to wait at the airport until roads were clear enough to take them to their destinations.

An audible groan from the passengers followed, and so the captain offered an alternative: 'We could always fly on to Toulouse instead,' he suggested. Once again, groans could be heard the length and breadth of the cabin. The captain then suggested we put it to the vote, and to our relief the referendum found in favour of Toulouse, where we easily found a hotel. We subsequently discovered that passengers from other flights who had landed at Montpellier had spent the night in a waterlogged athletics stadium.

The following morning after breakfast we drove to the little town of Argens-Minervois, where our boat was moored. It was a *péniche*, the standard hire boat for the French canals – roomy, comfortable, well-equipped. Pru was very impressed. 'It's like a palace,' she said on entering. Unfortunately, I did not share my wife's enthusiasm for our vessel as every time I had driven a *péniche* in the past I'd had difficulty steering it in a straight line.

'I'm sure you'll be fine this time, my love,' said Pru.

'Will I?' I replied. 'I hope you're right.'

France's history of working canals stretches back almost four centuries and in all that time one name stands out above all others: Pierre-Paul Riquet. Not only did Riquet create the Midi, but he was also the inspiration behind our own canal system and was known as the Godfather of all Canals. While the Midi was being planned and excavated, Riquet took residence at the Château de Paraza, which is situated on the banks of the Midi. Pru and I were invited by the owner to look around and stood at Riquet's bedroom window looking out at the canal, as he must have done 350 years ago while the work was going on.

Our host showed us some original surveyors' plans of the canal, and as we studied them he generously plied us with some very old – and very potent – brandy, which Pru tackled gamely but in the end admitted defeat – '666', it was called, and I think I know why.

'It's just too strong,' said Pru.

'Here, give it me,' I said gallantly.

Later that day we were served a delicate dinner of lamb's brain fritters, but Pru wasn't awfully keen on that, either. Once again, I did the decent thing.

While I had been looking forward to immersing myself in the history of canals, the voyage was leading Pru back into her own past. Increasingly, her early memories were becoming clearer than anything recent, like those of being in France as a young woman. When she was young, Pru had had a French au pair for a time who, as well as teaching her the language, had also imparted to Pru a great deal of knowledge about the country's culture and history. Eventually, Pru went over to stay with the family of her au pair, which obviously helped to enhance her acquaintance with the country. Many years later, Pru fell in love with a Frenchman and very nearly married him, so there was quite a bit going on really.

The next morning, fortified with coffee and a croissant to erase the memories of last night's lamb's brain fritters, Pru began to tell me something of her attachment to her French fiancé. While studying Japanese demonology, he had wanted to take Pru out to Tokyo with him. 'I was very much in love with him,' she said. 'Somehow, though, the call of the homeland swung the balance, and I ended up with you instead.'

Later that day Pru decided that she wanted to take a turn at the helm. As crew, she is responsible for, among other things, the locks and making tea, but with very few locks on the Midi and with her skipper being perfectly capable of making the tea, that was fine.

'Are you absolutely sure you want to try this?' I asked her. 'These things are terribly hard to navigate. You've seen how many bumps we've had.'

'How many you've had,' she said smiling. 'I also felt them! I'll be fine, my love. Come on. Move over.'

The first few minutes of Pru being at the helm were slightly fraught and she arrived at the conclusion almost immediately that our craft had a mind of its own. 'I can actually steer a boat,' she said as our vessel sat almost horizontal across the Midi, though fortunately with no other vessels in sight.

As Pru continued battling with our *péniche* (she eventually got the hang of it), I sat down beside her on the gunwale and started reading a book I'd bought on the history of the Midi.

'Another visitor to the canal was Thomas Jefferson,' I said to Pru, after having read a few chapters. 'Before he became President, of course.'

As the United States ambassador to France at the time, Jefferson had toured the Midi in the summer of 1787 and according to the book he'd had rather a good time of it.

'The boat advances at a slow pace and rhythm,' Jefferson wrote of his journey. 'More often, I walk along the tow path, stimulated by the song of the nightingales in the shade of the double row of trees. The weather is also favourable. The journey continues under cloudless skies and on crystal clear waters. Oh, the sun of the Midi, there is no substitute. If I happen to die in Paris, may my body be sent here to be exposed to its rains.'

Pru and me have encountered some fairly unusual things on canals over the years and shortly after our Thomas Jefferson discovery, something came into earshot that, had you asked us to make a list of sounds that you weren't expecting to hear along the Canal du Midi, might well have been situated somewhere towards the top.

'Tim, I'm sure I can hear bagpipes,' said Pru suddenly.

'You can't hear anything usually,' I countered jokingly. 'Have you got your ears in?'

'I have, and I can,' she said. 'I can hear bagpipes.'

After tuning in to my immediate soundscape, I too could hear bagpipes.

'Good lord, I think you're right,' I said.

'I told you,' said Pru, who was evidently rather pleased with herself.

A few moments later we saw in the distance a narrow-boat moored on the opposite side of the canal. At the helm of the vessel stood a man with a red face holding a set of bagpipes and playing 'Scotland the Brave'. We both shouted 'Bravo!' as we passed and gave the chap a wave.

'Canals,' said Pru. 'Always full of surprises.'

Slightly less of a surprise on the Midi was the difficulty we had negotiating the Fonseranes Locks. There are eight locks in total spaced over a distance of 300 metres, which allow boats to be raised to a height of 21.5 metres. Leonardo da Vinci invented the water lock, but it was Riquet who transformed his design into a work of art. The Fonseranes Locks are all oval-shaped and are really quite exquisite. Beautiful as they undoubtedly are, I don't mind admitting that as we approached the locks I was somewhat daunted by what lay ahead of us. We'd negotiated difficult locks before, but never in such a large and hard-to-handle vessel as this. We were going to have to have our wits about us.

Unlike the British, who view the art of queueing almost as a gift, I think, and especially on our domestic waterways, the French are rather less patient and think nothing of trying to push in. As Pru and me waited for the signal to move forward into the first lock another boat began to appear alongside us, which had me ready for a confrontation. 'I might have to ask you to translate a few words,' I said to Pru. 'Have you got your ears in?'

'What?'

'I said, HAVE YOU GOT YOUR EARS IN?'

'No, I must have forgotten. Sorry.'

'Oh, bloody hell!'

Regardless of any *affrontements* that may or may not have been about to take place, I needed Pru to be at the top of her game, and as locks are always rather noisy, her not having her ears in was not the news I'd been hoping for.

Fortunately, before the interlopers could push in, the lock-keeper, an absolutely charming lady who ruled with a rod of iron, instructed them to get back in line on pain of a rather agonising death.

'*Merci beaucoup, madame,*' I yelled. My God, I was relieved. The last thing I needed before tackling eight locks in a boat I found hard to handle with a mate who couldn't hear was a barney with an impatient Frenchman.

After receiving the green light to move forward into the lock we immediately encountered a problem. The lock gates were automated, which confused my mate. On top of this, with tens of thousands of gallons of water now on the move the noise levels had gone up somewhat, which made communication almost impossible.

'Wait till the gates are open then cast off,' I shouted, as the gates began to open.

'What?'

'Wait till the gates are open then cast off!'

'What?'

'WAIT TILL THE GATES ARE OPEN THEN CAST OFF!'

We got there in the end but the moment we sailed into the next lock we went straight into the wall.

'BUGGER!'

I remember quite vividly staring down at the remaining locks and thinking, *I'm not sure if I can do this!* Fortunately, with the help of the lock keeper, things gradually became a little easier.

'Wine?' I said, as we finally left the last lock and made our way to Béziers.

'Yes please,' said Pru. 'I'll have a bucket full.'

The following day heralded the final leg of our journey and was the part that we had most been looking forward to.

'What time are they arriving?' asked Pru after breakfast.

'About midday, I think.'

'Oh good. I can't wait to see them.'

Joe, Clem and Felix had driven all the way from their home near Lyon to join us and ever since the start of our journey Pru had talked about little else. With Joe and his family living in France, we had to take every opportunity to be together, and especially as Pru's condition was not going to get any better. When he asked me how

I thought Pru had been since the last time he saw her, I informed Joe that his mother had become slightly more forgetful.

'You mean the ears?' he said.

'And the handbag,' I replied.

Pru's handbag has always been quite famous in our family, and I have often likened it to a camel's stomach: three layers, each containing a different kind of absolute necessity – medical (plasters and such like), vanity (lipstick and mascara, etc.) and miscellaneous (your guess is as good as mine).

As Joe and I continued talking we came to the conclusion that the things that were on Pru's mind the most were her experiences before marrying me. 'Which is clearly where it all went wrong,' we said, after arriving at the same conclusion.

As if to prove our point, while Joe and I were chatting about Pru at the tiller, she was just behind us at the stern talking to Clement and Felix about her former French fiancé. The two boys hadn't been aware of this man's existence until then, and Pru went into great detail about a conversation they had had in Paris at the top of the tower at Notre-Dame about whether or not she would marry him and follow him out to Japan. She then told Clem and Felix that as she and her fiancé were standing there talking, she suddenly heard the voice of a little English girl, who was asking her mother if there were many more stairs to climb. 'Then, around the corner came two girls who lived quite close to my parents in darkest Surrey,' she said. 'And I suddenly thought, oh bugger, I can't marry a Frenchman.' Felix then made the point that if Pru had married the Frenchman he wouldn't be here. 'Either that or I'd be speaking Japanese,' he said.

Despite us all being separated by the English Channel, and also by a not inconsiderable amount of land, the fact that Joe lives in France and has a French family has been an undoubted source of joy to Pru and has helped her keep in touch with her past.

The end of our journey was heralded by the sight of the majestic Mediterranean Sea and as we passed from the Midi to the Med I couldn't help but be impressed by the fact that Riquet had actually achieved his incredibly grand ambition of linking two mighty oceans. He had allowed nothing to dim his passion, even his advancing years.

'Do you know how old Riquet was when he began work on the Canal du Midi?' I asked Pru. 'He was fifty-nine years old. Isn't that incredible?'

'I sympathize,' she said. 'I just want to go on working till the day I drop. Life can begin at fifty.'

'Or beyond,' I said.

'Or beyond,' Pru agreed.

The Shannon-Erne Waterway

When I let slip during a planning meeting one day that my mother was Irish, the producer's eyes suddenly lit up and by the end of the meeting we had agreed that we would visit Ireland as part of the next series of *Great Canal Journeys*. Up to now, we'd concentrated mainly on Pru's background (we'd looked into her Yorkshire forebears, her aforementioned French romance, followed by her Scottish romance – so many romances! – and her Surrey childhood and had visited the house where she was born) and so this was seen as an opportunity to redress the balance somewhat.

What the producer didn't tell me was that after we had decided to explore some of Ireland's many beautiful waterways, they had engaged the services of a genealogist, who would meet me during filming and look into my family's background. I left Wandsworth believing myself to be a member of an averagely competent theatrical family and did not expect to return as the apparent descendant of an aristocratic Anglo-Irish bloodline. Following a canal can lead you into surprising waters but this was on an altogether different scale.

Apart from a few professional visits to Dublin and to Wexford, I had not been back to the Old Country since my childhood, when my mother used to take my sister and I to County Wicklow from time to time. Does the

Emerald Isle include Northern Ireland? I hope so: I have performed in Belfast several times, and filmed in the area, and one of the prospects that excited me about exploring the canals there was to be able to cross from South to North on 'water that knows no boundaries'.

The history of waterways in the Republic of Ireland is, alas, not a happy one. Only two major canals survived the collapse of commercial traffic: the Grand and its rival the Royal, which both stretch from Dublin to the River Shannon by different routes. Each experienced severe economic and physical problems throughout the twentieth century, although a series of restoration programmes are now underway.

The route we decided to peruse, the Shannon-Erne Waterway, reopened in 1994 and is in fact a series of lakes connected by rivers and the odd bit of canal. In our not especially narrow but adequately comfortable narrowboat, *Maeve*, which measured eight feet six inches in breadth, we followed the Lough Erne Canal, and crossed the invisible line from Northern Ireland to the Republic. Lough Erne is known as one of the least commercially successful canals in history. Costing a whopping £25 million to build in today's money, its opening in 1860 coincided with the arrival of the railways, making it instantly obsolete. The canal operated for nine years in total but saw just eight paying boats in that time, generating a total income of, in today's money, £2,000. It then closed and remained that way for the next 126 years.

We were joined for part of our journey on the Lough Erne by Frank McCabe, the lengthsman of the canal, who is responsible for the towpath and the locks. Frank told us how the canal's construction was hampered by starvation in the terrible potato famine of the 1840s when many of the labourers were too weakened by hunger to work. A million people died during the famine, and a further million emigrated abroad, mostly to America. Frank himself had found evidence of the famine on his property by discovering what were known as 'famine pots' – large jars that were used by the government soup kitchens to distribute food to the starving. Far too often, however, it was a case of too little food, too late.

Reconstruction of the canal, which created a lost link between the north and south, was an idea born out of the Peace Process and was backed by both the Irish and British governments. 'I never realized as I was growing up,' said Frank, 'that this canal would become a symbol of hope.'

Although it rained quite solidly throughout our first day, after reaching our mooring for the night near the charming town of Leitrim we discovered the perfect antidote to the weather by accepting an invitation to Carthy's Bar, a pub in the town, where I seem to remember I drank quite a lot of Guinness. Pru had a go at some traditional Irish dancing, and I was invited to sing a local song called 'Lovely Leitrim Shore'.

Later that evening we were visited by a *seanchaí*, a professional storyteller dealing in Irish folk legends and stories that have been orally handed down through the generations. Pru was keen to find out more about Irish fairies, and the *seanchaí* explained that they are in no way related to the elusive creatures with gossamer wings so beloved by Victorian illustrators.

'In the Irish tradition, fairy folk could be just like you or me,' he told us.

'And do they have special powers?' Pru asked hopefully.

'They do,' he said. 'They steal away small baby boys, which is mentioned in a poem by Yeats called "The Stolen Child". *Come away, O human child, with a faery hand in hand.*'

'Oh dear,' said Pru.

This apparently explains why, in some early black-and-white photographs of rural Irish families, small boys are occasionally dressed up as little girls. To fool the fairies.

'But they can also bring good luck and fortune,' he reassured her.

'That's a relief.'

As the evening skies closed over *Maeve's* cabin, we lit some candles and our *seanchaí* produced a bottle of Irish whiskey. As we drank, our conversation turned to ghost stories. Had we ever had experiences of the supernatural? we were asked. Well, there has just been one occasion when I'd felt in the presence of a ghostly manifestation – not a single human presence, but a community from the past.

While appearing in a play at the Birmingham Hippodrome many years ago, I stayed with some friends of ours who owned a very old manor house in rural Warwickshire. One evening, after returning there from the theatre, I realized that my hosts had gone to bed. Fortunately, they had left a key to the front door where I could find it.

As I picked it up I felt an extraordinary blast of cold air on the back of my neck. I was mystified: it was a warm summer's evening and behind me lay nothing but open fields. As I gazed in the direction from where the cold air had come from, I saw a light that appeared to be flickering on the horizon, and, with it, what felt like a powerful current of hatred. I lost no time in opening the heavy oak door and shutting it safely behind me.

At breakfast the next morning, I told my hostess of my experience and, evidently not surprised, she told me the whole story.

'Where you saw the light,' she said, 'there used to be a village that fell victim to the plague and the Lord of the Manor, who lived here, gave orders for the village to be burned to the ground.'

The Lord of the Manor's instruction was accepted philosophically by the villagers, but what offended them was that he removed the great oak door from the church and installed it on the front of the Manor. I was with the villagers!

The next morning, we made our way to Crom Castle, home of the Earls of Erne for the last two hundred years. Part way through our journey Pru appeared, holding a couple of whiskies.

'What have you got there?' I asked her.

'A medicinal draft for the skipper,' said my trusty mate. 'And one for yourself, of course.'

'Of course!'

Crom Castle is extremely remote but in its heyday it was a social hub for the county set. Founded by a Scots settler at the start of the seventeenth century, it was also home to over one hundred estate workers and their families. The estate is set over a series of islands and the only way you could get around was by boat. It's still the same today and a delightful young chap from the National Trust, who now own the Castle Crom estate, gave Pru and I a tour on board a hundred-year-old vessel called a Crom Cot, which had been used by the estate in its heyday. A longish boat with a shallow keel that allows it to land on stony shores, the Crom Cot we were travelling on had been used to transport the estate worker's children to school each morning. It was part of a lost world, as was a beautiful folly we visited where newly married estate workers had been permitted to spend one night for their honeymoon.

'Would you like a second honeymoon here?' Pru asked me.

'Well, it would certainly be private,' I replied. 'No waiters sidling up to me and saying, "I think the lady has already retired, sir."'

From Castle Crom we made our way to Enniskillen, and on the way Pru appeared with two more gigantic whiskies. In thanks and celebration, I gave her a rendition of 'When I Was a Lad' from *HMS Pinafore*, a production of which I had directed and appeared in on a British tour several years ago and again in New Zealand. Pru was very impressed and even helped out with the returns.

> I cleaned the windows and I washed the floor and I
> polished up the handle on the big front door.
> (He polished up the handle of the big front door.)
> I polished up the handle so carefully that now I am the
> ruler of the Queen's Navy.
> (He polished up the handle so carefully that now he is
> the ruler of the Queen's Navy.)

Great fun.

It was in Enniskillen that I met Frank, the genealogist

who had been charged by the production company to do some research and uncover the full story of my links with Ireland. My mother Olive had been born in Dublin and my grandparents were Anglo-Irish. In fact, it was my mother's father who had started the family tradition of acting. My grandfather's stage name was C. W. Carleton-Crowe (it looked very good on the posters) and I, knowing my mother's maiden name was Crowe, assumed that he'd probably added the Carleton as a pretention. Frank informed me that this wasn't in fact the case, and that my grandfather's mother's maiden name was Carleton. He went on to say that she came from a family of some distinction, who had settled in Fermanagh. What's more, my ancestral home, which my family had built in 1613, stood just above on the shore of the lough that we were due to pass through that very afternoon.

We found the house, and met the present owner, a genial doctor called John Williams. It felt really uncanny, first of all to have been introduced to a whole family you never knew you had, in a place that you'd never been to, and then to find yourself sailing directly past the actual house in which that family had lived for four hundred years.

Pru was quite respectful towards me when she learned of my elevated lineage.

'I thought I'd married a penniless actor,' she said. 'But it appears I might have married into landed gentry.'

It soon wore off, though.

Finally, a word of advice, if I may. If you ever happen to visit Ireland with Pru and are put in charge of a boat, do not, whatever you do, allow her to pour the whiskies.

A Swedish Saga

I t had been decided that for series four of *Great Canal Journeys* we would venture to Sweden, a land of vast forests and island-strewn coasts. The idea was to cross the country from west to east in two episodes: one to cover our voyage across the western part of the country, from Gothenburg through the Trollhätte Canal and over Lake Vänern on to the Göta Canal; and the second to take us towards Stockholm and the Swedish archipelago.

For me personally, the prospect of visiting Sweden for the first time was tremendously exciting, and in the days leading up to us leaving I was, according to Pru, rather like a small child on Christmas morning. Pru was also looking forward to our adventure but, not being quite as nomadic as I am, she had managed to temper her enthusiasm.

Sweden is a land mostly of water, with islands all down its coast and a great number of inland lakes. The Göta Canal, to which we were principally drawn, links two of those lakes and was created to enable vessels to travel from the Baltic in the east to Kattegat in the west. It took sixty thousand men twenty-two years to dig the canal, and when it first opened in 1822 it was the greatest feat of engineering the country had ever seen.

The Göta Canal has fifty-eight locks to navigate, and I'd been made aware before travelling that part of the canal had been christened the 'Divorce Ditch' after the navigational difficulties encountered by some married boaters. Hmm. Given mine and Pru's history in these situations I thought it best we have a conversation about it before we took to water.

'Darling, there's something I need to tell you.'

'You're not divorcing me, are you?'

'Not unless you'd like to me to.'

'Not yet. Can I let you know?'

'Of course. Now look, I've just been told that there are no fewer than fifty-eight locks on the Göta and that part of the canal has been christened the "Divorce Ditch".'

'So you *do* want a divorce then?'

'No, I'm just informing you that we will have to be at the top of our game and that whatever happens you must remember to put your ears in.'

'Sorry?'

'Oh dear.'

We started off in style from Gothenburg aboard the *Juno*, a handsome, originally steam-powered vessel, the world's oldest registered passenger ship. She was launched in 1874, rebuilt in 1904 and converted for diesel in 1956. The full journey from Gothenburg to Stockholm takes four days and three nights, but we were going only as far as Sjötorp, with one overnight stay in a rather minute double cabin, and a double only in the sense that it had upper and lower bunks.

'Getting down in the middle of the night when it's dark is going to be interesting,' I said to Pru.

When I woke the following morning, having managed to refrain from having to 'go', it appeared that poor Pru had lost her sea-legs.

'Are you all right, my darling? You don't look at all well.'

'I'll be OK. I just need to rest for a while. You go on to breakfast. I'll be fine later.'

A few hours later Pru was feeling more like her old self again and after packing our things we transferred to our hired thirty-six-foot cabin cruiser and set out along the Göta. At Forsvik, a wonderful surprise was awaiting me: a Victorian paddle steamer! The *Eric Nordevall II* is a replica of the ship that sank in Lake Vättern in 1856. The wreck was discovered in 1980, and it was decided to build a perfect reproduction, powered by a single vertical cylinder and fired up, as in the original, by wood rather than coal. We came aboard for an hour's sail, which was bliss for me; and Pru had a nice time too with the vessel's young captain, very dishy in his nineteenth-century tailcoat. She's a terrible flirt, you know.

There is a floating sauna at Karlsborg, and I persuaded Pru to try it. 'Are you sure you've never been in a sauna before?' I asked her beforehand.

'I think I'd remember if I had,' she said. 'They're rather hot, aren't they?'

As we both disrobed I was reminded of a health club I once belonged to (what on earth was I thinking of?) whose patrons included a quite famous comedian with a very bad wig. He knew it was terrible and would go into the sauna only if he could sit on the highest step so that nobody could see the top of his head. I can sit anywhere I like in a sauna as I've never had that problem. We went in and it's safe to say that after just a few minutes I could tell that saunas weren't really Pru's thing.

'Do you feel Swedish?' I asked her.

'Oh, terribly Swedish. How long do we have to be in here for?'

'As long as you can stand it really.'

'Oh!'

In order to try to take Pru's mind off the heat and steam, which I believe might have been interfering with her hair and make-up that she'd spent rather a long time on that morning, I informed Pru that in ancient Rome the Senate used to meet in a sauna regularly and strip off.

'Being stripped off cut through an awful lot of political conversations,' I told her, 'which, if they had been fully clothed, would have gone on for a very long time. So, when you were naked you could speak your mind.'

'Bare body, bare soul,' Pru said.

'Exactly.'

After about twenty minutes, which was rather a good effort, I thought, and during which time we had each decided not to use the freezing cold plunge pool, I was reminded of one of the reasons why I fell in love with Pru in the first place.

'So, do you feel invigorated?' I asked her.

'Yes!'

'A new woman?'

'Why, do you want one?' she said, as quick as a flash.

Her memory might have been fading, but her sense of humour certainly wasn't.

Later that day, as we approached the end of the canal, we came across the famous Berg Locks, the final flight of the infamous Divorce Ditch. Until now we'd managed OK, primarily because there'd been plenty of lock-keepers on hand. With no guarantee of there being any here I wondered if we'd survive it – physically, mentally and conjugally?

In actual fact, we did – calmly and methodically, just passing the ropes through the correct rings, being civil to each other, and in fact enjoying the adventure.

'Why haven't we always done it like this?' I said to Pru after we'd navigated the final lock.

'Well, for a start, I remembered to put my ears in!' she said. 'Normal service will resume when I forget again.'

'Probably.'

It was here that we passed on to part two of our Swedish Odyssey, which was to take us across Lake Mälaren to Drottningholm Palace and Stockholm, and the islands beyond. Our new boat was very grand and had a huge bed that was set triangularly across the cabin.

'Have you ever slept triangularly before?' Pru asked me.

'I'm not sure,' I replied. 'There's a first time for every-thing.'

We went through Södertälje Canal onto the lake created, according to Norse mythology, by the goddess Gefjon when the Swedish king Gylfi promised her as much land as four oxen could plough in a day and a night. Cunning Gefjon used special oxen from the Land of the Giants, who uprooted the land and dragged it into the sea, leaving a space that became Lake Mälaren.

The experience of sailing across a lake is different from following the course of a river or canal, where you are looking at the bank and observing nature at close quarters. On a big lake such detail is usually too far away to see, and you are left to your own thoughts.

But how good are Pru and me at reading each other

under such circumstances? As actors, we have to learn to make audiences aware of our thoughts when necessary and without the assistance of language; but that's not the same as being able to read someone else's mind when they are silent and alone with their thoughts. As I sat on the bridge of our boat, steering across Lake Mälaren, Pru was just a few yards away and all of a sudden it occurred to me that I hadn't the slightest idea what was going on in her head. Was it the pleasure of just being here in the moment or was it reminding her of something in the past? Or was she perhaps thinking about the future?

We eventually arrived on the island of Björkö, which in the eighth century had been a Viking settlement. We hoped to find out the truth about Swedish Norsemen and had our very own Viking guide called Andreas. Pru's first Viking impressions were obviously favourable as for the first hour she did little else but smile at him.

'I say, you're very polite for a Viking,' she said. 'And you're terribly dashing.'

Andreas accepted Pru's compliments gracefully, and as she insisted on taking his arm whenever something even resembling an obstacle came into view, we made our way to a Viking cemetery where at least 3,000 people had been buried beneath the earth. According to Pru's new best friend, both male and female Vikings were often buried clutching their combs.

'Combs in the graves of warriors?' said Pru, doubtfully.

Ha! Her enthusiasm was waning.

From there we walked to the highest point of the island so that Andreas could show us the traditional Viking routes from Björkö to Stockholm and the Baltic Sea.

Halfway up, I stumbled once or twice and so looked around for some assistance. Alas, Pru had already forgiven the male half of the Viking population for being vain and, as I stood there on the hill bent double, she and Andreas strolled on arm-in-arm staring dreamily into each other's eyes.

'You're obviously very used to guiding ladies up here,' I heard Pru say.

Later that day we got to ride in a traditional Viking long-boat (although quite a small one) and while I rowed alongside some of our other fellow passengers, Pru read us a verse from the *Sturlunga* saga, an Icelandic Viking poem:

'"You must climb up onto the keel, Cold is the sea spray's feel, Let not your courage bend, Here your life must end." – Did you hear that, Tim? – "Old man, keep your upper lip firm, Though your head be bowed by the storm, Death comes to us all at last."'

'Well, thanks very much.'

One of the highlights of the second leg of our journey was a visit to the Drottningholm Palace Theatre, which is a sacred place for actors. Built in 1766, the same year as the Bristol Old Vic, it has remained virtually unchanged for over 250 years and is a theatrical time capsule. In addition to various dressing rooms, the theatre also has a number of bedrooms that were used by the actors. Take a bow then go to bed. What a marvellous idea.

Drottningholm's heyday was during the reign of the King Gustav III, who was so keen on the theatre that he both directed and performed in plays himself. That all came to a tragic end, however, in 1972, when, during a masked ball at the Theatre Royal in Stockholm, the king was assassinated. After that the theatre was boarded up and forgotten for the next 129 years, until it was rediscovered in 1921 in almost perfect condition.

At the end of the tour, we were invited to tread the boards for a few minutes and because the theatre was once famous for presenting French drama, I suggested that Pru might like to recite a bit of Molière.

'*Le Bourgeois Gentilhomme*?'

'OK, why not?'

And that was it, she was off. It was marvellous watching Pru in full flight on a stage again. She was amazing.

'All right, your turn,' she said.

'OK, how about something from *Richard II*?'

> Let's talk of graves, of worms, and epitaphs.
> Make dust our paper and with rainy eyes.
> Write sorrow on the bosom of the earth.

The acoustic is just magnificent in the theatre and I'm afraid I got carried away and continued for some minutes.

On this journey there were so many places to stop, explore and film, but we just didn't have enough time. And remember, not everything that's recorded in a programme like this makes it to the final edit. In fact, they haven't shown us any of the out-takes from *Canal Journeys* up to now, and I'm not sure I'd like to see them. I believe, though, that we somehow managed to capture something of the atmosphere of this remarkable country and we certainly hope to go back again one day.

A Venetian Adventure

I n Venice, mass tourism has become a very real and constant threat to the city's existence and far outweighs the natural peril of being washed away to sea. In addition, many of the residents situated in the old part of the city can no longer afford to live there because of over-inflated real-estate prices. It's all incredibly sad. The worst offenders with regards to tourists are the gigantic cruise ships. Docking in the beautiful Venetian lagoon, they disgorge a vast number of passengers who, because they are fed and watered aboard, don't even contribute to the local economy, save for the odd souvenir. The Venetian authorities are unapologetic about welcoming these huge vessels, more's the pity, as Venice apparently keeps the entire Adriatic cruise industry afloat, providing tens of thousands of jobs. I found out quite recently that things are so bad these days that even the city's UNESCO World Heritage status is under threat.

When Pru and I arrived in Venice with the *Canal Journeys* crew, we attempted to buck the trend by *not* behaving like tourists. The original plan suggested by the production company had been to take the Orient Express to Verona, and then approach Venice via the Brenta Canal, which would have been incredibly touristy, but given the situation we decided not to come by rail. Instead we flew to Venice and spent our first night in the beautiful city of

Mira, which is situated on the mainland. The next morning we went to the ancient town of Dolo, where a boat was waiting to take us along the Brenta Canal.

Our boat immediately met with Pru's approval. 'Very nice,' she said. 'Didn't the Venetian nobles regularly come on this canal?'

'Yes, they did,' I confirmed. 'But they would have travelled in even more luxurious vessels called *burchiellos*, which, more often than not, were adorned with velvet and gold leaf.'

I assumed that my lesson in Italian maritime history might have fallen on deaf ears as Pru had wandered off, but I was wrong.

'I don't suppose they had a fridge in their *burchiello*,' she said, waving a bottle of chilled wine she'd found.

'No, I don't suppose they did,' I replied. 'Then again, the Venetians have always claimed that for every four kilometres of canal you need one litre of wine, so they obviously managed somehow.'

The Brenta canal boasts six elegant locks that are thought to have been designed by Leonardo da Vinci. Unfortunately, they lay upstream of our journey, so we had to make do with the impressive number of very grand houses that were built along the waterway as a result of the repeal of an early law forbidding Venetians to build on the mainland. One of these houses is an elegant Palladian villa called the Villa Foscari – also known as *La Malcontenta* – that was built in the late 1550s for the ancient noble Foscari family, who have owned it ever since. We were privileged to meet Antonio Foscari, who rescued the place from neglect in 1973 and restored it to its original condition.

'Which of the wives was *malcontenta*?' Pru asked me as we arrived at the villa.

'Why do you assume it was one of the wives?' I asked her.

'Because it's malcontent-*a* and not malcontent-*or*,' she said.

That was me told. 'Well,' I replied. 'I expect she was very malcontent at being shut away for thirty years for having an affair.'

'Was she really?' said Pru. 'Good heavens. That's a bit unfortunate.'

Actually it was indeed quite unfortunate, as in those days it was considered perfectly normal for a Venetian wife to take a lover.

Pru and me had visited Venice a couple of times before (which was one reason I'd been keen on us returning, as I thought it might evoke some happy memories for Pru) but we had never approached it from the mainland. As we emerged from the canal into the lagoon, we looked out into the distance and watched the gradual appearance through the haze of this magical island resting in the sea. It was an unforgettable experience.

We at last bullied our way into a mooring (how well we know that problem) and disembarked onto the Piazza San Marco, the social, religious and, of course, touristic centre of Venice. At the Caffè Florian, patronized at different times by Byron, Goldoni, Goethe, Dickens and Proust, we were told of the strong aphrodisiac properties of hot chocolate, habitually ordered by Giacomo Casanova for his companions.

'Did you know they've been serving coffee and hot chocolate here since before you were born?' I said to Pru as we entered.

'Really? How long's that?'

'Ooh, about 1720.'

'Charming!'

Since arriving in Venice, Pru seemed to have had a permanent smile on her face, and her infectious lust for life had become more palpable than ever. Venice was having the desired effect, that's for sure, although I hadn't expected it to be quite so potent. As we were making our way carefully to our next appointment Pru suddenly, and without warning, started singing some of the libretto from *The Barber of Seville*.

'Bravo!' I said, once she'd finished. 'Where on earth did that come from?'

'Oh, I don't know, somewhere,' she replied, with a broad and beautiful smile.

I had played the title role in a production *King Lear* in 1971 at Venice's world-famous Teatro la Fenice as part of that year's Venice Biennale. Considered too modern for Milan, Verdi's *La Traviata* and *Rigoletto* had both premiered there, a fact that had not been lost on me at the time. A quarter of a century later in 1996, this most beautiful of theatres had been completely destroyed by a fire and had had to be completely reconstructed.

It took two years and ninety million Euros to resurrect the opera house's mid-nineteenth century heyday. 'What do you think Pru?' I asked as we entered the auditorium. It was my first time there in almost half a century and it felt exactly the same.

'It's incredible,' she said. 'You're so lucky to have performed here.'

An altogether different kind of theatrical experience awaited us at our next appointment, which was at the famous historical costumiers, Nicolao Atelier, where the actor Alessandro Bressanello dressed us in traditional costumes of the Commedia dell'Arte and improvised some scenes with us. It's a very actor-based kind of theatre; there is no place for writers or directors. But Carlo Goldoni, while using familiar Commedia situations, developed them in a more formal style, with the playwright always in control. Commedia troupes were actually the first in Europe to employ women to play female parts, we discovered, a device that proved so popular that sometimes scenes were included that encouraged girls to appear completely naked. Critics were not impressed by this (the playwright Ben Jonson described one female Commedia performer as a 'tumbling whore') and the Catholic church even less so. Indeed, the inclusion of women was deemed so scandalous by the Vatican that actors were not allowed to be buried in its cemeteries. That last fact garnered a gasp from Pru and me.

After having done our level best to remain a cut above the uncouth tourists, we finally succumbed to riding in a gondola, that timeless Venetian image. It was late at night, when the Grand Canal was deserted, and it was wonderful sailing in the moonlight. Just the splash of our gondolier's oar, and his song echoing from the walls of the silent palaces – it doesn't get much better than that. Pru was the happiest I'd seen her in years, and I was quite contented myself. This was turning out to be a marvellous trip.

The following morning, as the throngs of tourists began to appear, we wondered how many of them were aware of the secret behind the city's soaring spires and elegant squares. The reason for us considering such a question was because we were about to visit the Arsenale, the great shipyard at which, in the eleventh century, shipwrights, using separate workshops for carpenters, sailmakers, pitch-boilers, ropemakers and so on, would construct up to three large ships in a single day. The present enlarged complex was built in 1320.

Dante, in *The Divine Comedy*, pays tribute to the tireless workforce in his portrayal of one of his eight circles of hell:

> As in the Arsenal of the Venetians
> Boils in the winter the tenacious pitch
> [. . .]
> One hammers at the prow, one at the stern,
> This one makes oars, and that one cordage twists,
> Another mends the mainsail and the mizzen.
>
> Thus, not by fire, but by the art divine,
> Was boiling down below a dense pitch
> Which upon every side the bank belimed.

We went over to the island of Burano, where we met two attractive young women who were the local champion rowers. In their boat, which is called a *puparin*, they stand facing forwards with an oar each – one in the centre and one at the stern – which makes it easier to spot the sandbanks and sail along at an incredible rate. The girls kindly asked me if I'd like to have a go, but I thought I'd leave it to the experts. Puparins are perfect for fishing the shallow waters of the lagoon but were clearly not designed for transporting two nervy actors. Pru didn't say as much, but I think she was quite relieved.

The Final Voyage

By 2019, Pru and me had made no fewer than nine series of *Great Canal Journeys*, comprising no fewer than thirty-two episodes. As well as continuing to explore our domestic waterways, we also visited Amsterdam, the Marne-Rhine Canal, Rio Darro in Portugal, Lake Maggiore in Italy, Rideau Canal in Canada, Kerela in India, the River Nile in Egypt and the Paraná Delta in Argentina.

Of the twenty-one episodes from series four to series nine, thirteen covered waterways outside the United Kingdom, and with neither of us getting any younger and Pru's condition obviously worsening, although still quite gradually, we decided to make just two more episodes before calling it a day. Ideas for future trips were becoming more and more outlandish and in addition to the reasons I've just mentioned, I also felt that the series had lost its way slightly. Our original *modus operandi* with *Great Canal Journeys* had been to explore and celebrate some of Britain's most beautiful waterways, but we didn't really do much of that anymore. It was a shame, of course, but the time was right to move on.

For a new television series to last five years is quite rare these days, so I'm told, and one that's fronted by a couple of octogenarian actors about a subject that has never been what you might call fashionable, even rarer. During our tenure we had visited a great many interesting and beautiful places. We'd also met hundreds of fascinating people along the way and had made dozens of new friends. I should also mention the positive effect the show has had on the tourist industry here in Great Britain. We're really rather proud of that.

Our final two episodes, it was decided, would see us exploring Vietnam and Cambodia under the title 'An Asian Odyssey'. When we started filming the episodes, Pru was eighty-seven and I was eighty-five. Saving your most audacious adventure till last might have seemed a little foolhardy to some people, but not to us. Once again, Pru had a smile as wide as the Mekong Delta and I too couldn't wait to get started. We never dreamed that at our age we might be sailing in the South China Sea. It was going to be an incredible experience.

We started our journey in Hạ Long Bay, which is on the northeast coast of Vietnam and comprises no fewer than 11,000 miles of waterways. Although her sense of humour and lust for life were still very much intact, Pru's memory and her confidence had become noticeably reduced since the last series and I knew that Juliet and I would have to take extra special care of her.

Having Juliet with us made all the difference, not just to how Pru was feeling, but to how I was feeling too. By this time, we'd already made eighteen trips together and each one had brought Juliet and I closer. We'd obviously had a great deal of catching up to do and, although nothing could ever bring back those days we had lost from her childhood, the time we had spent together travelling had been joyous.

Our first port of call was one of the many floating villages they have in Hạ Long Bay, although there are far fewer these days than there used to be. Living off the rich fishing grounds created by the unique habitat, the villagers' way of life has changed very little across the centuries. We had tea with a family who had lived there for three generations. In fact, each of them had been born there and never left, so they had no idea what it was like living on land. 'We enjoy the peace and quiet,' one of them said to us. 'And we don't know any different.' As much as Pru and me enjoy spending time on the water, the promise of us being able to put our feet on *terra firma* at some stage is quite essential.

Early the next morning we arrived in central Hanoi where, in one of the parks, a large group of septuagenarian and octogenarian women were doing their morning exercises. On seeing our cameras they asked Pru if she would like to join them, and she jumped at the chance.

'Come on, darling, join in,' she said while performing a rather strange exercise that resembled something our grandchildren had made us do to a song called 'Heads, Shoulders, Knees and Toes'.

Rather stupidly, I decided to give it a go, and after touching my toes once or twice Pru suggested that we start our own group on Wandsworth Common. Fortunately, a minute or two later she had run out of steam and so all thoughts of forming our own group were forgotten. 'Coffee?' I suggested.

After fortifying ourselves with caffeine we hopped into a rickshaw to be taken on a tour around the old part of Hanoi.

'Are these safe?' Pru asked as we climbed on board.

'Probably not,' I replied.

Sure enough, it became evident very quickly that nobody had ever created a Highway Code in Vietnam and we spent the majority of our journey with our eyes closed, although when we could bear to open them the parts we saw were beautiful.

After happily alighting from the rickshaw we were taken by a guide around one of the many street markets, where Pru wanted to buy at least one of everything.

'Magic market,' she said after I'd bought her a Vietnamese lucky charm. The cost of this charm had been 120,000 Vietnamese dong which, when the guide had informed me of this, had almost made Pru fall over.

'A hundred and twenty thousand?' she exclaimed. 'That's an awful lot of anything!'

'It's about four pounds,' said the guide.

'Really? Oh, that's all right then.'

If truth be known, I think Pru was slightly disappointed.

Next up we took a sleeper train to Ho Chi Minh City, or Saigon as it once was called. Fortunately, our room had two beds that were adjacent to each other this time and despite it not being up to Orient Express standards it was quite comfortable. As we began to journey the thousand or so miles that separated us from the city, I asked Pru about the Vietnam War.

'Do you remember it happening?'

'All I remember is marching against it,' she said. 'I remember that very well. Make love, not war.'

We agreed, as millions had before us, that it had been a cruel and futile war.

327

Something more positive that occurred to us as we made our way to the city was what a wonderful time we were both having. We were each aware that we might not have many more adventures ahead of us, so we were determined to enjoy every moment.

After reaching Ho Chi Minh City we were straight back on the water again and I could tell immediately that Pru was happier. She'd become a little bit unstable on land, and I'd been keeping a very close eye on her. While now living the vast majority of her life in the here and now, some of the moments she was experiencing were evidently very special to her and she started telling me what a wonderful life she'd had.

'It's not over yet,' I said to her. 'Come on, we have a job to do here.'

'Aye aye, sir.'

A highlight for both us during our trip across Vietnam was visiting one of the amazing tailors they have where you can get a made-to-measure suit in a matter of hours. I think Pru might have lured me there under false pretences; the original plan had been to buy me a new lightweight jacket as the one I had with me had collected a stain or two.

As I was being served by one of the very helpful assistants, Pru had started looking at some fabrics for female garments and kept on glancing over at me hopefully.

'Can we get something for Pru?' I asked the assistant, and in earshot of my sardonically expectant wife.

'Really?' said Pru, rushing over. 'Oh, that's magic. Which one shall I choose?'

And therein lay a slight problem. There must have been

many hundreds of fabric designs at the tailors and although she was evidently thrilled at the prospect of having a dress made especially for her in just a few hours, Pru was having difficulty choosing. I obviously had to remain stationary while I was having my jacket fitted, but I could hear her going through them all. 'No – no – not that one – not that one – not that one – definitely not that one. Don't like that one, or that. That one's a bit too bridal for me.' And so it went on. And on!

After eventually choosing her fabric, Pru decided to have it made into a *áo dài*, a Vietnamese dress that was once worn by both men and women and had been inspired by Paris fashion. They're still worn on special occasions in Vietnam and, as we were having such a nice time, it seemed appropriate.

Pru looked absolutely amazing in her *áo dài* and according to her my new jacket made me look slightly slimmer, which I was rather happy with. By the time we left the tailors it was dark and so we made our way back to the river. There's an ancient tradition in Vietnam that takes place every full moon where villagers visit their nearest river and set lanterns onto the water in memory of a loved one. As with many such traditions, this has now been adopted by people who are visiting the country and, as we were doing just that, we hired a chap to take us on the river. Pru sent her lantern onto the water first, for Bim and John, and then I sent one for Harry and Olla. As the two lanterns slowly disappeared from view we blew each one of them a kiss and sat back.

'Thank you for a lovely life,' Pru said to me suddenly.

'It's a pleasure,' I said, taking her hand. 'So have I had a lovely life. Thank you.'

I don't mind admitting that by the time we arrived back from Cambodia a week later we were exhausted and barely moved for a fortnight, thus validating our decision to call time on things. Everything had taken a little bit longer than it had the previous series, and the period it took us to recover was no different. The going away bit was fine, it was everything else that took it out of us.

'Are you sure you're OK about us saying goodbye to *Canal Journeys*?' I asked Pru, while we had our feet up.

'Oh, I think so,' she said. 'I'm absolutely exhausted.'

'And you realize what this means, of course?'

'No?'

'It means we can get back to our own boat.'

'Of course. Isn't that marvellous. I've missed her.'

'A few leisurely days on the Oxford Canal will do us both the power of good. Back to where it all started.'

'Where what all started?'

'Our first narrowboat holiday. Don't you remember?'

'I think so.'

'We can stop off in Oxford and visit the Eastgate Hotel if you like.'

Fin

Epilogue

G iven our terribly advanced ages, not to mention our situation, you might be expecting the finale of our book to be written like some kind of tear-stained retrospective. A sentimental coda, bringing everything nicely to a close before Pru and me sit back in our comfy high-seated chairs, have a cup of tea or some cocoa and wait for whatever crumbs of activity life might have left for us to enjoy.

Not a bit of it.

You didn't really expect that, did you? Regardless of what's happening, we always make sure we have plenty to do and since our final two episodes of *Great Canal Journeys* were transmitted in 2019, we've had a lot on. Pru's had to take things a little bit easier but as well as looking after our garden, which she still takes very seriously and does very well, she accompanies me to plays and to concerts; and whenever I'm away working, which I still get asked to do occasionally, she'll spend time with friends or family.

Work's actually been quite kind to me since the end of *Canal Journeys*. You remember I filmed those episodes of *Dad's Army*? Well, after that I was asked to appear in a television series called *Gentleman Jack*, which you might have heard of, alongside the very talented actor Suranne Jones. That show has been terribly popular and is probably what I get asked about most at the moment. Well, that and Pru.

Regardless of what show or play somebody might want to quiz me about, whether it be a person in the street or a journalist, the first thing they always ask is: 'How's Pru?'

'She's fine, thanks,' I say. 'She'll either be in the garden deadheading, talking to a friend or reading a book.'

I forget who it was – it was either Joe or Sam, I think – but halfway through filming the second series of *Gentleman Jack* one of them called me up and reminded me that Pru was approaching ninety.

'On the twenty-second of June,' I said quickly. 'She was born in 1932. Good lord, you're right! What are we going to do?'

We thought long and hard about how we might best commemorate Pru's milestone, and in the end we decided to have a party at home. There were two reasons for this; first, Pru simply adores the place and it's undoubtedly where she is happiest, and second, given the amount of people we'd have to invite, being in familiar surroundings would make things much less confusing for her. And for me, come to think of it.

Despite it taking place in June and so officially summer, good weather could not be guaranteed so we hired a marquee and held the party outdoors but indoors, if you see what I mean. Also, because Pru can become quite tired in the afternoon we chose to make it an early affair so she would be able to spend plenty of time with our guests. Sam and Joe made the most marvellous speeches, and although she didn't recognize everyone immediately, Pru had the jolliest of times. She also looked quite beautiful, just as she always does.

She and Juliet spent hours getting ready in our bedroom

and when Pru finally emerged, had I not known her, I would have mistaken her for a woman of sixty. I once said in an interview that because we've spent so much time apart, we're always very pleased to see each other. The former might have been redressed just recently, but the latter hasn't changed one bit. When I see Pru, I feel happy. Happy, and very grateful.

I sometimes ponder the question of how our relationship has changed over the years and I always reach the same conclusion: that it hasn't, very much. We're obviously older and more worldly-wise, but instead of having grown apart, which is sadly what happens to some couples, we've gradually become as one. We've become Tim and Pru.

So, what else has been going on? Well, in the autumn of 2022 we went on a two-week cruise around the Greek islands together, which was rather fun. We took somebody with us to help look after Pru and spent a fortnight doing what we do best – exploring interesting and beautiful places, meeting new people and enjoying each other's company. Some folks are rather shocked when they learn that we're still taking cruises and such like, but to paraphrase what I believe to be a popular idiom these days, if one doesn't get on and use it, one is probably going to lose it. Well, we're not quite ready for that yet.

There's one more event I think I should mention and that's our impending sixtieth wedding anniversary, which will take place on 26 October 2023. For our fortieth and fiftieth wedding anniversaries we hired the PS *Waverley*, which is the last seagoing passenger-carrying paddle steamer in the world. Both parties took place on the River Thames, and we even arranged to have Tower Bridge open especially for us so we could pass through on our way to the Thames Barrier and back.

At one of these events, having been asked to make a speech, Joe stood up and said simply, 'Mummy, thank you for having me, and Daddy, thank you for coming.'

Silence reigned for about five seconds afterwards before suddenly, in unison, everybody present went into hysterics and remained there for a good five minutes. Joe was sitting next to the Dean of Southwark at the time, who laughed louder than anyone. He's quite a wit, our Joe.

We haven't decided what we're going to do yet for our sixtieth, but whatever we go with you can guarantee that the two main ingredients will be people and laughter. In fact, that's probably what we live for these days, with a bit of travel and the odd glass of wine thrown in.

I fear that very soon we shall have to part company, dear reader, as alas, we have arrived at the point where Pru and me spend the majority of our lives these days – the here and now. Whereas I wouldn't wish her condition on anybody, there is undoubtedly something to be said for spending more time in the present moment, blissfully unencumbered by regrets of things we haven't done or things we fear might happen.

'The present moment is all that actually exists,' a very wise friend said to me around the time of Pru's diagnosis.

'I suppose so,' I replied.

At the time it didn't resonate but as Pru's condition worsened I began to appreciate that, in her case, that's all there is. I would naturally give anything to have the old Pru back, but the fact that she doesn't have to worry about anything very much for more than a few seconds at a time is a crumb of comfort. She's also very well physically, which is a huge blessing.

I am often asked what I miss most about Pru before her condition got the better of her, and because I am the male of the species and from a certain generation, I always tend to brush over the subject. Now we are all together and because I think it is relevant to the book, I will attempt to elucidate, although briefly. Had I the impetus to do so, I could probably write reams on the subject, but what good would that do? The truth is that I miss her companionship; the companionship of my best friend. Pru and me used to tackle myriad subjects head-on, and if we ever locked horns, which we often did, no quarter would be given, and especially not by Pru. I miss going to see a play or a concert with her and being able to talk about it afterwards. We do still attend such events, but by the time we've left the theatre or concert hall, Pru will have forgotten what she's seen. She still enjoys going, though, which is important.

What I miss most of all, I think, is us no longer being able to share our hopes and fears with one another. You can have a conversation or go to the theatre with anybody, but you cannot bare your soul to just anyone.

The aforementioned regrets are tempered by the fact that Pru is happy and knows that she is loved. We also have a large and caring family, plenty of friends who fortunately haven't died yet, and a house and garden that Pru adores and feels safe in. Most of all, we have each other, and will for years to come with any luck.

I do hope you have enjoyed our time together. I most certainly have, as has Pru. She insisted on helping choose the photographs herein and while leafing through them together a multitude of brief and either sketchy or terribly vivid memories were unearthed. It was a joyous experience and is one we shall repeat.

As I write, Pru has just finished recording a section of the audio for her show, *An Evening with Queen Victoria*. The recording, which took place at our home, lasted slightly longer than it might have done twenty years ago, but she did a marvellous job. In order not to distract her, I waited in the next room and listened with the door slightly ajar. I shudder to think how many times I have heard Pru reading from a script over the years – many thousands, probably – and hearing her do so again after what must have been several years was a real tonic.

'Did I do all right?' she asked the engineer afterwards.

'You were wonderful, Pru,' he said.

'He's right, my darling, you were.'

It would have lasted no more than a few seconds, but just for a moment, Pru was able to experience some professional pride once again, not to mention a drop of well-earned and very sincere adulation.

'Can we do it again?' she asked.

'I've no idea,' I replied. 'I suppose so. Why, would you like to?'

'Rather. It's been just like old times. See, I can still do it.'

'I never doubted that for a moment.'

'You still love me then?'

'Of course I still love you. You know I do.'

'No divorce then?'

'No divorce.'

'Lord, that's a relief.'

'I'll tell you what,' I said, pouring us both a glass of wine. 'Why don't I take out an advert somewhere and see if I can get you some more work?'

'Oh, darling! Please say you will.'

There you are then. Two slightly weathered but ludicrously experienced voiceover artists for hire (we come as a pair, I'm afraid). Reasonable rates. All enquiries, care of Tim and Pru, Wandsworth.

Thank you for reading, and we wish all of you much love and happiness.

Acknowledgements

I would like to thank the following people who helped in the making of this book:

To Tim Bates, Samantha Brace and all at Peters Fraser + Dunlop for their guidance and support.

To Louise Moore and Fenella Bates for their enthusiasm and belief in the book right from the start, and to all at Penguin Michael Joseph for their hard work in bringing it to life, including Paula Flanagan, Beatrix McIntyre, Emma Henderson, Sukhmani Bhakar, Gaby Young, Stella Newing, Lily Riddett, Rosemary O'Dowd, Francisca Monteiro and Helen Eka.

To James Hogg, for his ability to become a much loved and important member of the family.

To Tania Annesley for her impeccable organization and assistance.

To Juliet, Sam, Joe, and all the grandchildren.

And finally, to Pru. This book might be told through my eyes, but over the last sixty-plus years my eyes have, more often than not, been pointing in her direction. I am an extraordinarily lucky man.